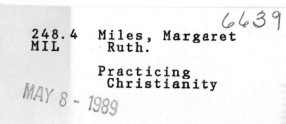
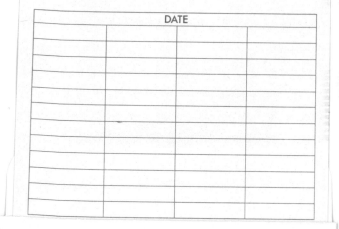

# Practicing Christianity

*inardescimus et imus*
*Augustine* Confessions *13.9*

# PRACTICING CHRISTIANITY

## Critical Perspectives for an Embodied Spirituality

*Margaret R. Miles*

6639

CROSSROAD · NEW YORK

1988

The Crossroad Publishing Company
370 Lexington Avenue, New York, N.Y. 10017

Printed in the United States of America

*Library of Congress Cataloging-in-Publication Data*
Miles, Margaret Ruth.
Practicing Christianity.

Bibliography: p.
Includes index.
1. Spirituality—History of doctrines.   2. Spiritual
life.   I. Title.
BV4490.M53   1988        248.4        88-20274
ISBN 0-8245-0904-8

For my students in the Fall 1986 "Patterns in the Practice of Christianity" course at Harvard Divinity School, who, by their enagagement with these matters, convinced me that, in a world full of books, this book still needed to be written, and that committed attention to life experience and to rigorous thought need not be antithetical.

# Contents

# Illustrations

# Preface

How did historical people learn to shape their lives around Christian ideas, attitudes, and values? There were many sources of instruction: liturgies, sermons, religious visual images, religious drama, and hymns. But perhaps the most important source was the devotional manuals that achieved the wide popular interest indicated by their frequent publication in the centuries after they were written. The resources, as well as what modern people usually consider the horrors, of Christian tradition are most directly accessible, not in the philosophical theology of the past, but in devotional manuals, the best-seller, self-help literature of the Christian West. Theological writings exhibit neither the wealth of practical advice nor the blatantly dualistic, individualistic, and privatistic focus that characterizes the literature of Christian devotion. This literature provides the twentieth-century historian of Christianity with remarkably rich evidence for laypersons' training in Christianity.

The devotional manuals I have explored for information about the practices that translated Christian ideas, attitudes, and values into lifestyle and imbedded Christianity in people's bodies and relationships are among the most popular of the tradition: the fourteenth-century *Meditations on the Life of Christ*, Thomas à Kempis's *Imitation of Christ*, John Bunyan's *Pilgrim's Progress*, the nineteenth-century Russian Orthodox *Way of a Pilgrim*, Erasmus's *Enchiridion*, and Francis de Sales' *Introduction to the Devout Life*, to name only a few.

My interest in the literature of Christian devotion is partly personal and partly academic. As a child growing up in a fundamentalist Baptist parsonage, my imagination was awakened and stimulated—for better *and* for worse, as I now think—by an illustrated copy of *The Pilgrim's Progress* that was always on my bedside table. Moreover, as a scholar I am committed to learning whatever I can about the so-called ordinary people of the Christian West. The historical evidence that comes closest to telling me about them is the visual images and books that were accessible to people who had no theological education. Devotional manuals informed the fragile lives of people of the past; they told and showed them how to navigate the slippery banks and rushing waters of life's deep and unmapped river. I sense their lives as I read devotional manuals and I puzzle over ultimately unanswerable questions: How did these manuals affect the people who read and reread them? Did these books contribute to people's awareness of the singular preciousness and beauty of human lives? Or did their insistent reminders of death, eternity, and judgment bleach the vividness from earth's colors and block people's recognition of the divine worth of human love?

I have not been able finally to answer these questions, but I have developed a respect for the historical people who undertook to live examined and cultivated (chosen) lives. I have also learned not to presume to judge for historical people, whose complex circumstances I do not see in full, what ideas, attitudes, and values they *should* have held. But I too am a Christian, and so I am addressed by devotional manuals. I can neither read them with detachment, nor can I simply adopt their advice. Some of their methods and practices seem to me misguided; some seem potentially quite dangerous in the context of the world in which I live. If it means something to me to identify myself as within Christian tradition, however, I must scrutinize, analyze, and evaluate the complex inheritance to which I am heir. A hermeneutic of generosity regarding the choices made about their lives by historical people must not preclude a hermeneutic of suspicion in the present toward the instructions in the practice of Christianity given by devotional manuals. To adopt a critical approach seems to me to take seriously manuals that were not written to be read for anachronistic interest, but for personal use.

My reading of historical devotional manuals, then, is an active and disobedient reading, in the sense that I am alert to what is unintended, accidental, or so thoroughly assumed that it appears "natural" within the text's argument. Implications, effects, and rhetorical strategies are also clues to what underlies the text, namely, a problem to be addressed or, perhaps, an experience for which a method is proposed. These textual signals help me simultaneously to understand the author's project more clearly and to assess its usefulness to me in the world in which I live and in the light of what I hold most dear.

Finally, I am a historical theologian with contemporary interests rather than a contemporary theologian building a theological system for the present. The historical evidence I have read offers suggestions for contemporary reinterpretations of Christian tradition that I will sketch rather than a comprehensive theory that I will argue. Also, because I am accustomed to working with students and colleagues at the Harvard Divinity School who have diverse ecclesiastical affiliations, I do not picture, as I write, a single denominational community in which devotional instructions from the Christian past might function. I will therefore suggest, propose, and sometimes argue, interpretations of the Christian traditions that will necessarily be assigned different weights by people with different perspectives, interests, concerns and perceptions of what constitutes the main danger faced by the global community in the last decades of the twentieth century. Instead of designing a theology, I will try to demonstrate a method for evaluating the present usefulness of historical instruction in the practice of Christianity.

My parents are to be thanked for showing me the possibility of a life not organized by "whatever happens," but by what one can *do* with whatever happens. My husband, Owen C. Thomas of the Episcopal Divinity School in Cambridge, Massachusetts, first suggested that I teach and write on this topic, a topic I had thought too personal to explore in public. And I am indebted to Harriet Crabtree for valuable bibliographical suggestions.

# 1

# Introduction: Taking One's Life in One's Own Hands

*People know what they do; they frequently know why they do what they do; but what they don't know is what what they do does.*

*Michel Foucault[1]*

The care and cultivation of an interior life has fascinated human beings for many centuries. Certainly, human life contains an irreducibly high incidence of gratuitous conditions and events, but the possibility of shaping one's subjectivity and one's life in society within the wider parameter of the unpredictable—variously named as fate, the will of God, luck, or simply "life"—continues to intrigue thoughtful people. Socrates may have overstated his plea for self-awareness and conscious choice when he said, "The unexamined life [*anexetastos bios*] is not worth living."[2] But the alternative—reliance on the social conditioning provided by one's culture—has frequently been experienced as confining or even as dangerous.

Socrates advocated the pursuit of philosophy as the access to an examined life. But others have said that it is not only one's involuted psyche and disorderly and contradictory ideas that require attention. Scrutiny of the habitual practices that inevitably affect consciousness and behavior has also been repeatedly recommended and exercised. In *The Care of the Self* Michel Foucault described a *cura sui,* developed in the first two centuries of the common era, that produced "an accentuation of the relation of oneself to oneself." This *cura sui*

> took the form of an attitude, a mode of behavior; it became instilled in ways of living; it evolved into procedures, practices, and formulas that people reflected on, developed, perfected, and taught.[3]

Regimes involving diet, management of sex, physical exercise, and

1

meditation or prayer were used to gather and focus attention and energy and to give a heightened sense of agency and responsibility, a new "relation of oneself to oneself."

Practices that regulate and shape one's life have, in the history of the world, often been used by individuals or groups of people who have had the economic resources to ensure the necessary leisure for exercising a more-or-less full-time cultivation of body and mind. But less privileged people have also woven disciplined regimens into the fabric of busy lives. In Western Christianity a voluminous literature of manuals of instruction in the practice of Christianity—"self-help" manuals—existed. These manuals do not often argue theological issues; the advice they give is usually concerned with changing their readers' behavior. Altering habits, they assumed, can change perceptions and ideas; insight is at least as likely to follow change as change is to follow insight. "Practice" is whatever people do, and thinking is as much a practice as is ritual or daily routine. If one wishes to understand how the Christian tradition has been practiced rather than to understand only the ideas associated with Christianity, one must reconstruct the interweaving of ideas and activities that have characterized the practice of Christianity in the past.[4]

In addition, the person who wishes not only to understand historical Christianity but also to design a Christian practice for the present will find it equally important to analyze the world within which a contemporary practice of Christianity must be formulated. Thus our task is simultaneously historical and constructive; the past must inform the present, and our analysis of the present situation must lead to a critical evaluation of traditional values and practices. The guiding principle of this book is that the history of Christianity represents a rich resource for contemporary Christians; it also contains ideas, values, and practices that are deeply problematic in the context of the nuclear world.

Two features of the contemporary Western world make it especially urgent for twentieth-century Christians to examine our practice of Christianity. First, we live in an entertainment culture. The communication media assign to individuals the role of spectator, or passive voyeur. Without the television set, few of us can bear to sit quietly in our rooms, the activity Pascal said was a necessary condition for beginning to know oneself. Moreover, along with providing entertainment, the communication media condition attitudes and behavior, create our self-images, and create and shape desire by advertising consumer goods. All cultures, of course, have socialized their members to think and act in ways that support the social, economic, and political arrangements, but until recently none has possessed the technology necessary to inform, entertain, and condition massive populations continuously and cumulatively. In response to the passivity induced by an entertainment culture, an enormous literature of secular self-help has been produced in North America in the past decade. But curiously, this literature has not been effective in its advocacy of self-awareness and active choice. Rather, secular self-help manuals seem to have had the cumulative effect of confusing us with their contradictory theories, claims, and instructions.

Another urgent incentive for twentieth-century Christians to examine Christianity is our precarious existence in a nuclear world. Human beings have always lived in peril, vulnerable at any and every moment to accident, disease, and, ultimately and inevitably, death. But the possibility that humans could exterminate the human race and destroy life on the planet has existed only in approximately the last forty years. I will have more to say about the complex political, environmental, and social conditions condensed in the term "nuclear world." For now it is enough to suggest that the nuclear threat, together with cultural conditioning to passivity, has created a situation unique in the history of the world: "The temptation to lie down is very great,"[5] *and* the urgency of awareness and activity has never been greater.

It is my conviction that historical Christians who learned, under vastly different circumstances from ours, methods for "taking their lives in their own hands," in the best sense of the phrase, can inspire us to do the same. However, cultivation of one's self or soul cannot be an end in itself in a nuclear world. The contemporary practice of Christianity cannot have as its goal individual happiness or even, in the traditional term, individual salvation. Rather, in the nuclear world, an "examined life" is a moral responsibility. A life before God in our time requires a degree of social responsibility far greater than that recognized by most historical Christian writers.

This book will endeavor to engage the reader in both reflection on traditional instructions in living a Christian life and consideration of traditional Christian practices and values in relation to contemporary experience. Its task is threefold: to explore a variety of historical interpretations of what constitutes Christian living; to analyze the values—implicit or explicit—that inform these interpretations; and to develop a critical method for constructing a contemporary practice of Christianity. The reader must expect, then, not only to entertain ideas but also to evaluate the usefulness of traditional instructions for Christian practice in the last decades of the twentieth century.

What are the resources and some of the problems that we will encounter in examining historical Christian practices from a contemporary critical perspective? The primary source material for historical information about the practice of Christianity is the literature of Christian devotion, the best sellers of Christian traditions, the most popular and influential devotional instructions of an approximately two-thousand-year period, from early Christian writings to the early modern period, across a wide geographical distribution. For the time period before the age of printed manuals, I have selected the devotional instructions given by the most influential Christian writers; for the time after the sixteenth century, I have used manuals whose popularity is demonstrated by their appearance in many editions in the following centuries. These manuals were frequently not only the most popular among their genre but also the best-selling literature of any genre in their time.

My choice of the literature of practical instruction as primary evidence of historical Christianity represents a protest against the preference of historians and theologians for works of philosophical theology as sources of information about historical Christianity. The intellectual tradition of Christianity—the doctrines that summarize the essential ideas of Christian faith, and the philosophical and theological explanations and development of these ideas—has been understood as the primary access to the Christianity of the past. Identification of Christian tradition with philosophical theology, however, results in a picture of the past that is both elitist and sexist; Christian intellectuals of the past were usually the most uncharacteristic members of their communities, men whose social, cultural, and educational privilege permitted them the leisure to read and write, to think and discuss. The great majority of historical Christians had a much more pressing and immediate need for the orientation afforded by Christian ideas and practice than for intellectual precision. The exigencies of the lives of Christian laypersons placed stern demands on their religious provisions.

Most of the devotional manuals that will be discussed in this book were written for Christian lay people. They characteristically forego sophisticated theological arguments because they address people who have no specialized education in Christian theology. Although a few of the manuals that will be discussed were initially written for monastic audiences, their wide circulation and popular appeal in the centuries following their original publication can be documented by the number of manuscripts that scholars have found or, in the centuries following the invention of the printing press, by the number and volume of their editions. Also, devotional manuals originally written for monastic audiences often became models for lay people as well as for those with full-time religious vocations.

I have chosen the historical resources available to Christian lay people, however, for a reason more urgent than the intrinsic interest of such works. The ideal Christian life has often been thought of as the monastic life, while laypersons were seen as practicing at best a diluted version of that ideal life. Theologies of the laity have occasionally attempted to correct this model of a two-class system of Christians, but efforts to demonstrate the important place of lay people in Christian churches have not been as influential as the hierarchical distinction between "full-time" and "part-time" Christians, between clergy and monks on the one hand, and laity on the other.[6]

Manuals written for, and/or used by, Christian lay people will enable us to reconstruct the ideas and activities that informed and focused the practice of Christianity in Christian communities. But written texts were not the only means of communication among predominantly illiterate communities in the Christian West. Most people, we need to remind ourselves, did not receive their religious information from books. In addition to sermons, scripture readings, and religious drama, they received a rich and varied range of religious messages from religious images on walls and altars of their parish churches. Religious images told stories, provided models of devotional engagement, and focused the emotional lives of Christians; they were part of the media of historical Christianity, accessible to all people in Christian communities on a daily basis. Until the sixteenth century, when iconoclasm in some branches of the Protestant Reformation created churches with bare walls and altars, religious images instructed Christians in the practice of Christianity. Even intellectuals acknowledged being moved, taught, and shaped by them.

Although this book will not extensively explore religious images in liturgical settings,[7] we will notice that many devotional manuals were illustrated. John Bunyan's *Pilgrim's Progress,* perhaps the most popular Christian devotional manual of all time in the Christian West, was liberally illustrated with woodcuts that encouraged the reader to visualize the pilgrimage of the protagonist, Christian, and his companions toward the Heavenly City in order to imitate it. The influence of illustrations on people whose imaginations were not crowded with a glut of media images must not be ignored as we reconstruct historical instructions in the practice of Christianity.

In short, if we want to understand the history of Christianity, not as the history of a few philosophically inclined educated men but as the struggle of Christian people to live a Christian life, we will need different historical evidence than the theological treatises that have provided the intellectual histories of Christianity. Most people created a meaningful life in Christian communities by the use of religious messages interpreted for them by sermons, paintings, religious drama, and devotional manuals—the media of people of the past. The overriding concern of most historical Christians was primarily a practical concern: how to live a Christian life in the face of the expectation of an inevitable judgment in which their destiny of everlasting reward or punishment would be decided by an omniscient and unbiased judge (see fig. 1). Historians have not yet explored rigorously enough the effect of such a belief on people of the past; because most modern historians do not subscribe to this belief, we tend to discount it as the strongly motivating and organizing pressure it was for those who did.

A methodological point follows from the claim that pressing practical interests rather than theology or doctrine motivated historical Christians: identification of the complex of theological ideas that supported religious practices is not adequate to explain the properly *religious* aspect of that practice. The affective intensity—the passion—with which historical Christians prayed, served the sick and the poor, journeyed on pilgrimage, and solicited mystical communion with Christ cannot be "explained" by the theological rationale accompanying these practices. Attempting to explain religious phenomena by theological ideas is a category error that has been repeatedly committed by historians and historical theologians. The result is that people of the past are, in modern eyes, reduced to the ideas we think they held. Their vividness, their intensity, their passion, and their irreducible alienness has been glossed over. In fact, people of the past did what they did for complex and perhaps ultimately inscrutable reasons—reasons that we may be more or less successful in reconstructing. Their fasts, pilgrimages, persecution of dissidents, rituals, and visions were not primarily the result of their study of theology, but represent their enactment of religious provisions that enabled them to comprehend their lives and make choices about them, to achieve self-esteem, to manage social arrangements, and ultimately, they hoped, to achieve eternal salvation. Although religious practices cannot be explained by identifying the theological ideas that rationalize them, theology and religious practice are interrelated; practical advice assumes a conceptual framework within which the advice specifies the practices that embody the world view, idea of God, and religious values of its author.

Moreover, manuals of instruction in the practice of Christianity are frequently more explicit about their agendas than are theological texts. Since, by definition, the authors of instructional writing are concerned to promote activities and attitudes that enable the reader to live fruitfully as a Christian, manuals are characteristically more explicit than theological texts in identifying the fears or longings that should motivate and stimulate the reader or hearer. They make the connection between the theoretical and the practical explicit—aspects of human life that are, in fact, never disconnected, except, perhaps, in academic analysis.[8] Manuals permit us to recognize what the author held dear and advocated for readers; by identifying the author's assumptions and values, we can

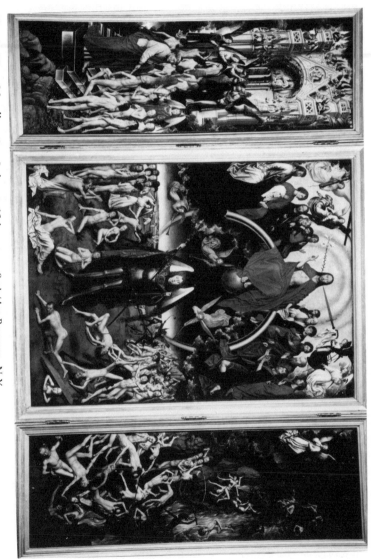

Fig. 1. Hans Memling, *Last Judgment*, 15th century. Scala/Art Resource, N.Y.

evaluate more readily the usefulness of the author's instructions for the twentieth century.

Historical manuals of instruction in the practice of Christianity comprise a very diverse literature, not only in instructions given but also in literary quality. The fact that it is such a large and diverse body of writing makes it clear that do-it-yourself manuals on how to live a Christian life were attractive to a large number of people. Each manual has a strong and vivid interpretation of Christianity, a way of construing the world and human life that is passionately held and articulately expressed. The authors of devotional manuals, clergy and monks, women and men, are people who had accepted the trouble, the discomfort, and frequently, the pain of a quest for self-knowledge, who had explored their own and others' predilections and aversions, and had discovered or created methods they found helpful for moving toward a more centered and loving life. Their methods can sometimes give us suggestions for our own practice of Christianity, but, more importantly, we can always learn from their struggle: their *work,* not necessarily their conclusions, can be our models and guides for our own activity of designing a contemporary practice of Christianity.

Historical devotional manuals, however, are frequently difficult reading for twentieth-century Christians. They often contain advice that contradicts our own clearest self-knowledge. Symeon, the so-called New Theologian of the Eastern Orthodox Church, for example, describes the essence of the practice of Christianity as "fleeing the world and ridding oneself of passions." One must act, he wrote, "as though he had wholly lost his own life."9 Advice like this sounds diametrically opposed to our twentieth-century preference for affirming "passions," senses, and our own lives. Before we could evaluate the usefulness, for us, of Symeon's advice, we would need to look very carefully at what Symeon meant by "passions" and "fleeing the world." But his energetic, committed effort to craft an interior life in faithfulness to his understanding of God, the world, and his own nature can be a challenge and inspiration for us.

Nevertheless, in trying to understand with some precision what Symeon and others meant by their key terms, I will not endeavor to render their alien perceptions of the world and their pious practices completely comfortable and agreeable to us. Even after we have used a hermeneutic of generosity in a strenuous effort to grasp the insight the author wishes to communicate, we will frequently find that there are aspects of historical authors' thought that stubbornly refuse to fit our interpretations, but must be allowed to remain alien. In these instances we will need to ask how the author's values differ from those of many twentieth-century Christians so that misunderstanding or nonnegotiable disagreement persists between the text and the twentieth-century interpreter. A host of intriguing questions arises when we approach manuals of instruction with the aim both of understanding historical people better and evaluating whether the manual's values, methods, and goals are useful and useable in the twentieth century.

Another difficulty arises when different—and sometimes opposite—instructions occur in different devotional manuals. We will indeed find a variety of different proposals in these manuals for organizing a Christian life; different ideas and practices are placed at the center of importance, and there are even contradictory recommendations in different manuals as to which practices should be done at all. The diversity of these proposals can also help us to recognize that a Christian life may be much more one of self-conscious, ongoing alertness to the need for correcting one's particular propensities—"temptations," historical Christians called them—than a matter of discovering universal prescriptions, equally useful and pressing on everyone who undertakes to live as a Christian.

We will ask, then, for what sort of person in what historical circumstances the author's prescription was designed. That is, in very concrete terms, *who*—man or woman, of what age, class, physical condition, or occupation—might profit from these instructions. The manual itself may imply or state its ideal reader, but it seldom describes her. Rather, devotional manuals claim implicitly or explicitly to be universally valid. Their universalizing rhetoric even operates to steer the reader away from questions about the gender, social location, education, and state of health of the manual's ideal reader. It makes a great difference, for example, whether the ideal reader is in excellent health or is desperately ill; different practices, visual images, and ideas will be appropriate to people in these conditions. Yet many devotional manuals seem to assume that the normative human condition, the condition one must conceptually, if not physically, create is to imagine oneself at the point of death.

Questions concerning the historical location of authors and original readers of devotional manuals do not assume or imply the complete relativism of all advice on the practice of Christianity. I do not advocate or formulate a historicism that reduces all meaning to the conditions under which it arose. It is, however, possible *both* to understand the text as part of a complex historical situation which has shaped the style and content of the writing *and* to find that some of the insights formulated under this historical pressure are relevant and useful for me in *my* historical situation, while some are not. The effort to historicize a written document becomes an evasion of engagement with the document's content only when one refuses to entertain the possibility that there might be some "detachable" insight, some meaning that could be translated or reinterpreted in such a way that by it I am helped to understand my life. Reconstruction of the historical situation of the author of a devotional manual, then, does not preclude present use of the author's insights, but enables us to understand the manual more fully, to reconstruct it as a living text, functioning in a human life or lives, a text embodied in the Christian communities in which it was read and valued.

Educated twentieth-century people, however, are probably not so much tempted by our predilection for contextualizing normative statements as by our ability to entertain different analyses without trying to decide which provides the most accurate and fruitful account in the context of ourselves and our world. It is the moment of appropriation that we evade. This "openness" is frequently an appropriate stance; we see many situations in both personal and public arenas "through a glass darkly." But this praiseworthy reluctance to form strong opinions on matters we do not see with clarity can also become an escape from self-knowledge. There is a more-or-less accessible *truth* about one's interior life. Like one's body, one's psyche (soul or self) actually exists in a particular state of health or malnutrition—of equilibrium or disequilibrium. This condition can, with work, be discerned, addressed, and either maintained or treated. All instruction in the practice of Christianity assumed the possibility of accurate discernment and treatment.

For twentieth-century people, alerted to the existence of gender assumptions in our own society, there is a further difficulty in reading the authors of devotional manuals. The use of male language is pervasive in devotional literature. The male language of these texts is symptomatic of the male perspective that has dominated historical writing.[10] Valerie Saiving has written:

> Of course it would be ridiculous to deny that there is a structure of experience common to both men and women, so that we may legitimately speak of "the human situation" without reference to sexual identity. The only question is whether we have described the human situation accurately by taking into account the experience of both sexes.[11]

The universalized male perspective of the historical societies from which devotional literature came affects the assumptions, agendas, and particular advice given by particular manuals.

Whether the male language of historical texts should be translated as neutral or inclusive language is a perplexing question. The universalization of a male perspective is an endemic problem in historical Christian literaure, a problem that cannot be made to disappear by the relatively simple device of inclusive translation. I therefore do not automatically translate historical texts euphemistically; to do so would be to mask the consistent gender bias of historical Christianity, a bias that must be allowed to show. A *historical* decision is required concerning the legitimacy of translating inclusively: if the author understands himself or herself to be addressing men, and/or if the text reveals the author's assumption that the male is normative, male language must remain.

Historical people—women and men—did not have a twentieth-century sensitivity to issues of gender conditioning, the author's social location, and the inevitable operation of power relations, of course, and it is certainly important to understand the concerns and interests that *consciously* motivated their projects. Nevertheless, if their instructions in the practice of Christianity are to be read—as they intended—as offering serious advice for the cultivation of a spiritual life and a religious practice, we must not *only* read them for historical knowledge—for anachronistic curiosity—but we must bring to them the questions and issues to which our own personal and cultural experience has sensitized us.

My usage in the terminology of gender analysis may be evident by now: "sex" in relation to male and female human beings denotes no more than biological difference. "Gender," on the other hand, indicates the social conditioning of masculinity and femininity.[12] I assume that it will never be known if, or to what extent, biological differences of women and men determine behavior; we will never find individuals who have not received gender conditioning because there is no society that has not developed a host of strategies for training individuals to gender roles and expectations.[13]

The purpose of examining the ways in which gender assumptions and the universalization of a male perspective have influenced devotional writing in the Christian traditions is not, then, to assume that an ideal society in which all roles and opportunities are equally open to all could exist. Nor is it anachronistically to castigate historical authors for their lack of sensitivity to a late twentieth-century issue. Rather, alertness to the influence of gender assumptions in religious texts will help us to understand the effect as well as the intent of historical texts. We will ask: How does a text both reflect and reinforce the relative values, roles, and expectations of women and men in the culture for which it was originally written?

To readers who are concerned with "orthodoxy," the acknowledgment that one can—and must—evaluate, judge, and reject some aspects of Christian tradition may appear dangerous. A closer examination of historical Christianity, however, will make us aware that all that is genuinely nontraditional about the task of sorting useful from peripheral or even dangerous ideas, images, and practices is the explicit acknowledgment that we are doing so. Religious leaders of the past found, focused, and emphasized aspects of Christian faith that they found useful and useable; then, instead of critiquing and rejecting other aspects, they simply ignored them. But they adjusted the weight, the central focus, and the emotional intensity of Christian faith in radically new ways that responded to the religious needs of their contemporaries. The activity of continuous reappropriation *is* what it means to participate in a tradition. The strategy employed by most theologians of the past to mask their innovations was their claim to be simply identifying the "true" Christianity, the Christianity of "the early church." There is, in short, no way to avoid the critical appropriation of Christian tradition; the only choice is whether to do so explicitly or implicitly.

Moreover, there is no value-free appropriation; a complex of personal and cultural values is always engaged in interpretation. Historical authors in the Christian traditions frequently claimed a God's-eye view based on scriptural or ecclesiastical authority. Yet the claim to be speaking for God often concealed a socially and institutionally privileged voice. Women, Blacks, and Third World people have only recently participated in theological discussion in critical masses. This pluralism has created a new awareness that *all* human beings speak from a perspective that both informs and limits our analyses and evaluations, our descriptions and prescriptions. Under these conditions—the "universal" condition of human speech—we can speak *about* God but no one can speak *for God*.

Finally, a critical appropriation of Christian tradition requires that the interpreter relate her theological agenda to the world in which she lives and speaks. Only when we know how an author perceives the contemporary world can we agree or disagree in an informed way with her theological prescriptions for that world. For example, I have referred to the contemporary world in which theological discourse is conducted as the "nuclear world." The fact that we exist in a global crisis unique in the history of the world seems to me the most pressing aspect of the present that needs to be taken into account by present religious practices. Yet the "nuclear world" is perhaps only the most vivid symptom that presents itself. The capacity to exterminate the human race and destroy the biosphere may be the bottom line of the global crisis, but it functions, in my usage, to represent a complex of interrelated geopolitical policies and world problems such as hunger, population, ecology, exploitation and oppression of all kinds, and unjust distribution of wealth. Unless the relationship of Christian practice to the "nuclear world" can be demonstrated, we are in danger either of cultivating a dead religion or of participating in religious practices that are narcissistic and escapist. Moreover, the fact that nuclear weapons were invented in the predominantly

Christian West places a responsibility on people whose lives have been fundamentally shaped by Christianity to examine the tradition both for its destructive aspects and for its resources for the present.

The nuclear world is at least partly the product of a tradition in which human bodies have not been sufficiently valued in spite of doctrines of creation, Incarnation, and resurrection of the body that would seem to affirm human body-selves. Oddly, these central tenets of Christian faith do not seem as characteristic of Christianity as centuries of practical advice to deny, despise, and even to damage one's body in harsh ascetic practices. The notion of human transcendence over the material conditions of human life has created some endemic problems in Christian tradition, problems that perhaps have only become fully visible and urgently pressing in the contemporary world.

One might ask, why look for resources for a nuclear world in a tradition that has fostered attitudes of contempt for living bodies and the natural world? It is my conviction that, just as human beings do not personally choose the problems we inherit, we similarly cannot create *ex nihilo* the tools with which to confront the problems we have inherited. People do not create in the same way that the Hebrew Bible describes God's creation—out of nothing. Our creativity—a real creativity—can be exercised by finding and pressing into service tools that are unused or underdeveloped in Christian tradition. As participants in a very small world, as members of an endangered species, we have a responsibility to suggest any resources—ideas, images, or practices—that can be identified in Christian tradition for addressing the mammoth problems of the nuclear world.

These may be resources that perhaps have never been given adequate expression in images or articulated in such a way that people find them compelling. Or perhaps, like the doctrines I mentioned above, they have been given forceful historical expression but their contemporary relevance and significance need to be specified. In addition to surveying the history of Christianity for resources relevant to the nuclear world, we also need to explore the religious significance of contemporary activities we usually think of as secular—political engagement, peace and justice activism, and participation in the women's movement or in environmental concern groups. And we must incorporate suggestions from other religious traditions that have valued the natural world more consistently and articulately than has Christianity. Our attitude in seeking resources within Christianity cannot be one of confident assurance that the resources of a tradition that has contributed to the creation of a nuclear world will be effective in relieving its pressing needs. Rather our attitude must be one of stubborn courage in the face of what appear to be overwhelming obstacles and peril.

The Anglo-Saxon epic poem *Beowulf*[14] provides a metaphor that describes the creativity with which historical resources must be identified
and used in present crises. As the epic begins, Beowulf, the warrior hero,
is called upon to rid the community of a monster who regularly appears at
night when Beowulf's fighting men are asleep, snatching several of them
to carry off to devour in her[15] watery home deep in a virtually bottomless
lake. In order to do battle with the monster, Beowulf arms himself with
his trusted sword. At this point the poem proceeds to spend several less
than edifying pages listing the sword's credentials by naming the noble,
fearless, and mighty warriors it has killed. The narrative continues:
Beowulf trails the monster to her den in the bottom of the bottomless
lake, raises his sword to strike her, and finds to his horror that it melts in
his hand. Desperate, he looks around for a weapon, grabs various imple-
ments and cooking utensils off the wall—literally "off the wall"—and
manages to kill the monster.

What the story articulates—perhaps more vividly than is necessary for
purposes of making my point—is that weapons or tools that have served
well on other historical occasions may not be the best ones with which to
do present work. Tools with which to understand and address our world
may be provided within Christian tradition, but they may not be those
which have dominated the tradition. Or, they may not have been the
favored ideas and images of the *people* who have dominated historical
communities.

The first section of this book will explore the three metaphors for
Christian life most frequently developed in devotional literature: Christian
life as the imitation of Christ, as pilgrimage, and as ascent. I will discuss
historical interpretations of each of these metaphors, asking at the conclusion of the discussion of each whether the metaphor seems fruitful for
twentieth-century North American Christians. The second section of the
book will examine some characteristic Christian activities, like prayer,
service, and ascetic disciplines. As in the first section, I will describe a
wide range of instructions about the relative importance and practice of
each activity, asking in the conclusion of each chapter whether these
traditional Christian activities address contemporary needs. The third
section of the book will discuss some issues arising from the practice of
Christianity that are problematic to many twentieth-century Christians. A
certain amount of repetition of the themes and metaphors is inevitable in a
discussion of devotional manuals. The overlapping of ideas, metaphors,
and illustrations in devotional literature reveals not only the common goal

of inciting readers to the energetic pursuit of Christian life but also their authors' respect for the effectiveness of traditional conventions and stylistic strategies. I will begin by discussing metaphors that commanded a strong consensus as the most accurate and vivid scenarios within which to imagine and conduct Christian life.

# Part One

# Metaphors of
# Christian Life

# Introduction to Part One

*Religion has been efficacious because it is* not *theology, because it makes abstract principles concrete, incarnating Good and Evil, Satan as villain, Christ as hero.*

*Roger R. Rollin[1]*

In order to live a Christian life, one must first imagine such a life, must visualize what it might look like, might feel like. In the history of Christianity, metaphors have been a primary device for providing a setting and lending vividness to the ideas and practices that embody Christian life. Metaphors govern understanding by suggesting that an unknown and ineffable entity, life, can best be understood as an activity one knows something about—pilgrimage, for example. This comparison of an unknown to a known entity, Sallie McFague writes, is "the way language and more basically, thought works."[2] The power of metaphor cannot be overestimated; metaphors are not ornament, but meaning itself, and one metaphor cannot be substituted for another without significant change in meaning.

In the twentieth century, for example, the metaphor of revolutionary struggle informs the Christian practice of thousands of base communities in Central and South America. In Christianity understood as revolutionary struggle, people worship, pray, study scripture, and participate in sacraments in order to achieve the communal solidarity and empowerment necessary for acting in society to bring about political change. A generation ago, another metaphor, the metaphor of exodus—God's leading of an oppressed people to freedom—informed the deeply religious civil rights movement in the United States. Both of these metaphors, revolutionary struggle and exodus, highlight engagement and action, vigorous participation in the public world of politics and society.

Before the twentieth century, metaphors usually focused less on struggle against unjust social arrangements and oppressive governments than on individual struggle to renounce the social world. Society and the "transient" rewards of the social world have frequently been understood as enemies of a Christian life. The monastic movement that gathered mo-

19

mentum in the fourth century, for example, was initially a lay movement of literal withdrawal from family and society for purposes of seeking self-knowledge, the intermediate goal and the road to the ultimate goal, the kingdom of God. For monks, the metaphor of ascent, pictured as climbing a ladder, interpreted progress in Christian life as increments of distance from the cares and delights of the earth. This metaphor assumes the context of a stable life in which one can assess progress; it is not as congruent with a busy life in a rapidly changing world. Moreover, featuring removal from "the world," and assuming a full-time practice as it does, this metaphor has not been as useful as some others for people who undertake to live a life that is "in the world, but not of the world." Pilgrimage, moving through the world of human societies as through a strange and alien place, perhaps has been the most frequently used metaphor of Christian life for lay people. Before the sixteenth century, however, pilgrimage was not primarily a metaphor, but was a literal practice by which people achieved a fundamental dehabituation from their accustomed environment. The metaphor's suggestive power lies in its insistence that interwoven in the daily life of a person who undertakes to live as a Christian is an element of detachment from the business of secular life. The weakness of pilgrimage as metaphor from a twentieth-century perspective is that it does not provide an impetus or a rationale for social action.

Similarly, the metaphor of Christian life as warfare has strengths and weaknesses: understanding Christian life as war certainly presents forcefully the need for watchfulness and energetic engagement, but it has also been used to present the world—other people, the natural world, even one's own body—as hostile and threatening. It fails to evoke love for creation and for living creatures in their beauty and goodness. Yet the metaphor of Christian life as war has been an influential one in historical Christianity; it has functioned both as a structuring image in devotional literature, and as a leitmotiv woven through other metaphors.

# 2

# An Image of the Image:
# Imitation of Christ

*And because God is love, and the Son likewise, whoever is of God is love; he requires in us something like himself, so that through this love which is in Christ Jesus, we may be allied to God who is love, as if in a sort of blood relationship through the name of love.*

*Origen,* On the Song of Songs, *Prologue*

Perhaps the most frequently developed traditional metaphor is Christian life as imitation of Christ. Interpretations of what it means to imitate Christ vary widely, and we will explore a range of these interpretations, from Saint Francis of Assisi's literal participation in the suffering of the crucified Christ to less flamboyant imitations of the virtues of Christ's life and ministry. Let us begin, however, by considering the theology that underlies this model of Christian life.

How is it possible for human beings to imitate Christ? The foundation of advocacy of the imitation of Christ is the scriptural statement that human beings were created in the image of God. If humanity was made in God's image, the actualization of human nature lies in developing this similarity to the divine. An actualized likeness to God, however, was lost in the sin of Adam and Eve, so that all that remains is the faint image. The image is built-in, indestructible, a lifelong characteristic of human beings. Nevertheless, although the image of God cannot be completely lost, neither can it be developed without divine help due to its badly warped condition, the result of human sin. Patristic authors like Athanasius used the image of a damaged painting to describe the state of the image in sinful humanity. [1]

Gregory of Nyssa also used the image of human nature as a partly obliterated painting in his treatise *On Perfection*: Christ, because of his love for humanity, became himself an "image of the invisible God"; he took on physical form, modeling "a beauty in accord with the character of the Archetype."

> Just as when we are learning the art of painting, the teacher puts before us on the panel a beautifully executed model, and it is necessary for each student to imitate in every way the beauty of that model on his own panel, so that the panels of all will be adorned in accordance with the beauty that was set before them: in the same way, since every person is the painter of his own life, and choice is the craftsman of the work, and the virtues are the paints for executing the image, . . . one must prepare the pure colors of the virtues, mixing them with each other according to some artistic formula for beauty, so that we become an image of the image.[2]

Christ reveals, in living flesh, what God is so that human beings can see, in this translation of divinity into body, the possibility of rehabilitation—as one restores an old and damaged painting to freshness of line and vividness of color—of the image of God in oneself.

Diverse interpretations of what it means to imitate Christ appear in instructional manuals in the practice of Christianity. We will explore several representative descriptions: Thomas à Kempis's *Imitation of Christ,* Gregory of Nyssa's *On Perfection, The Little Flowers of St. Francis,* and the illustrated fourteenth-century manuscript *Meditations on the Life of Christ.* Each urges the imitation of Christ but describes the practices informing such an imitation differently.

*The Imitation of Christ* was the most popular devotional text of the fifteenth century and one of the most popular manuals in the history of Christianity. It was written by a monk, Thomas à Kempis (1380–1471), who was involved in the late medieval popular religious movement, the *Devotio Moderna,* or New Devotion. Although it was founded by monks of the Brethren of the Common Life under the direction of Gerhard Groote (1340–84), the New Devotion quickly became a lay movement, inspiring gatherings of hundreds of groups of people in the Netherlands and eventually reaching into southern Europe. Motivated by the then novel idea that life in the world did not necessarily exclude one from being a real Christian but could become itself a spiritual discipline, the New Devotion had no vows. The movement was simultaneously a rejection of the "full-time" model of Christian practice, a denial that one could only engage in a complete religious life in the setting of a monastery or convent, and an attempt to describe what a different kind of full-time engagement in Christian life might look like for people who worked, loved, and lived "in the world." Members were expected to continue their accustomed lives, informed by communal study and discussion of scripture and prayer. Education was important to the movement, and free education accompanied the spread of the New Devotion. The revolutionary potential of the idea of an ordinary life as spiritual discipline is attested by the rapid growth of the movement. By shaping the inner life of the individual around meditation on the life and passion of Christ, the imitation of Christ could be achieved in the midst of the most demanding of lives.

*The Imitation of Christ* is typical of Christian self-help manuals in its greater concern with issues surrounding practice than with theology or doctrine. Defining imitation of Christ as meditation on the life of Jesus, Thomas describes meditation, not as a mental exercise, but as "making one's whole life conform to the pattern of Christ's life." By "Christ's life," he means his interior life, not Christ's external deeds. Book 1, "Some Thoughts to help with the Spiritual Life," takes up some standard devotional themes of his time: "having a humble opinion of oneself"; "avoiding excessive familiarity"; "the miseries of our human state"; and "considering one's death." Book 2 continues with "Some Advice on the Inner Life," but book 3, specifically addressed to "Spiritual Comfort" comprises the bulk of *The Imitation.* Here Thomas argues that the only true comfort is to be found in "spurning the whole world and becoming the servant of God."[3] *The Imitation* concludes, in book 4, with "A Reverent Recommendation to Holy Communion" in which Thomas describes the preparatory meditations and penances that can make participation in the sacrament a strongly felt experience.

From *The Imitation of Christ* we can gain some understanding of how an unaccustomed pressure was brought to bear on individuals in order to create a new relation "of the self to the self," a new relation of the individual to the group, and a new sense of relationship to God. The New Devotion represented, in its own time, a skillful reconstruction of the "self," an intensification of Christian life that *produced* the "self" it addressed. In *The Imitation* the individual is no longer seen as primarily a social entity, gripped by conditioning, limited by economic and political restraints, but as a unique self constituted by listening and speaking to God. The forceful pressure on the individual to exchange her or his "natural' predilections toward a comfortable life for a life focused on relationship to God was balanced in the severity of its demands by the support and counsel of a group of similarly engaged people.

Much of the advice of *The Imitation* is not congenial to twentieth-century people. Thomas à Kempis spoke in violent imagery of "crushing one's natural feelings," of "killing the old impulses"; he names as enemies the passions, emotions, desires, and even one's own body. "The highest and most profitable form of study is to understand one's inmost nature and despise it," he wrote. This rhetoric attempts to demonstrate the value of a chosen, consciously shaped, cultivated Christian life in contrast to a life thoroughly programmed by cultural conditioning. Thomas's use of the word *natural* also needs careful interpretation: in context he seems to mean that feelings that seem to appear "naturally" are not to be regarded as either inevitable or normative, but can be changed.

Twentieth-century people, many of whom have learned that one's socialization or cultural conditioning is frequently inadequate and confining, and have set out to change habitual responses, can perhaps understand Thomas à Kempis's project even if the violence of his language makes us recoil and the enemies he names are not our perceived enemies. Anyone who has tried to change her conditioning in order to cultivate a richer life, a wider repertoire of responses to people and events, and a greater energy for love and work knows both how difficult it is to change settled habits, attitudes, and feelings *and* that it can be done. Reading Thomas à Kempis with a hermeneutic of generosity requires that we bring to his advice the experience we have that matches the sense of intensity and urgency we get from his rhetoric.[4]

In *The Imitation* we find some of the ideas of Christian tradition that most trouble twentieth-century people. For example:

> It is a wretched thing to have to live on earth; life here becomes steadily more distasteful to anyone who is longing to be more spiritual, for such a person is always seeing more clearly and feeling more deeply the shortcomings of our mortal state; for eating and drinking, waking and sleeping, resting and working, and submitting to all that our body demands, proves a great hardship and misery to the devout person, who longs to have done with it all and be freed from all sin. The needs of the body in this world are certainly a great burden to the inner self.[5]

These statements raise an issue that reappears in devotional manuals throughout Christian tradition. Statements of *metaphysical* dualism[6] are precluded in Christian tradition by the central doctrines of creation and the Incarnation of Christ, doctrines that affirm the value and integrity of bodies and the "sensible world." Yet one of the most powerful strategies of a cultivated life—not only in Christian tradition but also in the philosophical schools of antiquity as well as in other religions—was to regard one's body as the site of immoderate appetites and unwelcome desires and to design ascetic practices that discipline the body. Alienating a part of the self in order to focus on other parts or functions left underdeveloped by socialization is one of the constant tools of those upwardly mobile in the religious life.

Most often the body has been identified as the part of human being responsible for dangerous insubordination. Historical people feared that the body contained potential for uncontrollable betrayal of the whole person by a part of the person. Old people whose bodies no longer function well and sick people whose bodies prevent them from caring for their own physical needs and doing the things they enjoy may understand more readily than those in robust good health the antagonism toward the body often exhibited by historical texts. This identification of the reader most likely to be sympathetic to Thomas à Kempis's identification of "the enemy" may not make it any more useful for twentieth-century people. It can, however, at least suggest that the context we need for understanding *The Imitation* is the helplessness of medieval people in the face of illness and accident and their inability effectively to alleviate pain. The pandemic plague that swept Europe in the generation before Thomas à Kempis was born and continued to flare in various locations about once in every generation for the next several centuries also provides an essential piece of the setting for his instructions.

Another feature of *The Imitation* that may distress modern readers is the implied individualism of Thomas à Kempis's instructions. Other people may help or hinder the one who seeks to cultivate a Christian life. Instructions to flee crowds, seek solitude, and, on occasion, to spurn family and friends appear as a leitmotiv: "If you give up unnecessary conversation, idle walking about, and listening to news and talk, you will find plenty of time which you can devote to good meditation."[7] On the other hand, communal study, prayer, and discussion of Christian life was the New Devotion's major strategy for converting lives. In this context, Thomas cannot overestimate the importance of generosity in one's regard for others; other people can be indispensable for support and challenge; if necessary, they can even be understood as spiritual discipline: if everyone were perfect, we should have nothing

> to bear from other people for the sake of God. As it is, he has made things the way they are so that we may learn to bear the burden of another's failings. There is no one free from weakness, no one without a load to carry, no one who is self-sufficient, no one who can dispense with others' help; and so it is our duty to support each other, to comfort each other, to help, guide and advise each other.[8]

Thomas's insistence on a double hermeneutic of suspicion and generosity in "reading" other people's behavior and intentions may seem to us inconsistent with his steady advice to "despise" oneself. We know that we usually suffer more from thinking too harshly, rather than too highly, of ourselves. We recognize the impossibility of loving others if we do not love ourselves. From a twentieth-century perspective, the gospel command, "Love your neighbor as yourself," might read as a statement of fact: "[You do] love your neighbor as yourself," rather than as an injunction. If we take Thomas's instruction to "despise" the self too literally as a psychological disposition, we will miss the point of practical importance: despising the socialized "self" is, for Thomas à Kempis, the best kind of care for "oneself," an attention to the aspect of the self that is capable of listening and speaking to God at the expense of the phenomenal, conditioned self.

Much more could be said about *The Imitation of Christ,* and we will return to this enormously popular manual in discussing other issues. Our purpose here is to recover a range of historical interpretations of what it meant to understand Christian life as an imitation of Christ. Thomas à Kempis defines the imitation of Christ as a meditation on the inner life of Jesus. By meditation, one's life begins to conform to "the pattern of Christ's life." Since the inner life of the historical Jesus is not readily accessible, and since Thomas does not, in *The Imitation,* exegete the Gospels for suggestions about Jesus' inner life, Thomas's translation of Jesus' inner life into attitudes, practices, and lifestyle was dependent on two sources: Christian tradition—especially the monastic devotional tradition of which he was a part—and his own experience in cultivating a Christian life. *The Imitation,* though it was written as part of a movement of lay devotion and was used by lay people, still explicitly addresses monks; implicitly, however, it assumes the usefulness of the instructions for all who wish to live a full-time Christian life, whether in a monastery or in the world.

Saint Gregory of Nyssa (d. 395) was a bishop in Cappadocia, the brother of Saint Basil and friend of Saint Gregory Nazianzus. The influence of his thought on the Eastern Orthodox Christian churches has been profound. Gregory considered spiritual perfection, or deification, to be the goal of Christian life and to be attainable in this world by the earnest seeker. Deification is the doctrine that human beings can, through liturgy, participation in the sacraments, and devotional piety share in the divine energy brought into the world of human experience by the Incarnation of Christ. Although intellectual knowledge of God beyond what has been revealed in scripture is not possible for human beings, through human cooperation with God—synergy—full participation in the divine energy of love is a present possibility for Christians.

Gregory of Nyssa's definition of the imitation of Christ appears in his treatise *On Perfection.* Human beings, created in God's image, can learn by imitation of Christ, who participated fully in both the divine and the human realms, how to actualize the image of God. Gregory lists the attributes of Christ, analyzing those that human beings can imitate, and those that cannot be imitated; the latter should be worshiped:

> The marks of the true Christian are all those we know in connection with Christ. Those that we have capacity for we imitate, and those which our nature does not approximate by imitation, we reverence and worship. Thus, it is necessary for the Christian life to illustrate all the interpretive terms signifying Christ, some through imitation, others through worship.[9]

Gregory divides Christ's attributes into two kinds: attributes associated with wisdom and those associated with power. Both kinds of attributes are accessible to Christians. Christ as peace, as light, as redemption, as life, and as spiritual nourishment makes the reality of these characteristics available to the one who bears Christ's name. Gregory's proposal for the imitation of Christ, then, focuses on scriptural—especially Pauline—accounts of Christ's wisdom and power, and the Christian's realization that his participation in Christ's life and body permits him to share Christ's attributes. Gregory carefully limits his account of the imitation of Christ to what is revealed in scripture, abstaining from "theories concerning the divine nature."[10]

Like *The Imitation of Christ,* Gregory is concerned not only with right belief but with a practice of Christianity that steadily weaves one's body and life into the divine life. Gregory recognizes that

> Human nature is not simple, but . . . there is an intelligible part mixed with a sensual part and . . . a particular type of nurture is needed for each of the elements in us, sensible food to strengthen our bodies, and spiritual food for the well-being of our souls.[11]

The two aspects of human being must both be engaged in a Christian life: "The beauty of the chief cornerstone [Christ] sets off our building when our dual existence, straight and true, is harmoniously set up according to the right rule of life by the plumb line of the virtues, having nothing in itself that is bent or crooked."[12] Platonic influence on Gregory is evident in his awareness that a development of mind is not sufficient apart from engagement of the body; Plato had written: "Never exercise the body without the mind, or the mind without the body."[13]

Gregory's method is scholarly and biblical, but it is also passionate. Yet Gregory names the passions as the factor of human life that is most likely to alienate the Christian from God. Why write a passionate treatise about the evil of the passions? Why understand Christ as "passionless," and the source of passionlessness in contradiction to Gospel accounts of Christ's anger, sadness, and compassion? A partial answer to these questions lies in an enriched understanding of the Greek word *apatheia*.

*Apatheia* is an extraordinarily difficult word to translate, and the English word *passionlessness* is a misleading translation in terms of twentieth-century connotations. *Apatheia* took different nuances of meaning from the different contexts in which it was used, and can mean lack of feeling, or insensibility, freedom from emotion, detachment and tranquility, or—as frequently in Christian usage—freedom from sin.[14] Gregory was careful to explain his use of the term in *On Perfection*. Freedom from sin is the meaning of *apatheia* here; the one who rejects, by his way of living, any of Christ's attributes (truth, justice, holiness, etc.) becomes as much a sinner as if he had denied Christ himself, Gregory wrote. Christian life consists, for Gregory of Nyssa, precisely in the Christian's embodiment of "intellectual beauty," so that the inner and outer person cooperate without conflict. When there is no "civil war" between body and soul, "the graceful bearing of our life coincides with our thoughts which are put into motion in accordance with Christ."[15]

Gregory of Nyssa's *On Perfection* presents a design for a particular kind of Christian life, that of an educated intellectual, skilled in study and contemplation. By identifying distractions from one's chosen life as caused by "passions," Gregory did not intend to preclude integrated passion. Indeed, as a Christian Platonist he understood that all intellectual endeavor must be motivated by an original passionate interest in the world of the senses.[16] However, passion that remains stuck on the surface of the sensible world, passionate interest that cannot move more deeply into sensual objects in order to contemplate their origin in the intelligible world (for the Platonist) or in their creator (for the Christian), becomes the enemy of the cultivated life. It is important to notice that it is not the sensible world itself that is dangerous or threatening, but the inability of the passionate lover of sensual objects to move beyond their surfaces into contemplation of the implications of their existence.

Francis of Assisi (1181/2-1226) introduced into Christian tradition the most dramatic interpretation of the imitation of Christ. He was the first saint reputed to have received the stigmata, a "marvelous imprint of the passion of Christ in his flesh," an event witnessed and reported by his disciple and friend, Brother Leo (see fig. 2).[17]

Francis's distinctive practice of Christianity was organized around the poverty, humility, powerlessness, and vulnerability of the historical Jesus: "He was always thinking about Jesus," his first biographer wrote, "Jesus was in his mouth, in his ears, in his eyes, in his hands; Jesus was in his whole being."[18] Although Francis's physical participation in the crucifix-

Fig. 2. Giotto, *St. Francis Receives the Stigmata,* 14th century. Scala/Art Resource, N.Y.

ion of Christ was only the ultimate result of his long imitation of Christ's life and ministry, the stigmata have, understandably, received a greater share of attention than his less dramatic daily imitation of Christ.

The late fourteenth-century *Little Flowers of St. Francis,* a compilation of earlier documents, reports Brother Leo's account of Francis's stigmatization. As Francis was praying in a solitary place on Mount Alverna, he experienced a vision of Christ in which he conversed with Christ at length. When the vision disappeared:

> it left a most intense ardor and flame of divine love in the heart of St. Francis, and it left a marvelous image and imprint of the Passion of Christ in his flesh. For soon there began to appear in the hands and feet of St. Francis the marks of nails such as he had just seen in the body of Jesus Crucified, who had appeared to him in the form of a Seraph. For his hands and feet seemed to be pierced through the center with nails, the heads of which were in the palms of his hands and in the upper part of his feet outside the flesh, and their points extended through the back of the hands and the soles of the feet so far that they seemed to be bent and beaten back in such a way that underneath their bent and beaten-back point—all of which stood out from the flesh—it would have been easy to put the finger of one's hand as through a ring. And the heads of the nails were round and black. Likewise in his right side appeared the wound of a blow from a spear, which was open, red, and bloody, and from which blood often issued from the holy breast of St. Francis. [19]

The enormous popularity of Saint Francis in his own time guaranteed that his version of the imitation of Christ became one of the marks of sainthood in the Christian West for the next several centuries. Francis's celebrated love for, and power over, the natural world, his embrace of poverty in a time of steadily increasing commercialism, and his frequent visions and ecstatic states made him perhaps the most popular saint of all time in the Christian West. Over the centuries between Francis's time and our own, many have claimed that they received the stigmata from Christ, including Catherine of Genoa, Gertrud of Delft, Veronica Giuliani, Therese Neumann (who died in 1962); Catherine of Siena and Teresa of Avila claimed to have invisible, but painful, stigmata. Even today, outside North America, there are reported cases of stigmatization that have a wide popular following.

The illustrated devotional manual *Meditations on the Life of Christ,* dating from the end of the thirteenth century, gives yet another interpretation of the imitation of Christ, the final one we will examine before discussing the present usefulness of each of these models. As in Saint

Francis's interpretation, it is the humanity of Christ that the anonymous author urges the reader to imitate. The imitation of Christ advocated in the text and pictured in the illustrations, however, is not the colorful and extreme practices of Francis, but a devotion more adapted to the daily lives of ordinary people. Here the imitation of Christ is described as the production of a deeply felt empathy with Christ and with the scriptural characters who surrounded Christ during his life on earth.

The necessary condition for feeling with the scriptural figures, the *Meditations* says, is to imagine oneself participating as an actor or an observer in the events of Christ's life; the necessary condition, in short, is "being there": "If you wish to profit you must be present at the same things that it is related that Christ did and said, joyfully and rightly, leaving behind all other cares and anxieties."[20]

But it is not enough simply to recall a verbal story; one must also place oneself in a visual setting. As another author contemporary with the author of the *Meditations* wrote, images

> move the mind more than descriptions; for deeds are placed before the eyes in paintings and thus appear to be actually carrying on. But in description, the deed is done as it were by hearsay, which affects the mind less when recalled to memory. Hence, also, it is that in churches we pay less reverence to books than to images and to pictures.[21]

Since the goal of the *Meditations on the Life of Christ* was to render scenes from the life of Christ vivid, the best way to accomplish this immediacy was to aid the visual imagination of the reader, already well trained to engage in religious practice by paintings in her parish church.[22] Illustrations for every narrative were planned for the manuscript of the *Meditations*.[23] With simple but eloquent gestures, the figures in these drawings express their deep devotion to Jesus. Their relationship to Christ, told more through image than through words in the *Meditations,* is presented as the model for all Christians. For the purpose of strengthening the reader's bond with Christ, Gospel stories are embellished to make them familiar and intimate. Extrapolation from scriptural narratives is limited only by the requirement that it must not "contradict the truth" or "oppose faith and morality." One illustration, for example, shows seven disciples sleeping in two straight rows—fully clothed and complete with halos, while Christ adjusts one disciple's blanket (see fig. 9). The text reads:

> Reflect thus and see Him as He calls them with longing, being kind, fraternal, benign, and helpful, leading them outwardly and inwardly and even taking them home to His mother and familiarly going to their houses.

He taught them, instructed them, and cared for them as a mother for her son. It is said that the Blessed Peter told how, when they were asleep in one place, the Lord rose at night and covered them; for He loved them most tenderly.[24]

The tender care of Christ for his disciples—and for the Christian so continually exhorted to put herself in their place—is made immediate and concrete by the embellishment of scriptural accounts and by skillful illustration. These devices enable the reader/viewer imaginatively to enter the earthly life of the historical Jesus. In its account of how a Christian should imitate Christ, the *Meditations* instructs the reader to imitate the emotional attachment of Jesus' family, friends, and disciples rather than the attributes, physical experiences, or inner life of Christ himself:

Oh, if you could see the Lady weeping between these words, but moderately and softly, and the Magdalen frantic about her Master and crying with deep sobs, perhaps you too would not restrain your tears.[25]

Interpretation of what it means to imitate Christ has, as we have seen, covered a wide range of conceptual schemes, attitudes, and practices— from imitation as primarily a physical and literal imitation of Christ's suffering to intellectual cultivation of the attributes and characteristics of Christ. After identifying some emphases that these instructions have in common—emphases I take to be representative of the literature of Christian devotion—we will consider whether the metaphor of the imitation of Christ seems useable and fruitful in the nuclear world.

A common theme in treatises that use imitation of Christ as their dominant metaphor is the creation and development of a self organized and unified by the practice of Christianity. "Keep watch on yourself, rouse yourself, remind yourself, and whatever happens to others, do not take your attention from yourself," *The Imitation of Christ* urges.[26] The fourteenth-century Dominican preacher and mystic Meister Eckhart wrote, "Begin, therefore, with yourself, and forget yourself."[27] The ambiguous use of the term translated "self" in contemporary English usage is puzzling until we recognize that the "self" cultivated by religious practices is not the socialized self, crusty with habits, imbedded in a society that shapes and conditions desire around available and approved objects and lifestyles. Rather, the self identified and strengthened in religious practice is the self in relationship to God. The goal of the practice of Christianity is to make *this* self strong enough to form the center around which the whole personality can be organized so that, as Gregory of Nyssa put it, the two aspects of the person, body and soul, can become one, and a "harmony of dissonant parts" can be achieved.[28]

It is important to remember that the imitation of Christ is not, even when contemplation is its major tool, simply a conceptual orientation or a mental attitude. The concreteness with which the metaphor is to be actualized, the precise instructions on practices that enable imitation of Christ, is demonstrated by the care with which Christian authors describe them. The self does not become a unity by imagining itself so, but by acting in a unified way in hundreds of large and small ways every day. Michel Foucault's description of the philosophical "care of the self" in the first Christian centuries could equally well describe the agenda of most devotional manuals throughout the Christian centuries:

> It is important to understand that this application to oneself does not require simply a general attitude, an unfocused attention. The term *epimeleia* [cultivation] designates not just a preoccupation but a whole set of occupations. . . . The time is not empty; it is filled with exercises, practical tasks, various activities. Taking care of oneself is not a rest cure.[29]

Manuals in the practice of Christianity advise a great number of practices from disciplines of the body (practices of diet and sexual abstinence) to prayer, meditation, reading, spiritual direction, conversation with "holy" friends, and so on. All of these practices have the goal of imbedding a preoccupation with the life of Christ in occupations, and ultimately, in a Christian's lifestyle.

In addition to the construction of a new self, devotional manuals often agree on strategies for identifying, exercising, and strengthening this self. In general, their agenda is to achieve an incremental intensification of religious experience, an intensification that is simultaneously a privatization of religious experience. Although communities of similarly engaged people may surround and support the seeking self, it is not *communities* that are addressed, but individuals. Only to the extent that an *individual* accepts a practice does she begin to experience the particular configuration of attraction and stern discipline that shapes the self in hitherto unimagined ways. Others may know about, may even practice, a program of development of a religious self, but the program itself is not teamwork, but an individual commitment and experience.

What were the specific strategies for focusing an unfamiliar aspect of the person for cultivation and development? Scrutiny of one's body and what one does *as* body was the first exercise of the religious life. Every historical person who was adept in the spiritual life understood the energy to be gotten from naming the body as a field of conflict. The advantage of attention to the body over engrossment in one's thoughts becomes apparent if we compare the example of a historical author who fastened his attention not on his body as the field of spiritual endeavor, but on his thoughts. In the seventeenth century, John Bunyan, in his autobiography, *Grace Abounding,* described the progress of his conversion. He suffered from excruciating agonies of thought, at every moment at the mercy of whatever thought came to him, and he considered himself damned if heretical or apostatizing thoughts occurred. Sometimes a consoling verse from scripture inhabited his mind; at the next, he would conceive a thought that he feared was itself a final nonnegotiable "sin against the holy ghost." Focus on the body—on what one does—even if this attention was sometimes excessive and compulsive, at least freed one from slavish self-identification with random thoughts.

In addition to a consensus on the need for the reorganization of personality around a religious "self," authors of manuals of instruction in the practice of Christianity, in the centuries before the Protestant reformations of the sixteenth century, agreed that the body is the most available and useable tool for increasing pressure for the formation of a spiritual life. Their instructions differ in how an exercise of the body is to be conceived and practiced. For orthodox Christian authors the body can never simply be enemy. The Christian doctrines of creation, Incarnation of Christ, and resurrection of the body ultimately preclude scapegoating the body. Yet it is an undeniable fact of human experience—in other religions as well as in Christianity—that abstinence from food and drink, sex, and sleep, as well as other disciplines can produce states in which the psyche is accessible and vulnerable, conditions necessary for work on the self. Philosophically inclined theologians of the past were often careful to state that such practices cast no doubt on the integrity and goodness of the body and created things.[30] However, authors of devotional manuals were not primarily theologians, and religious leaders of a more pastoral and practical bent tended to describe the distinction of body and soul in less nuanced terms, as a dichotomy in which one component was strengthened only at the direct expense of the other. "When the body is strong, the soul withers; when the soul is strong the body withers," one fourth-century desert ascetic wrote.[31] Although not many Christian authors were that direct in stating their sense of the hostility of body and soul, many of them described the experiential relation of body and soul in terms that were only slightly more honorific to the body.

The energy to be gotten from rendering the body a field of struggle external to the self but able to affect the self seemed, to the authors of devotional manuals, abundantly demonstrated in practice. Of the authors discussed in this chapter, only Gregory of Nyssa understood Christian life to involve no "civil war" between body and soul; other authors assumed that an inevitable struggle between body and soul will last until death. Even in Gregory's description, however, the unity of the "two principles" is brought about by the vigorous subjugation of the body to the soul's quest for perfection. Similarly, Saint Francis, his biographer reports, achieved the ecstatic states for which he was famous by "great abstinence and severity, mortifying his body and comforting his spirit by means of fervent prayers, watchings, and scourgings."[32] *The Imitation of Christ* also describes a direct relationship between physical suffering and spiritual comfort and growth:

> The more his body is reduced by suffering, the more his spirit is strengthened by inward grace. His desire to be moulded to the cross of Christ makes him long for trials and difficulties; and he finds such strength in this that he would not want to be delivered from his sorrow and distress if he could, since he believes that as he bears more and heavier burdens for God's sake, so he becomes more acceptable to him.[33]

We must not, however, confuse and conflate a range of different experience, all of which is referred to in devotional texts as "suffering." If we have in mind Saint Francis's fastings and scourgings when we read a statement like that of *The Imitation of Christ* above, we will omit an important distinction between self-imposed suffering and involuntary suffering. A later chapter will deal directly and in more detail with the complicated place of suffering in Christian life as described by historical authors; for now it is enough to point out the significance of the difference between suffering that can be neither prevented nor arrested and suffering that is deliberately and actively sought. In the quotation from *The Imitation of Christ,* for example, the author made it clear that he was writing about involuntary rather than self-imposed suffering—suffering that is inevitable and unavoidable in every life.

> Even if you arrange everything to suit your own views and wishes you will always find that you still have to suffer something, whether you want to or not. . . . If you do not suffer physical pain, you will have inward trials of the spirit; sometimes God will abandon you, sometimes your neighbor will give you something to bear, and worse still, you will often be a burden to yourself. No remedy or comfort will be able to deliver or relieve you, but you will have to bear it as long as God wills it so.[34]

As soon as we begin to look behind practices that produce intensified religious experience to the motivation for such practices, a curious feature of instructional manuals emerges. Christian authors describe the motiva-

tion for developing a religious self as made up of approximately equal parts
of love and fear. Almost to a text, devotional manuals reject the formula of
1 John 4:18: "There is no fear in love: but perfect love casts out fear;
because fear has torment. The one who fears is not made perfect in love."
Rather, they agree with Augustine's prayer: "To the extent that I do not
yet love, let me fear."[35] In devotional manuals, the affects of fear and love
lose the opposition given to them in 1 John and become similar in their
capacity for stimulation.

But what do fear and love, which initially seem so dissimilar, have in
common so that they can be described as equally energizing? Fear and love
are the most strongly concentrated and the most powerfully intense states
of the psyche. Only the emotions of fear and love are strong enough to
organize one's whole psychic structure around the object of one's fear or
love. Something essential about a human being is understood when the
object of his fear or love is known. Augustine wrote, "If you want to know
whether a person is good, do not ask what she believes or what she hopes,
but what she loves."[36] In the sixteenth century, Juan de Valdes, the
Spanish Roman Catholic reformer, wrote, "In everything you fear and
love, if strictly noticed, you will discover yourself there."[37] And in the
twentieth century, Freud developed a method for treating a distressed
psyche by systematically exploring the person's fear.

It is the project of a lifetime, as Augustine saw, to shift these masses of
compacted feeling, to change the "weight of the soul" from fear to love.[38]
In the meantime, if love for God is not yet sufficiently weighty to
motivate one, fear of God's judgment must serve as motivation. *The
Imitation of Christ* puts it this way:

> There is no reality except in loving God and serving him alone; and so the
> man who loves God with his whole heart does not fear death or punish-
> ment, judgment or hell, because perfect love enables us to come to God
> without fear; but it is no wonder if the man who still finds pleasure in
> sinning is afraid of death and judgment. All the same, it is a good thing if
> the fear of hell restrains you, if love cannot yet call you back from wrong.[39]

Ultimately love must motivate the Christian. Love, devotional manuals
agree, "brings about all things."[40] Yet the Christian cannot wait until his
love is fully developed; in fact, the practices associated with Christianity
are precisely the method for shifting the dominating motivation of the
soul from fear to love. But the initial impetus will probably come from
fear. And for generating and focusing fear, historical authors found that
nothing worked better than imagining one's own death and the judgment

to follow. "In all your doing and thinking," *The Imitation* instructs, "You should act on the assumption that you are going to die today":

> If you have ever seen a man die, recall that you too must travel the same road. In the morning, think that you will not reach the evening; when evening comes, do not venture to assume the morning will be yours. Always be ready; live in such a way that death can never find you unprepared.[41]

The devices we have discussed—the body as field of struggle, motivation by fear and love, the most powerful emotions of the psyche, and remembering one's own death—are leitmotivs of devotional manuals. They are not peculiar to the few devotional texts under discussion in this chapter, nor are they incidental to picturing an imitation of Christ. In addition, these techniques provide the force of the practical instructions.

None of the historical interpretations of the imitation of Christ that we have explored can be adopted without reinterpretation in the nuclear world. Neither the voluntary physical suffering of Saint Francis nor Gregory of Nyssa's cultivation of intellectual virtues and emotional tranquility offer viable resources for most twentieth-century Christians. Similarly, reliving the heightened emotions felt by the family and friends of the historical Jesus or contemplating and attempting to incorporate the inner life of Christ fail to recommend themselves as activities that offer concrete suggestions for the nuclear world. Moreover, there is an emphasis on individual struggle and achievement both imbedded in the metaphor itself and in devotional manuals' interpretations of the imitation of Christ. Nations and governments, political powers, and even ecclesiastical institutions probably cannot imitate Christ; rather, use of the metaphor requires individual appropriation. And focus on individual development as an end in itself is neither realistic nor desirable in a world in which the human race must somehow learn to live together in order to avoid dying together in a nuclear holocaust.

There are other problems with imagining Christian life as an imitation of Christ. To what extent was Christ's vocation unique? Christian tradition's insistence that Christ was not only fully human but also fully divine casts doubt on the possibility of imitating his characteristics. The dissimilarities between Christ's life and the lives of Christians seem greater than the connections. *His* death redeemed the world; the suffering and death of human beings do not. *His* self-sacrificial life, a life that led to martyrdom, was voluntary, tradition says, but countless people suffer both involuntarily and without "spiritual benefit." "Few people are improved by sickness," *The Imitation of Christ* remarks wryly.[42] Physical pain and illness should certainly not be sought in a world in which there is so much involuntary suffering.

Enormous problems arise when the model of Christian life as imitation of Christ is urged on women. Were women understood to be created in the image of God and therefore capable of imitation of Christ? This question was frequently raised and avidly disputed in the history of Christianity. It is not prompted by twentieth-century sensitivity, but by attention to the volume of discussion on gender issues in Christian tradition. The difficulty that Christian tradition has had in trying to decide whether women were created in the image of God may itself be deplorable, but perhaps not puzzling in Western societies that subordinated women to male authority and limited their access to education and the public sphere. On the one hand, as we will see, the argument reflects these social arrangements, but it also reinforces and supplements them, providing a rationale for continuing subjugation of women.

Augustine of Hippo launched the first full discussion of the question of whether women were created in the image of God in *On the Trinity*. Like earlier Christian authors, he held that the image of God was located, not in human beings as a whole or in whole human beings, but in a particular function of human being : rationality. Most Christian authors were in agreement that God's image does not appear in human bodies since God is not necessarily embodied.[43] And, looking about them and seeing that the educated intellectuals were all male, they declared—to a man—that rationality clearly existed most strongly in males. Most women, confined to housework and childbearing, were consumed with caring for the physical needs of their families and thus exhibited a kind of rationality not developed along lines recognizable to educated men. Therefore men seemed to exhibit more of God's image than women. Several authors took on the thorny question of whether a woman *as* woman, that is, unattached to any man, bears God's image. Augustine's answer is ambiguous and difficult to interpret. His answer depends on a woman's role rather than a woman's nature. Leaving aside the vexing issue of whether a woman's nature includes the image of God, he concludes that, because of her God-ordained role as helpmate for man, she does not contain within herself the image of God:

> The woman together with her husband is the image of God, so that the whole substance is one image. But when she is assigned as a helpmate, a function that pertains to her alone, then she is not the image of God, but as far as the man is concerned, he is by himself alone the image of God, just as

fully and completely as when he and the woman are joined together into one.[44]

The judgment that woman by herself is not created in the image of God, though sometimes argued with another outcome than Augustine's, was discussed in other genres in a less nuanced way. In the sixteenth century inquisitorial manual, the *Hammer of Witches,* for example, Christ's appearance in the male sex was described as privileging that sex. For example, men are not as likely as women to become involved with witchcraft:

> Blessed be the highest who has so far preserved the male sex from so great a crime; for since he was willing to be born and to suffer for us, therefore he has granted to men this privilege.[45]

Thomas Aquinas's discussion of the question of whether women were created in the image of God quotes Augustine. Although he repeats the gender assumptions of a patriarchal society, he articulates a different concern than that of theological precision; he expresses the importance of granting religious affirmation to women *as* women:

> Because the male sex exceeds the female sex, Christ assumed a man's nature. So that people would not think little of the female sex, it was fitting that he should take flesh from a woman. Hence Augustine says, "Despise not yourselves, men the son of God became a man; despise not yourselves, women, the son of God was born of a woman."[46]

But literary communications were not historical people's only source of information about how to imitate Christ. The religious images of medieval communities in the West also showed how Christ could be imitated. Thomas Aquinas's concern about the devotional needs of both women and men is evident in visual images. Scenes from the life of Christ and the life of the Virgin seem purposely designed to parallel one another and to provide gender-differentiated models for men's and women's devotional life. It is difficult and dangerous to attempt to assess the usefulness of the image of the virgin/mother Mary for women. We will need to look in more detail in another context at the question of whether images and stories of the Virgin functioned for women as messages of social control more than as empowerments.

Theological discussions over whether women were created in the image of God were not as important to most Christians as were the devotional models they received. Even in times when this question was being argued by theologians, not only were women implicitly included in injunctions to imitate Christ, but some of the most popular devotional manuals of the Christian centuries were specifically addressed to women, the *Meditations on the Life of Christ,* Juan de Valdez's *Christian Alphabet,* and Francis de Sales's *Introduction to the Devout Life,* to name only a few. Writers of devotional manuals who were more pastorally than theologically inclined clearly had no difficulty in recommending the model of Christ's life for women's emulation.[47] However, women were consistently directed to emulate, not Christ's qualities of intransigent self-possession, but his obedience, gentleness, and compassion for others.

Imitation of Christ, understood as self-sacrificing martyrdom, is a highly problematic model for women. Whether a male savior is beneficial to women[48] needs to be examined, not in terms of biological difference, but in relation to the gender-specific conditioning in Western societies. The adaptability of the model of imitation of Christ for purposes of social control—for both women and men—is obvious. Perhaps the imitation of a self-sacrificing Jesus has been a useful corrective for men, socialized to vigorous competition in societies oriented to male aggression. Self-sacrificing attention to the needs of others has, however, been part of the socialization of women, and therefore does not provide a correction to gender conditioning that encourages and rewards women's self-abnegation and single-minded attention to the needs of men and children. As Valerie Saiving, Judith Plaskow, and others have shown, women are tempted to neglect their own talents and gifts, depending on others for self-esteem, and to scatter time and energy in a variety of tasks rather than to sustain a focus on a central task.[49]

The imitation of Christ's gentleness, compassion, and self-sacrificial love is damaging to women in societies that demand of women, and socialize them to, such attitudes and behavior. If twentieth-century women are to find this metaphor useful, it will need to be on the basis of carefully selected characteristics of Christ that confront and challenge women's social conditioning rather than those that sustain it. Christ's anger at injustice, Christ's practices of self-remembering and centering, Christ's rejection of the social role expectations of his day, and the creativity with which Christ met difficult situations and answered awkward questions about himself and his ministry could be useful to women in the twentieth century.

Devotional manuals were frequently written by men and addressed to women. They represent men's ideas of how women should think and act. Giovanni Boccaccio, in *The Decameron*—definitely *not* a devotional text, but one that gives a lively sense of male and female roles in fourteenth-

century Italy—puts in the mouth of a beautiful young woman the following edifying sentiments:

> Women do not know how to reason in a group when they are without the
> guidance of some man who knows how to control them. We are fickle,
> quarrelsome, suspicious, timid, and fearful. . . . Men are truly the leaders
> of women, and without their guidance, our actions rarely end suc-
> cessfully.[50]

The spiritual guidance of women by men is certainly as well documented—and as problematic from a twentieth-century perspective—as is
men's management of the public realm and women's confinement to the
private.

We have noticed some of the strengths and weaknesses that various
interpretations of the imitation of Christ contain. We are now ready to
consider the usefulness of the metaphor of Christian life as the imitation of
Christ to twentieth-century Christians in the context of the nuclear world.
My first observation concerns devotional manuals' admonitions to vigorous
engagement in Christian life. The metaphor is simultaneously inspirational and flexible. Both of these qualities are advantages for twentieth-
century interpreters. No stronger metaphor can be found for Christian life
than to understand it as an imitation of Christ. Yet the metaphor itself
leaves open how one identifies the characteristic of the Christ one seeks to
emulate. Suppose, for example, that I think of myself as imitating a
historical human being who was incarnated for the purpose of demonstrating the central claim of Christianity, namely, that God *is* love. The
metaphor is still vague; the loving response in every human situation is
not immediately obvious. And Christian tradition contains many examples of questionable and even deplorable interpretations of what constitutes loving behavior. Augustine's famous injunction "Love, and do as
you will"[51] has been used too often as a rationalization for religious,
political, economic, and social oppression. If, then, the metaphor not only
*can* be abused, but has often *been* abused, does it hold any constructive
possibility for the present?

We can begin to answer this question by acknowledging that every
metaphor can be abused either by willful misuse, or by application in
situations in which it is destructive. The simultaneous value and danger of
metaphors lie in their capacity for interpretation and application in diverse
situations. Nothing in the metaphor itself guarantees its responsible use.
In order to use it fruitfully, the one using it must define it in relation to an
accurately analyzed present situation. The metaphor must enable both

constructive conceptual grasp and responsible action. Like other metaphors, the imitation of Christ must be carefully interpreted in relation to
particular situations. Every attitude and act has a context, and the
metaphor of Christian life as the imitation of Christ emphasizes the need
for an accurate "reading" of the context—as Christ himself had to discern
both the requirements of his own integrity and the essential features of the
context in which he acted. Christ's earthly life, according to Gospel
accounts, included moments of anger, distress, sadness, feelings of aban-
donment and self-doubt as well as the loving generosity that we—and
historical authors—seem to emphasize. Which of Christ's emotions, actions, or characteristics represents both an accurate interpretation of the
needs of my present situation and my own capacity to respond?

Imitation of Christ as a model for Christian life inspires and demands
strenuous engagement, hard work, rather than passivity. It raises questions; it does not provide answers. Yet its inspirational value is potentially
great. Because twentieth-century Christians live in a predominantly secular world, we frequently do not think of ourselves as purposely and
continually engaged in the creation of Christian life. The metaphor of
imitation of Christ can both challenge us to do so and can inspire us to
begin to ask ourselves: How might I imitate Christ in *this* moment?

# 3

---

# A Society of Aliens: Pilgrimage

*This world is not my home, I'm just a-passin' through;*
*My treasures are laid up somewhere beyond the blue.*
*The angels beckon me from heaven's open door,*
*And I can't feel at home in this world any more.*

*American Spiritual*

The second metaphor of Christian life that we will examine is that of Christian life as pilgrimage. Unlike Christian life as imitation of Christ, there was both a literal and a metaphorical use of this image: Christians both went on extended journeys to holy places, and—especially after the Protestant reformations of the sixteenth century—they stayed at home but conceived of their practice of Christianity as a long sojourn toward heaven, their native land. Both literal and metaphoric pilgrimage began to capture Christians' imaginations in the fourth century. Shortly before Augustine wrote his epic saga of the pilgrimage of Christian life, the *City of God,* Egeria, a Christian woman from northern Europe, traveled to Jerusalem and the holy places and recorded her impressions of what she saw in letters to her "sisters" at home.

The theology of Christian life as pilgrimage was first formulated by Augustine. In the *City of God* Augustine pictured the human race as divided into two cities, "for the present mingled together in body, but in heart separated."[1] Human beings participated in the "city of this world" or "City of God" according to the objects of their love and longing; if a person's love flows toward the possession of objects in the sensible world, he is a citizen of this world; if her love flows in the direction of God, she is a member of the city of God. A citizen of the heavenly city, however,

as long as he is in this mortal body, is a pilgrim in a foreign land, away from God; therefore he walks by faith and not by sight. . . . While this

43

Heavenly City is on pilgrimage in this world, she calls out citizens from all nations and so collects a society of aliens, speaking all languages.[2]

Augustine's metaphoric use of the idea of Christian life as pilgrimage provided the framework within which this metaphor was developed for the next fifteen hundred years. We will discuss some of the assumptions and implications of the metaphor of pilgrimage after we first examine pilgrimage as a literal practice.

By the 380s Christians in large numbers began to travel to the "Holy Land" to express and renew their devotion to Christ by placing themselves at the geographical locations of the major events of Christ's life. The first famous pilgrim to Jerusalem was Helena, mother of the emperor Constantine, who claimed to have discovered there a piece of the true cross; it was she who initiated popular interest in pilgrimage to the holy places. In addition to pilgrims who went on one or several long pilgrimages in a lifetime, some pilgrims adopted the life of continuous pilgrimage as a protest against a Christianity that had become socially acceptable and even, by the end of the fourth century, a convenient affiliation for the upwardly mobile. Many fourth-century pilgrims found pilgrimage exciting as well as edifying. In writings by and about them, the note of thirst for experience is strong; for example, Jerome writes of the wealthy pilgrim Paula and her entourage:

> Though they [pilgrims] deprived their bodies of material comforts, they delighted their souls with pilgrimage. They wanted to see everything with their own eyes and experience everything for themselves. . . . In visiting the holy places so great was the passion and enthusiasm she [Paula] felt for each, that she could never have torn herself away from one had she not been eager to visit the rest. Before the cross she threw herself down in adoration as though she beheld the Lord hanging on it; and when she entered the tomb which was the scene of the resurrection she kissed the stone which the angel had rolled away from the door. Indeed, so ardent was her faith that she kissed the very spot on which the Lord's body had lain, like one athirst for the river which she has longed for.[3]

In the 380s the pilgrim Egeria also traveled to Jerusalem from northern Spain.[4] Her travel diaries, written to tell a community of women of her experiences, are the earliest extant description of the Holy Week and Easter liturgies of Jerusalem. Her letters repeatedly set aside the descriptive mode and focus on her own excitement in being "on the spot," in her direct experience of "places mentioned in the Bible":

I know I should never cease to give thanks to God, but I thank him especially for this wonderful experience he has given me, beyond anything I could expect or deserve. I am far from worthy to have visited all these holy places.[5]

Egeria thought of the "holy places" as visible witnesses to the truth of the biblical account of Christ's life. Her journal describes a practice that is the opposite of mentally visualizing oneself as an observer and participant in the events of Christ's life; she describes her vivid experiences as the result of her presence at the holy places; her physical presence "on the spot" brought her mind, spontaneously and immediately, to contemplation of the scenes that occurred there.[6]

Egeria's description of Lent and Easter in Jerusalem emphasizes the engagement of senses and emotions in the liturgies that marked the events of the passion of Christ. She describes traveling from site to site—from church to church, erected at the places of Christ's arrest, trial, crucifixion, and tomb—literally following the stations of the cross. Nor were Egeria's pilgrimages over once she had seen these sights; her life was one of perpetual pilgrimage:

> So, loving ladies, light of my heart, this is where I am writing to you. My present plan is, in the name of Christ our God, to travel to Asia since I want to make a pilgrimage to Ephesus and the martyrium of the blessed apostle John. If after that I am still alive and able to visit the holy places, I will either tell you about them face to face, or at any rate write to you about them if my plan changes. In any case, ladies, light of my heart, whether I am "in the body" or "out of the body," do not forget me.[7]

The development of the Christian practice of pilgrimage from its origins in the fourth century to its peak of popularity in the later Middle Ages cannot be told here. It had become, by the fifteenth century, a frequently questioned practice; by then its widespread popularity had led to abuses in which pilgrimage had sometimes lost its religious austerity and had become, on occasion, the sort of lark recounted in Chaucer's *Canterbury Tales*. By the seventeenth century, largely under the influence of one devotional manual, *The Pilgrim's Progress*, pilgrimage had become a major metaphor for Christian life in Protestant circles; literal pilgrimage has continued to be practiced for inspiration and renewal in most Roman Catholic countries.

At its peak of popularity in the Middle Ages, a pilgrimage might be undertaken for any of several reasons. A pilgrimage might be penitential, either self-imposed, assigned by a confessor, or stipulated by a civil judge in recompense for a crime; even capital offenses were often punished by judicial pilgrimage.[8] But most medieval pilgrimages were undertaken for reasons similar to those of Egeria centuries before, namely, for the excitement of physical proximity to martyr's shrines and the holy bones they contained, the sites of miracles one could witness with one's own eyes.

Preparations for a medieval pilgrimage emphasized the seriousness and potential danger of a major pilgrimage. The pilgrim acquired the pilgrim's dress, a long, coarse tunic with a large cross, staff, and a pack in which food and other essential items were carried, along with a little money. Ideally, the pilgrim was exhorted to bring no money in order to dramatize her dependence on the charity of others.[9] The pilgrim's clothing and equipment were blessed by a priest. Before setting out, the pilgrim also made a will and made amends with anyone to whom he owed anything or with whom he had unhappy relations. Finally, he might secure a safe-conduct document for passage through territories reputed to be dangerous, even though the effectiveness of these first "passports" was anything but guaranteed in practice.

In addition to emphasizing the religious seriousness of pilgrimage, these elaborate preparations were a recognition of the danger of such an endeavor. Sickness caused by contaminated food and water as well as by unaccustomed exertion were an almost inevitable feature of pilgrimage. A twelfth-century *Guide for Pilgrims to Santiago* lists common dangers: wild animals, bad roads, natural catastrophes, and bandits. One fourteenth-century observer wrote that half the pilgrims who set out for Rome in 1350 were robbed or killed on the way.[10] Even attendance in churches along pilgrimage routes on the feast days could be hazardous: Abbot Suger, in urging the need for expansion of the Church of Saint-Denis, cites the terrible crush of pilgrims, sometimes causing fatalities, on feast days; in 1120 a fire broke out in the Church of Sainte-Madeleine on the feast day of Saint Mary Magdalen in which 1,127 pilgrims were burned to death. In addition, the constant problem of finding food for themselves and fodder for animals, though predictable rather than catastrophic, was endemic to pilgrimage. The most dangerous pilgrimage was to Jerusalem; many pilgrims walked three thousand miles or endured six weeks in tiny—and sometimes doomed—boats in order to reach Jerusalem. In the fourteenth century, the pilgrim Margery Kempe described a sea voyage to Jerusalem whose conditions were little improved from those of centuries before.[11] Together with the grave religious consequences of not conducting a pilgrimage with the right inner commitment, these formidable conditions constituted both physical and spiritual dangers.

There were also moral dangers. Pilgrims traveled in groups, both for self-defense and for mutual help and amusement. Sermons were their only organized recreation, but apparently pilgrims found more lively amusements, since rumors of pilgrims' misbehavior have reached to our own time; it is clear that dehabituation from accustomed lifestyles could be morally uninhibiting as frequently as it could be spiritually reviving. We should also remember, however, that abuses, rather than the unremarkable "uses" of religious practices, tend to be noticed and written down. Nevertheless, even during the times of greatest interest in pilgrimage, medieval authors repeatedly expressed concern over the frequency with which pilgrimage was treated as an escape from both the problems and the moral strictures of daily life at home.

Medieval doubts about the value of pilgrimage were not aimed simply at potential moral dangers; pilgrimages were also questioned on theological grounds. At the end of the fourth century, in his treatise *On Pilgrimage* Gregory of Nyssa wrote, "When the Lord invites the blest to their inheritance in the kingdom of heaven, He does not include a pilgrimage to Jerusalem among their good deeds."[12] In the fourteenth century, Berthold of Ratisbon wrote: "What is the point of going all the way to Compostela to see some bones, for the real St. James is not there, but in heaven. Also, all you have to do to enter into the presence of God is to go to the parish church."[13] Nevertheless, people went on pilgrimage in great numbers for at least a thousand years of Christian history, motivated by a desire to expiate sins and to experience or witness miracles. We must remember that fear of hell was cultivated—vividly described and visually depicted—in the daily communications of their societies, sermons and paintings. Moreover, in a time when people died suddenly of injuries we now consider minor, intense interest in saints, miracles, and relics as the only recourse to healing available to them seemed less irrational. Such interests seemed theologically valid to people who were routinely taught that their God became flesh and shared the vulnerable human condition of embodiment with its susceptibility to accident, disease, pain, and death, and could thus be expected to empathize with them and heal their frequent illnesses and pains.

Even the most uneventful pilgrimage resulted in physical and emotional change of the most thoroughgoing sort; the pilgrim was completely removed from accustomed environment and relationships, work, nourishment, and habitual behavior. In addition, pilgrimage was a strong experiential reminder that the unpredictability of human life is not adequately represented by a sedentary lifestyle. Travel over dusty countrysides, steep and slippery mountain passes, through woods, and over hills and valleys was a more accurate representation of human life. Different geography created awareness of the diverse landscapes of the soul, the rocks, sunlight, green growth, and dust of emotional life. Life as spiritual pilgrimage to a destination—the most insistent message of medieval Christianity—was rendered concretely knowable for medieval Christians by pilgrimage. Twentieth-century people who keep appointment books, plan for retirement, and nourish the life of the imagination on media images can maintain illusions of immortality very alien to the medieval pilgrim. Life as pilgrimage can be acknowledged intellectually but not grasped emotionally and psychologically without experiences that make evident and immediate the brevity and unpredictability of human life.

Sometimes pilgrimage also resulted in physical cures that seemed miraculous to medieval people. The belief that physical diseases had spiritual causes was a strong incentive to experience the cure of a disease once spiritual restitution had been made. Despite physical dangers, the potential physical benefits of pilgrimage frequently were worth the risk, according to medieval sources. Certainly a range of illnesses we might now regard as psychosomatic were often cured by the sight of a powerful relic. In addition, many events we might think of as circumstantial—the reconciliation of a family feud, the sudden change of heart of a man bent on revenge—seemed miraculous to medieval people, due to their expectation of God's direct activity in the world. In the sixth century, Gregory of Tours lists among the miracles he had experienced: recovery from toothaches, headaches, pimples, and indigestion. In short, there are strong reasons for crediting medieval reports of the spiritual and even the physical benefits of pilgrimages.

In the sixteenth century, when pilgrimage began to be practiced less, some gains and losses occurred as practice became metaphor. Before we can evaluate these, we must consider the metaphor of Christian life as pilgrimage as it was mapped in the "most popular work of Christian spirituality ever written in English,"[14] John Bunyan's *Pilgrim's Progress.* Since its first publication in 1678, it has been translated into over a hundred languages in subsequent centuries and has appeared in hundreds of editions, most of them illustrated.

John Bunyan (1628–88) was born in a family he described as "being of that rank which is meanest and most despised."[15] He was an itinerant tinker, or mender of pots, when he became a member of the Particular Baptists, one of the myriad of religious sects in seventeenth-century England. After years of spiritual torment over whether his attention to religion had occurred "too late" for efficacious repentance and redemption,[16] and anxiety that perhaps the "day of grace" was "past and gone,"[17] Bunyan at last experienced conversion and began to preach. He was elected minister, without training or formal ordination, of a congregation in Bedford. He was imprisoned in 1660 for religious dissent and released only in 1672. While he was in prison, under conditions of filth and

Fig. 3. Christian Speaks with Mr. Worldly Wiseman, illustration from the first edition of *The Pilgrim's Progress*, 1678.

undernourishment, he wrote *The Pilgrim's Progress,* an extended allegory of the journey of the protagonist, Christian, through the terrors and trials of the world to the Celestial City. Leaving the City of Destruction in order to "escape from the wrath to come,"[18] as well as from the "lusts, pleasures, and profits of this world,"[19] Christian journeys through the Slough of Despond, Vanity Fair, Doubting Castle, and other places named for their capacity to either encourage or prevent his progress. He meets many people on the way who either aid or impede him: Evangelist, Mr. Facing-both-ways, Worldly Wiseman (see fig. 3), the Interpreter, Greatheart, Ignorance, Mr. Talkative, Madame Bubble, Vain-hope, Mrs. Know-nothing, and others. The end or goal of Christian's pilgrimage occurs when, passing through the Valley of the Shadow of Death, he and his companion, Hopeful, come at last to the gates of the Celestial City, where they are met by shining angels and ushered into heaven, accompanied by "melodious noise," and into the presence of the King.[20]

Part two of *The Pilgrim's Progress,* published eight years after the first, describes the journey of Christiana, Christian's wife, and her children, over the same route that Christian took earlier to the Celestial City. Sixteenth-century gender assumptions make for some revealing variations in Bunyan's account of Christian's and Christiana's experiences as they crossed the same terrain, at different times. For example, when the Interpreter describes to Christian what to expect on the road he will travel, he characterizes the pilgrimage in the vigorous metaphor of a fight.[21] When Christiana meets the Interpreter, he instructs her about her journey with the following object lesson:

> So he [took] them into a slaughter-house where was the butcher killing a sheep: and behold, the sheep was quiet, and took her death patiently. Then said the Interpreter, You must learn of this sheep to suffer, and to put up with wrongs without murmurings or complaints. Behold how quietly she takes her death, and, without objecting, she suffereth her skin to be pulled over her ears.[22]

The example seems an odd one for illustrating the necessary attitudinal stance for Christian life, but it makes evident the flexibility of the metaphor of pilgrimage for adapting to—rather than altering—existing gender roles. Although Christiana's choice to undertake the strenuous pilgrimage might have been used to challenge women to take responsibility for developing an individuated life, a centered self-before-God, *The Pilgrim's Progress* leaves intact—indeed strongly reinforces—women's socialization.

The vivid images of *The Pilgrim's Progress,* in which the natural world, cities, and human beings are externalizations of the pilgrim's inner struggles, temptations, comforts, and assistance, informed all future use of the metaphor of Christian life as pilgrimage in the English-speaking world. Let us first explore some of the differences between pilgrimage as a literal practice and pilgrimage as metaphor.

In the practice of pilgrimage, dehabituation is a means to the end of a renewed and intensified religious experience. Removing the context and habits of daily living results in the revivification of experience: altered physical conditions produce an altered—a more alert and sensitive—consciousness. It was clear to the medieval pilgrim through her or his physical experience that journeying through the world was a way to expose oneself to learning the actual condition of human life: that human life is constantly difficult and dangerous. Pilgrimage as metaphor also features an imaginary reconstruction of the intensified experience of a dangerous "trip." But in the tranformation from practice to metaphor some fundamental changes occurred. When pilgrimage became metaphor, there was no longer a physical dehabituation; none of the habits of daily life were altered. Rather, the metaphor's effectiveness depends on imaginatively producing a sense of distance from the ordinary world. One must imagine one's past and future life in the scenario of *The Pilgrim's Progress*. The medieval pilgrim's physical vulnerability and discomfort in unfamiliar surroundings are translated into a metaphor in which the world is "wilderness." The world is seen as a place of "many mountains, rocks, and rough places," Jonathan Edwards, the eighteenth-century New England Puritan preacher said in a sermon on "The Christian Pilgrim." Edwards's evaluation of the world of human experience resulted from carrying the metaphor of pilgrimage to its logical conclusion: "It was never designed by God that this world should be our home."[23]

Let us now examine some implications of the metaphor of Christian life as pilgrimage as they appear in Bunyan's narrative and in several other authors who use this metaphor. First, the metaphor requires a separation of the spiritual world (the goal and reward) from the world of everyday experience (the arena of preparation and struggle). Anything valued in the visible world must be valued primarily, if not solely, for its capability to move one forward on one's journey to "the Celestial City." "Let us not love the world," Augustine wrote, "We must rather labor in it that it seduce us not than fear it lest it perish."[24] Only what stimulates increased longing for our destination is to be valued; other "goods" are to be used, but not enjoyed for their own beauty or goodness. "We should set our *hearts* [italics his] on heaven," Jonathan Edwards said:

Though surrounded with outward enjoyments, and settled in families with desirable friends and relations; though we have companions whose society is delightful, and children in whom we see many promising qualifications; though we live by good neighbors and are generally beloved where known; yet we ought not to take our rest in these things as our portion. . . . We ought to possess, enjoy, and use them, with no other view but readily to quit them, whenever we are called to it, and to change them willingly and cheerfully for heaven.[25]

Separation of the *process* from the *goal* or completion of human life, together with the assignment of asymmetrical value to each can, and often did, result in a devaluing of other people, one's "fellow pilgrims" in life. And it is inevitably one's nearest and dearest who are seen to represent the greatest impediment to "pilgrimage." Christian, determined to set out from the doomed City of Destruction is detained by his wife and children who, on learning that he was leaving,

began to cry after him to return; but the man put his fingers in his ears, and ran on, crying, Life! life! eternal life!. So he looked not behind him, but fled towards the middle of the plain.[26]

If we look beneath the surface of instructions to regard others as "mere shadows," however, we can detect a reason for this advice. Edwards, for example, says that for purposes of "moderation in mourning," it is important to think of others as on their own pilgrimage, a pilgrimage that has reached its goal and reward when they die. Furthermore, Edwards adds, we will see them again. The deaths of those one loves, a potential cause of cataclysmic grief and disorientation, are somewhat more manageable if loved ones are thought of as pursuing their own trajectory rather than as appendages of one's own life. The metaphor of pilgrimage, when applied to others' lives as well as to one's own, can help to make the transience of life bearable; finitude can be accepted as a meaningful condition of human life rather than as outrage and injury: "This is the way to have death comfortable to us," Edwards wrote.[27]

We will need to say more about the treatment of death associated with Christian life as pilgrimage in the concluding section of this chapter. Here it is important to notice that underlying rhetoric that sounds to us like a denial of death and disparagement of loved ones is the encouragement of attitudes toward death that render it less overwhelming. This strategy for managing death might seem more attractive to twentieth-century people with similar anxieties and griefs, if we did not have technologies that make death seem less continuously threatening. Modern medical ability to keep death at bay is somewhat greater than that of historical people; at least most twentieth-century North Americans do not die from small injuries or from formerly fatal diseases that can now be cured by anti-biotics. Moreover, when death occurs, we are able to keep it out of sight much more than could people of the past. Authors of devotional texts maximized the difficulties and pains of human life in order to minimize the terror of death—one's own death or the deaths of loved ones.

A further result of the separation and asymmetrical valuing of this world and the next is frequently encountered in devotional manuals that picture Christian life as pilgrimage. Well-being in this life was frequently described as inversely correlated with spiritual health:

> When it is well with you, when all earthly things smile on you, none of your dear ones has died, no drought nor hail nor bitterness has assailed your vineyard, your cask has not turned sour, your cattle have not failed to give increase, you have not been dishonored in any high dignity of this world in which you were placed, your friends all around you live and keep their friendship for you, your children obey you, your slaves tremble before you, your wife lives in harmony with you, your house is called happy—then find affliction, if in any way you can, that, having found affliction, you may call upon the name of the Lord.[28]

Instructions to trust adversity are not unique to the metaphor of Christian life as pilgrimage. The imitation of Christ also pictures the "way of the cross" as fruitful for learning from the inevitable difficulties of life. From a twentieth-century perspective, historical manuals seem to over-state the point when they insist on the *desirability* of trouble as "learning experience."[29] But there is a coherent and cogent rationale in devotional literature for regarding troubles as trustworthy. Troubles are simply "trials," sent by God, who knows "what we are able to bear," and will send only the afflictions that ultimately strengthen a Christian. Scriptural passages state that God's overruling providence of Christians includes sending troubles when these are necessary for reformation, punishment, or "pruning." The advantage of this explanation is twofold: it encourages a sense of God's detailed and discerning engagement in a Christian's per-sonal life; and it pictures troubles as God-given and therefore not intended to overwhelm but to strengthen. An attitude of active learning can alter the effect of situations that seem at first to be nothing but human waste and loss.

Problems with belief in a God who sends adversity on Christians, however, are somewhat more complex. The image of God as a father who "chastens those he loves" can encourage not only trust but also helpless dependence on an all-powerful God who will ultimately save human beings from themselves and the nuclear world we have created, but perhaps only in some millennium that will occur *after* a nuclear holocaust. The image of God as simultaneously "loving," punishing, and, in the end, redeeming tends to minimize the dramatic need for discernment and responsibility in the nuclear world. We can acknowledge some advantages in regarding personal and communal "troubles" as God-sent without finding the idea of God as a powerful and wise parent an ideal image for twentieth-century Christians. The nuclear world desperately needs images, metaphors, and models that underscore and strengthen a sense of gratitude and responsibility—gratitude for the fragile and threatened natural world, and responsibility in working for its perpetuation. Thus this scriptural image—one that has had a strong attraction in Christian tradition—appears to entail risks in the context of the nuclear world. In the late twentieth-century, Christian adulthood, a balance of attitudes of gratitude and responsibility, not infancy and dependency needs to be cultivated and strengthened. Moreover, in a social world in which domestic violence has reached epidemic proportions and is on the increase, an image of God as all-powerful father can connote to many people a battering God rather than a God who protects and shields us from the effects of our childish irresponsibility.[30]

Several other results of imagining Christian life as pilgrimage require our consideration if we are to determine whether this metaphor can retain its traditional usefulness in a nuclear world. First, treatments of death in devotional manuals like *The Pilgrim's Progress* need to be reexamined. We have seen that people of the past found it important to minimize the fear of death. But the instinct to minimize the pain of an unavoidable certainty, we may feel, has gone too far when it is not content with minimizing, but actually glorifies death. Bunyan's description of the death of Christian and his companion, for example, is rhetorically inverted to present death as precisely the opposite of its usual experiential content, a triumph instead of a painful defeat. In the midst of reading Bunyan's triumphal description, a modern reader may even have difficulty remembering that *death* is the actual subject of the passage:

> These two men went in at the gate; and lo! as they entered, they were transfigured; and they had raiment put on that shone like gold. There were also [people] that met them with harps and crowns and gave them to them. . . . Then I heard that all the bells in the city rang for joy . . . I looked in after them and behold the city shone like the sun; the streets also were paved with gold; and in them walked many men with crowns on their heads, palms in their hands, and golden harps, to sing praises withal. . . . And after that they shut up the gates; which, when I had seen, I wished myself among them.[31]

In order to understand passages like this in their historical setting, we need to consider again the "higher profile" of death in historical periods in which the dying were usually cared for, and the dead prepared for burial, in their homes and by their loved ones. We must also remember that, for the vast majority of historical Christians, a future existence in heaven or hell was a vivid reality. Those who used the pilgrimage metaphor did not consider pilgrimage optional or "advisory," but, as Edwards wrote: "if our lives be not a journey towards heaven, they will be a journey to hell."[32]

Philippe Ariès, in his *Western Attitudes toward Death*, has suggested another interpretation of what often seems to the twentieth-century reader a "morbid preoccupation with death" in historical devotional writing. Ariès's thesis is that dying and dead bodies in the home and in everyday life did not make death terrible and horrifying to people; rather, it is the erasure of death from modern people's direct experience that creates fantasies of terror surrounding death: hiding death makes it fearsome. Familiarity with death, Ariès claims, creates "a form of acceptance of the order of nature."[33] In analyzing devotional texts that seem preoccupied with death, then, it is important not to project onto people of the past the "morbidity" of the present—a time in which we remove death from sight by professionalization of care for the dying and the dead. Death was, for historical people, on the one hand, a physical reality that strengthened a sense of interdependence among generations: the woman caring for her dying father knew that one day her daughter would care for her in the same ways. On the other hand, frequent reminders of death in sermons, hymns, and devotional texts were not intended to depress, but to generate energy and motivation for intentional living; the inevitable reality of the approach of one's own death was the single strongest incentive to living well.

Reminders of death in devotional treatises are also related to another major theme of this literature. Jonathan Edwards's first practical "direction" for understanding one's life as pilgrimage is: "Labor to get a sense of the vanity of this world; on account of the little satisfaction that is to be enjoyed here: its short continuance, and unserviceableness when we most stand in need of help, *viz.* on a death-bed."[34] The absolute ontological priority of eternity over time in devotional manuals was ultimately supported by consideration of the relative lengths of the present and future lives:

> The future world was designed to be our settled and everlasting abode. There it was intended that we should be fixed; and there alone is a lasting habitation and a lasting inheritance. The present state is short and transitory, but our state in the other world is everlasting. And as we are there at

first, so we must be without change. Our state in the future world, therefore, being eternal, is of so much greater importance than our state here, that all our concerns in this world should be wholly subordinated to it.[35]

In short, the metaphor of pilgrimage effectively highlights the transience of human life and the urgency of using it well. But transience is often exalted on the grounds that the world is worthless, or worse than worthless—filled with nothing but evils and temptations. The glorification of transience and death by historical texts is a dangerous teaching in the nuclear world.

The assumption that underlies evaluations of the world as worthless is that only what is permanent has value. Unless the "goods of this world" can become reminders of eternity, temporary things, no matter how delightful, nourishing, and stimulating, have little or no value in relation to eternal things. Happiness is too often presented in Christian tradition as illusory at best and, at worst, as distracting from the pilgrim's goal. "All the world," Christian tells his companions, "is in a state of condemnation,"[36] a sentiment that echoes, more than a thousand years later, Augustine's bitter statement, "The world is an enemy to the Christian."[37] Even though Augustine did not pursue his notion of the world's transience to the point of glorifying death,[38] his postponement of the perfection and completion of human nature until the next life effectively diminished the value of present life in order to generate and sustain longing for eternal life. The pleasures and delights of this world inevitably suffer by contrast with the permanent joys of paradise; in comparison with heaven, this world's rewards seem puny and fragile. The seventeenth-century German Pietist Johann Arndt, in his *True Christianity* wrote: "One is to consider pleasures as worthless, to draw oneself away from all that is high, glorious, pompous, powerful, and beautiful in the world."[39] And this advice was not intended for members of religious orders: there were none among the Lutheran congregations with which Arndt was familiar. *True Christianity* was the first devotional manual written for the Lutheran public.

In order to make sure that Christians recognized the preponderance of suffering in human life, Augustine emphasized the present inaccessibility of happiness. Although every human being without exception wishes to be happy,[40] in actuality a lion's share of suffering is the lot of the human race. Augustine catalogued his evidence in book 22 of the *City of God* that the human condition is primarily one of suffering. Woes range from the discipline one must undergo as a child in order to be socialized and educated ("How is it that what we learn with toil we forget with ease?") to the "pains that trouble all humankind": harsh weather, calamities, storms, terror of death, tempests, floods, earthquakes, political upheavals, the danger of being crushed by falling buildings, of being attacked by animals ("anyone walking anywhere is liable to sudden accidents"), assaults of demons, and "diseases for which the treatments and medicines themselves are instruments of torture."[41] Augustine interpreted suffering as evidence that the human race as a whole exists in a "state of punishment": "What else is the message of all the evils of humanity?" The ultimate purpose and benefit of suffering, according to most Christian authors, was its ability to dissolve a Christian's attachment to this world with its beauties and pleasures.

It is clear that Christian tradition has employed a variety of strategies for managing the deaths of others and one's own death: "Learn to give up the world before it gives you up," Arndt wrote.[42] We have also seen that the idea of death has been used as a stimulus for considering one's life a pilgrimage, a mirror in which the "vanity of the world" can be clearly seen. When we look at the context of world-renouncing rhetoric, it is possible to reformulate the incentives for speaking disparagingly of a frightening world. For example, Augustine certainly inhabited such a world. The *City of God* was written in the slippery world of the later Roman Empire, in the decade following the conquest and sack of Rome, and in a society without effective internal police, without secure food supply, and in constant peril of invasion. John Bunyan's situation was jeopardous to a similar degree, though in different particulars. The volatile political and religious situation in seventeenth-century England was especially dangerous to a radical dissenter like Bunyan, who spent at least seventeen of his sixty years in prison.

Similar contextualizing details of the social and political situations of other authors of devotional manuals could also be explored. The lives of most of the people of the past have been heavily burdened—in Hobbes's famous phrase, "solitary, poor, nasty, brutish, and short."[43] Until recently, however, no matter how personally or communally threatened people or nations were, no one could seriously contemplate the disappearance, not only of the world of human affairs, but of all forms of life; whatever else was perilously slippery, the natural world seemed indestructible to historical people. It did not seem in need of any defense or protection, and they gave it none.[44] Policies of "conquering and subduing" the natural world seemed to be appropriate under conditions of the presumed stability and inexhaustible supply of natural resources.

We no longer live in such a world. And therefore the rhetoric of Christian tradition, its metaphors and images, must be examined and reevaluated in the light of the fragile and threatened world of twentieth-

century experience. Although belittling the inherent value of the world
has been a time-honored strategy for psychological survival in situations of
threat and insecurity, it is not the only possible strategy to adopt in
dangerous times. "Everything terrifying," the German poet Rainer Maria
Rilke wrote, "is, in its deepest being, something helpless that wants our
help."[45] Instead of permitting ourselves the self-protecting device of
finding the joys of human life worthless in contrast to fantasized heavenly
delights, we must find the ideas and images that help us to risk intense
love and gratitude for the beauty and goodness of the earth. And we must
work hard to preserve it, even if we have no assurance of success; our efforts
may be too feeble and too late to save the world from nuclear destruction.
Nevertheless, "love is not inactive in a lover," Augustine said;[46] our love
for human life and for the vulnerable earth can stimulate us to work for its
preservation.

This brings us to another feature of the pilgrimage metaphor that looks
quite different to a twentieth-century perspective than it did to historical
Christians, namely, the individualism of the pilgrimage. A disturbing
sense of privilege—the religious privilege of the few "saved" in contrast to
the many damned—deeply informs the metaphor of Christian life as
pilgrimage, as it does the other dominant metaphors of Christian life.[47]

Devotional manuals insist that to think of one's life as pilgrimage it is
necessary to focus one's entire attention on oneself and one's own salvation.
How can we understand this focus on the individual and apparent lack of
interest in community? An individuation that we are inclined to read as
individualism was advocated in historical devotional manuals because
authors assumed—rightly or wrongly—that most of their readers felt
little initiative to change themselves and needed to be prodded. In spite of
explicit and forceful injunctions to forget others and focus on achieving
one's own salvation "without tarrying for any," however, metaphorical
pilgrimages like *The Pilgrim's Progress* as well as actual pilgrimages occurred in the company of others. In fact, the pilgrim's attitudes toward
others became the topic of detailed and lengthy discussions in devotional
manuals precisely because other people were understood as *connected* to
oneself. The problem addressed by manuals is the problem of the differentiation of an individual from family, friends, and society. In contrast to
modern discourse about relationship, in which the problem addressed is
the existential alienation and estrangement of individuals from one another, Bunyan's analysis of what was needed in the seventeenth century led
him to provide the scenario for individuation, not for renewed connection
among people. Similarly, after emphasizing the imperative of individual
decision and initiative and of keeping a psychic distance between oneself
and loved ones throughout his sermon on pilgrimage, Edwards acknowl-

edges in the last paragraph that "Christians help one another in going this journey." Even then, however, the danger of "company" seems in the forefront of his mind as he concludes the sermon with a warning against hindering one another.[48]

Despite these historical and textual considerations of reasons for focus on the individual in devotional texts, we must question its usefulness in the twentieth century. Devotional manuals have cumulatively formed modern consciousness to such an extent that that favorite character in fiction, "autonomous Western man," has come into being. In a nuclear world people who could die together must learn to live together as interdependent, acknowledging our need for mutuality rather than for individualistic competitiveness. But we must not ignore another consideration: this diagnosis that there is a contemporary need for strengthening connectedness does not acknowledge that, even in the twentieth century, not everyone needs to be reminded of connectedness rather than the importance of individuation. Although the phrase "autonomous Western man" has frequently been used to characterize post-Enlightenment people as a whole, in fact the phrase is not equally applicable to all people in Western societies. White, educated, professional men are more tempted to think of themselves as independent of others than are women, racial minorities, and those who live beneath the poverty level.

A feeling of powerlessness and passivity in regard to political, social, and economic change seems to have informed most historical Christian authors—a deep pessimism, perhaps based partly on their own discouraging experiences, and partly on a strong doctrine of original sin. The doctrine of original sin posits the pervasive and inevitable element of sin in every human choice and act, the dark undertow of all human life that leads irreversibly to death. Every human effort to change the world for the better is, according to this doctrine, doomed to failure. Attitudes of passivity and escapism were the result of such pessimism. If "this world is not my home," if nothing can be done to alleviate suffering or to feed the hungry or to avert natural catastrophe, then, historical Christians often reasoned, let us lay up our treasures "somewhere beyond the blue."

In the same manuals that advocate regarding other people as "mere shadows," readers are urged in the strongest possible terms to love them. Augustine's teaching has been influential on this issue also. Augustine's principle on how other people are related to one's Christian life was stated in *On Christine Doctrine:* "Among all these things only those are to be enjoyed which we have described as being eternal and immutable; others are to be used so that we may be able to enjoy those."[49] Other people, Augustine said, are to be "used," but not "enjoyed" as ends in themselves. Although "use" in modern parlance has come to connote a cavalier disregard for the other, in Augustine's usage, some things which are to be "used" must also be loved; his examples are: human beings, angels, and one's own body.[50] One can love while realizing that the child, woman, or man one loves is, like oneself, not a "blessed immortal," but fragile, vulnerable, and mortal. The best way to love a mortal being, Augustine said, is to include this person in the central concentrated river of one's love that flows ultimately toward God: "Whatever else appeals to the mind as being lovable should be directed into that channel into which the whole torrent of love flows."[51]

Augustine's famous injunction to "love the neighbor in God" has received many pejorative interpretations, and it is certainly possible to read in it a devaluation of the "neighbor" who is not to be loved for her or his own sake. It is also tempting to find the origin of almost countless historical devaluations of others in the traditional devotional manuals that followed Augustine's phraseology. Clearly, if Augustine did not intend any diminishment of other human beings, he was not careful enough to protect his statements from misunderstanding and misrepresentation. But let us reconsider his formula to see if there is perhaps a kernal of insight that might be of use to twentieth-century people, even though we would certainly want to find a happier expression than his. Augustine's treatise *On the Trinity* gives his clearest exposition of what he means by "loving the neighbor in God." He remarks first on the appropriateness of scriptural passages that "place one for both" in enjoining either love of God or love of neighbor:

> At times it [scripture] mentions only the love of God as in this passage: "We know that for those who love God all things work together unto good," . . . and so on in many other texts. For one who loves God must logically do what God commanded, and loves God just so much as he does so; therefore, he must also love his neighbor since God has commanded this. At other times, Scripture mentions only the love of our neighbor; . . . we find many passages in sacred Scripture where love of our neighbor alone seems to be commanded for perfection, and the love of God is passed over in silence. . . . But this also follows logically, for he who loves his neighbor must also love love above everything else. But "God is love, and he who abides in love abides in God." (*Trin.* 8.8.12)

The one who loves "knowingly or unknowingly"[52]—as opposed to one who grasps other human beings possessively in relationships—participates in the very activity which *is* God, for "God is love and the one who abides in love abides in God." It is, according to Augustine, impossible truly to love without such participation in God's love. The only other possibility of relationship with other human beings is what Augustine called *cupiditas,* compulsive manipulation of "the neighbor." In loving human relationships—admittedly rare in proportion to exploitive relationships—God is directly experienced. Augustine emphasized that only this kind of love, love of the neighbor in God, recognizes and preserves the consummate independent value of the neighbor. Furthermore, it is clearly possible to "desire" another human being too much, but it is not possible to love, in the proper sense of the word, too much: "Neither should we let this question disturb us, how much love we ought to spend upon our brother, how much upon God. . . . We love God and our neighbor from one and the same love."[53]

Augustine's precisely worded and closely reasoned description, however, did not come from a manual in the practice of Christianity, though it influenced the way many historical Christian authors wrote about what a Christian's attitude toward other people should be. Christian authors, in attempting to correct what they saw as a debilitating hemorrhage of attention and energy onto objects in the world and onto other people *as* objects, often exaggerated their descriptions of the necessity to ignore, disdain, and neglect everyone and everything in order to orient oneself solely to God. Yet traces of Augustine's meaning can still be found, even in authors that advocate "willing one thing." Johann Arndt wrote:

> The love of God and the love of neighbor are one thing and must not be divided. . . . The love of God, indeed, God himself, has fallen away from that man who does not find the love of neighbor in himself. . . . [God] does not wish to be loved by us aside from the love of our neighbor.[54]

In the nuclear world in which human beings are, in fact, one human community in life and death, love of "neighbors" takes on a newly critical meaning. If we are to find the metaphor of pilgrimage useable in the later twentieth century, we will need to reject historical suggestions that other people are to be seen merely as help or hindrance in one's individual pursuit of salvation. And we will need to face the question of whether a rehabilitated interpretation of what it means to "love the neighbor in God" can be useful when the phrase can be, and has been, abused and misunderstood so frequently in the past.

We have discussed various aspects of Christian life that have been featured in historical interpretations of Christian life as pilgrimage. We have also examined alternative interpretations within the metaphor. In conclusion, we must try to evaluate the usefulness of the metaphor as a whole for Christian life in the nuclear world. Does the metaphor contribute anything of importance to twentieth-century Christians in our threatened and threatening world? Some historical instructions, we have seen, are particularly dangerous when we scrutinize them in our own context: disparagements of human life in this world in relation to a presumed life-after-death; denial and glorification of death; and individualism that fantasizes independent agency and autonomy. We have also seen some historical interpretations that could be valuable in our world: for example, an emphasis on loving other people in a way that is not compulsive or possessive, but regards others as themselves "before God," engaged in their own pilgrimage. Moreover, in the practice of actual pilgrimage, a sense of the natural world as rich with spiritual meaning was stimulated; the dissolution of daily habits and habitual responses also suggested the need for dehabituating practices that relieve and refresh body and spirit.

We saw also that Augustine, in advocating that the Christian "use" rather than "enjoy" other people and objects in the world, still urged that others are to be loved. Nevertheless, the connotations of "use" in the modern world have become so cluttered with implications of devaluation that, if we were to state our attitude toward others in Augustine's terms, we must choose "enjoyment" as the most accurate description of our appreciation for the natural world, other living beings, and the natural world nearest home, human bodies. By urging that we understand our relationship to the natural world as Christians as one of "enjoyment," I do not advocate that we unthinkingly appropriate its pleasures and beauties. Moreover, the social "world" must also receive our continuous examination and criticism; we cannot simply "enjoy" a world of unjust social arrangements, unfair food distribution, exploitation and oppression. But we must, I urge, "enjoy" the natural world, other human beings, and the delightful objects of our physical senses to a degree and in a way that results in the spontaneous response of gratitude and responsibility; such enjoyment is a moral responsibility in the nuclear world.

Finally, pilgrimage as metaphor for Christian life can still retain in the twentieth century one of its most highly valued historical functions. Realization of the impermanence of the world of human experience, of one's own mortality and that of others, can produce a heightening and intensification of experience, a strong treasuring of the moment. Awareness of finitude can infinitely increase our delight in the kaleidoscope of sensible beauty provided daily by the natural world and the human community. Instead of making us long for a future life in contrast to which the one we know seems shabby, we will perhaps come to think of a future life as the fulfillment of a present world too colorful, too vibrant with meaning, too precious, to end—the continuation of a pilgrimage too engrossing and rewarding to have a final destination.

# 4

# Staying Is Nowhere: Ascent

*We go to God not by walking but by loving.*

*Augustine*[1]

The third influential metaphor for Christian life we will explore is Christian life as ascent to union with God. Unlike Christian life as pilgrimage, the metaphor of ascent was not based on a literal practice. Conceiving of Christian life as ascent can be combined with either pilgrimage or imitation of Christ, and is often interwoven with these other metaphors. In *The Pilgrim's Progress,* for example, Christian's progress is described, in both text and illustrations, as climbing "a mighty hill" to the Celestial City.[2] The scriptural bases of the metaphor are Moses' encounter with God on Mount Sinai, Jacob's vision of a ladder between heaven and earth, and Christ's transfiguration. All of these were events in which there was a meeting of the divine and the human realms. The Prologue of John Climacus's manual, *The Ladder of Divine Ascent,* describes the steps—practices and attitudes—by which a Christian may mount to heaven:

> To all who are diligent to have their names inscribed in the book of life in heaven, the present book points out the best path. Journeying by this way, we shall find that this book is an unerring guide to those who follow it, keeping them unharmed from every stumbling stone. And it sets before us a fixed ladder leading from things earthly to the Holy of Holies; it makes manifest the God of love, who stands upon its summit. . . . And so, I entreat you, let us climb with zeal and faith up this spiritual and heaven-scaling ladder.[3]

Two initial observations must be made on the metaphor of ascent as a model for laypersons' practice of Christianity. First, ascent has been imagined in two ways: a Christian's lifetime can be imaged as a gradual and cumulative climb toward heaven; or it can also—and particularly in devotional manuals—be used as an image of brief but intense mystical experiences. In this chapter I intend to discuss only the first use of the metaphor: ascent as description of a lifelong practice of Christianity. Sometimes, however, authors take advantage of the ambiguity of the model to picture the momentary mystical glimpse, the "vision of God," as a hint of the reward for a lifetime of faithful ascent. It is difficult, then, to separate the two uses of the metaphor of ascent.

Second, the metaphor of ascent was primarily designed as an image of monastic practice of Christianity. The instructional manuals in which this metaphor dominates—such as that of John Climacus—were usually not directed to lay people but were written to people whose lifestyles were designed to cultivate the personal and communal practice of Christianity. The image of Christian life as ascent is also to be found frequently in manuals written for laypersons, but it was tacitly understood or explicitly stated that lay people could not expect to climb as rapidly, to glimpse divine things as frequently and fully, as could those whose lives were carefully and continuously organized around exercises that prepared them for the ascent. Thus the metaphor of ascent was used in historical Christianity to support the view of monastic life as the ideal Christian life; by comparison, the effort to live a Christian life "in the world" was seen as a diluted, a less effective, version of monastic life. The full-time Christian life, "undistracted" by the cares of "this world," seemed, to most historical Christian authors, obviously the "higher" life.

Nevertheless, sermons and devotional manuals for lay people frequently urged them to think of their lives as an ascent to heaven. The practices of prayer, the exercise of the virtues, and loving service to others enabled lay Christians to ascend. Lay people were urged to *try* to climb the ladder toward God, even though they labor under severe constraints of time and energy. Since ascent was not, however, a primary metaphor for lay practice of Christianity, it will need to be analyzed as a monastic model, a model that was adopted and slightly adapted for lay usage. Moreover, its strengths *and* problems as a model for monastic life also carried over into its use by lay people.

The first strength of the metaphor is that although the steps or rungs of the ladder were variously described in different manuals, the stages of ascent were practices, not ideas. The metaphor thus entailed a concreteness not highlighted in the metaphors of Christian life as imitation of Christ or pilgrimage. John Climacus's instructions on how to ascend by following "the narrow way" list as necessary practices or life situations that can stimulate and encourage ascent:

mortification of the stomach, all-night standing, water in moderation, short rations of bread, the purifying draught of dishonour, sneers, derision, insults, the cutting out of one's own will, patience in annoyances, unmurmuring endurance of scorn, disregard of insults, and the habit, when wronged, of bearing it sturdily; when slandered, of not being indignant; when humiliated, not to be angry; when condemned, to be humble.[4]

We may wonder how a monk was to find these trying circumstances in the community of "brothers and fathers" addressed by John Climacus, but apparently trials were readily available, even in such a setting. Even so, life in the world must surely have offered many more opportunities for practicing tranquility of spirit and the virtues of humility and endurance in the face of temptations to anger or distress. In any case, the primary problem with John's instruction for twentieth-century people does not lie in its monastic setting, but in its lack of recognition that suppressed emotion causes physical and mental illness. Nevertheless, the emphasis on practice, rather than on concepts, called for a practical method rather than a conceptual scheme. If a Christian knows what she must *do* in order to achieve a highly valued experience, she is enabled, by this specification, to proceed to the experience with more confidence and with less waste of energy on confusion or perplexity. Prayer, scripture reading, tears of repentance, conversation with others on religious topics, meditation, and various ascetic disciplines were the tools for the ascent in all monastic manuals.[5]

Like the metaphors of pilgrimage and imitation of Christ, ascent emphasizes the possibility of individual change and growth in spiritual life; Gregory of Nyssa, in his exhortation to ascent, *The Life of Moses,* wrote:

We are in some manner our own parents, giving birth to ourselves by our own free choice, in accordance with whatever we wish to be.[6]

In order to stimulate the monk's effort, monastic manuals sometimes emphasized the efficacy of labor at the expense of adequate acknowledgment of reliance on grace. Benedict of Nursia (c. 480–547), author of an early monastic *Rule,* wrote:

If we wish to attain the pinnacle of the highest humility and quickly come to that heavenly exaltation to which the ascent is made by the humility of the present life, then we must, by our upward-striving works, erect the ladder which was revealed to Jacob in the dream.[7]

Manuals that use ascent as their dominant metaphor insist that the reader, as "sculptor, carving in your own heart,"[8] must vigorously undertake to chip away from one's life "every obstacle to the pure view of the hidden image."[9]

A second strength of the metaphor of ascent is that it emphasizes the connection between advance in Christianity and moral integrity. Separating what one *does* in one's relationships with others from what one can understand is a modern phenomenon, completely alien to historical Christianity. Thomas Aquinas, in his discussion of contemplation in the *Summa Theologiae,* poses the question of "whether the moral virtues pertain to the contemplative life." He answers that, although moral virtues are not part of the essence of contemplation, they are nevertheless an indispensable prerequisite for contemplative experience.

The danger of slipping and falling, by moral lapse or by laziness, is also heightened by the ascent metaphor. Ladder imagery renders more dramatic the possibility of sudden collapse and precipitous descent, not merely to one's starting place, but, as the frontispiece (fig. 4) in the original manuscript of John Climacus's manual shows, into the gaping mouth of hell, depicted as huge lips on the earth's surface.[10] Neither of the other major metaphors for Christian life describe so vividly the consequences of a relaxation of effort; yielding to temptation occasionally caused the pilgrim, Christian, to slow his pace, or even to retreat a few steps, but it did not land him in a worse position than before he began the long trek to the Celestial City. Similarly, failing to imitate Christ in one situation merely means that one must begin again. Not so with the metaphor of ascent. The Christian who slips does not usually descend to the rung below, but crashes ignominiously—in visual as well as in verbal image—to the very bottom, indeed, to beneath the earth.

Ascent imagery raises some issues that are central to determining the present usefulness of the metaphor. The lowest rung of the ladder is invariably occupied by "sensible things"; the goal of the ladder is union with God; the trajectory of the ascent, then, is away from the sensible world and toward an imageless "seeing." The method of the ascent is "renunciation of all earthly things," specified by John Climacus as "love, care, and worry about money, possessions, parents, worldly glory, friends, brothers, or anything at all on earth; . . . it is a great disgrace for us to worry about anything that cannot help us in the hour of our need, that is to say, in the hour of our death."[11] Did the authors who gave these instructions intend to deny the value of the sensible world? Or is this an effect—albeit an unfortunate one—of the text's rhetoric?

In order to answer this question, we must distinguish between metaphysical descriptions of the status of the sensible world and exhortations that aim at inspiring and energizing vigorous ascent. There are sometimes

Fig. 4. Frontispiece, St. John Climacus, *The Ladder of Divine Ascent*. St. Catherine's Monastery, Sinai.

strong differences or even contradictory statements within the same texts, depending on the specific context of statements about the sensible world. Typically, philosophical theology differs from practical instruction in describing the status of the sensible world more inclusively. In meta-physical descriptions, the sensible world is primarily the created world, a world that is itself a full demonstration of the infinite beauty of its creator. The sensible world thus requires and rewards a Christian's attention. In the sixth century an Eastern author, Pseudo-Dionysius, wrote:

> Any thinking person realizes that the appearances of beauty are signs of an invisible loveliness. The beautiful odors which strike the senses are repre-sentations of a conceptual diffusion. Material lights are images of the outpouring of an immaterial gift of light. [12]

In this description of the relationship of the sensible and spiritual worlds, the created world is not understood as a pale shadow of the spiritual world; it is rather the strongest and most direct evidence of its existence. Similarly, in Saint Bonaventure (1221–74), the biographer of Francis of Assisi and contemporary of Thomas Aquinas, the "steps of our ascension to God" are a natural part of the universe of human experience: "This universe of things is a stair by which we may ascend to God." [13]

Bonaventure describes a process by which, by more attentive engage-ment with corporeal objects, one can begin to move upward along "stairs" that lead progressively to a more and more rarified spiritual atmosphere. [14] Each "stair," however, must not merely be traversed, but must *inform* ascent to the next step. In metaphysical descriptions like Bonaventure's, one must explore "things" deeply and appreciatively rather than hastily traversing them to reach another level. Sensible objects themselves inform the climb to union with God. Augustine also described the contemplation of the sensible world in this way:

> And what is this God? I asked the earth and it answered: "I am not he," and all things that are on the earth confessed the same. I asked the sea and the deeps and the creeping things with living souls . . . I asked the blowing breezes . . . the heaven, the sun, the moon, the stars. . . . Tell me something about my God. And they cried out in a loud voice: "He made us.": *My question was in my contemplation of them, and their answer was in their beauty.* [15]

This quotation raises another consideration in relation to ascent imag-ery: the ambiguity of the use of the terms "lower" and "higher." "Lower" may frequently mean less valuable or beautiful or significant, as it ex-plicitly does in many devotional manuals. But the "lowest" step is also the foundation, the point of access, the necessary entrance to the ascent. Without the bottom rung, the "higher" rungs of the ladder would be inaccessible. Bonaventure wrote: "Since we must ascend Jacob's ladder before we descend, let us place the first step of the ascent at the bottom, holding up this whole sensible world before us as a mirror, through which we may rise to God."[16] Theologians often give careful and nuanced descriptions of the value of the sensible world for spiritual life.

In contrast to metaphysical descriptions of the status of the sensible world, manuals of practical instruction usually presented the natural world of bodies and senses as foil for purposes of urging neglect or rejection of the external world. This rhetoric should be understood as part of the intense pressure brought to bear on the cultivation of an interior life. Spiritual growth was envisioned as a struggle to turn one's attention and affection from objects in the world to God, the invisible "object." Because of the practical agenda of devotional manuals, because of their interest in specifying the practices that create the physical and emotional conditions for realizing ascent, these manuals are much more disparaging of the sensible world. Put simply, conceiving the social world, the natural world, and one's own body as enemies provided the provocation and energy for the performance of the mental and physical exercises by which one mounted to God.

We can recognize the effectiveness of this counterintuitive, counter-cultural interpretation of the body in placing pressure on a specifically spiritual development even while we may wholeheartedly regret the disparagement of the natural world and living bodies in Christian tradition. The human body, symbol and nearest representative of cultural conditioning, was the monk's most important tool for fashioning a spirit free of the accumulated sediment of the social world—a world not tailored to, or concerned with, the specific rigors of spiritual ascent. "Let no one, when he is young, listen to his enemies, the demons, when they say to him: 'Do not wear out your flesh, lest you make it sick and weak,'" wrote John Climacus.[17] With the tools of gentle ascetic practices, the monk achieved a dehabituation of the routines of daily life that maintain the spirit's sleep; by harsher asceticisms, he created, over time, a systematic deconditioning of his most fundamental and deeply ingrained cultural reactions and responses. Although we can acknowledge the effectiveness of training the body in order to strengthen the soul, however, the danger of contrasting the worth of the body with the far greater worth and dignity of the soul or spirit is more evident in the twentieth century than it was in historical Christianity.

In addition to implicit, and frequently explicit, disparagement of the body and the world of the senses in devotional manuals, more subtle issues arise from the implied placement of the diverse contents of human experience on a ladder, graded according to value, beauty, and relative inaccessibility. "Hierarchy" has become a pejorative term among twentieth-century people who have inherited the problems caused by unequal assignments of value to the natural world in relation to the spiritual world. A conceptual arrangement of the world of human experience in metaphysical and experiential hierarchies no longer seems to us to be obvious and "natural." For most historical Christians, however, it was a visible and experiential reality, continually reiterated in social and political arrangements. The visual images in parish churches also presented a spiritual hierarchy; in religious images, saints, prophets, scriptural and divine figures were each placed in the painting and marked by relative sizes and distinguishing colors according to their value and importance. The "natural" arrangement of people and things in hierarchies was taken for granted throughout most of Christian history.

Since the idea of a natural hierarchy intrinsic to the structure of the world is not as obvious today as it was to medieval people, it is especially important to attempt to understand why this conceptual arrangement recommended itself to them so strongly. Why have so many Christian authors wanted to identify, not only the practices that propel one into spiritual insight but also hierarchical levels of being, reality, and value in the universe that correspond to steps or stages of ascent?

There are two practical advantages of a conceptual scheme that places all the phenomena of human experience in a clearly defined rank order: first, in a world of experience that might well be interpreted as chaotic, psychological security is the immediate reward for thinking one knows the nonnegotiable relative place and worth of everything that can be perceived, thought, or imagined. Second, picturing oneself on a ladder of spiritual ascent through a universal hierarchy specifies a mode of access to the highest realities available to human beings. Even if a Christian understands herself to be operating on one of the lower rungs of the ladder, the possibility is always present of moving higher; an access road has been mapped. Historical people, thoroughly accustomed to social hierarchies they considered inevitable, put their attention on the sides—the uprights—of the ladder, rather than on the relative height of the various stairs; when attention is put on contiguousness and continuity, the ladder model reinforces the message of accessibility. The ladder's uprights *hold together,* as surely as they keep in their places, all the steps and the phenomena they represent. Thus the unity of all beings, and the approachability of the highest being, God, was the dominant historical interpretation of the ladder of ascent as a model of Christian life.

Pseudo-Dionysius, one of the most articulate and influential exponents of the universe as graded hierarchy, defined hierarchy as "a certain perfect arrangement, an image of the beauty of God which sacredly works out the mysteries of its own enlightenment in the orders and levels of understanding of the hierarchy." The function and "goal" of the hierarchical arrangement of the universe is "to enable beings to be as like as possible to God and to be at one with God":

> Hierarchy causes its members to be images of God in all respects, to be clear and spotless mirrors reflecting the glow of primordial light and indeed, of God himself. It ensures that when its members have received this divine splendour they can then pass on this light generously and in accordance with God's will. [18]

Clearly, Pseudo-Dionysius's interpretation of hierarchy emphasized the participation of all living beings in the power and goodness of being. Some, of course, participate more fully than others, and we will need to look more closely at this implication shortly. We will need to ask how the description of the material and spiritual worlds as hierarchically arranged has functioned to inform assumptions about social arrangements in the Christian West. But first, a historical point needs attention.

Fundamental differences of experience lie between twentieth-century people and our ancestors in the Christian West, differences that influence how the ladder metaphor will be interpreted. Even to begin to suggest the content of those differences would be a mammoth task; perhaps, though, some differences can be evoked. Although, for example, twentieth-century North Americans live in perpetual danger of nuclear holocaust, most of us do not experience personal and communal vulnerability with great immediacy and intensity; we construct the insecurity of our world imaginatively rather than experience it directly. In contrast to the existing *potential* for destruction, our daily lives are relatively secure. Food supply is not a daily worry; even if we do not have money with which to buy food, food is on the shelves of our grocery stores, though this may be minimally comforting to people who have no money. It is still markedly different from many historical situations, however, in which food supplies were unpredictable and intermittent. Postal services, protection of our homes by a police force, medical attention, and other services that modern people take for granted—whether or not we are content with their actual operation—were far from the daily experience of historical people. Twentieth-century people are judgmental of historical people's need for secure, even if inequitable, social arrangements and services without realizing that our cavalier attitude toward physical security assumes a degree of daily protection never available before very recent times.

Differences of interest, that is, of investment in securing what we need to make life livable, and, beyond that, what we want, largely determine differences of interpretation of the same image or metaphor. In terms of the ascent metaphor, everything depends on whether one's experience has directed one's attention to the uprights or to the stairs of the ladder. Placing ladder and ascent imagery in historical setting, however, does not resolve the question of whether a metaphor that hierarchically arranges the world of human experience is a fruitful one for modern use. Before this can be evaluated, we must look at a further result of the use of ladder imagery by historical people.

Twentieth-century recognition that power relations are an inevitable aspect of every human relationship has sensitized historians to power relations in the past. Yet different experiences and the sensitivities derived from them lie between the way historical people thought of state and institutional power, and the way power has come to be thought of in the present. Twentieth-century people tend to expect that those who hold power will inevitably abuse it; we find Lord Acton's statement, "Power tends to corrupt, and absolute power corrupts absolutely," axiomatic. In the classical world, however, power entailed responsibility for people's protection, and it was this meaning of power that dominated Christendom until Machiavelli's sixteenth-century description of irresponsible totalitarian power. [19] Abuses of power were not, of course, absent until Machiavelli described them as the norm; abuses were frequent and blatant, both in the late classical and the medieval world, but the expectation of power continued to be that power protected and enabled. Thus, while modern people tend to think of power as *power over,* until about the sixteenth century, most of the people of the past thought of power as *power to*—enabling power.

Nevertheless, as in our examination of hierarchy as a feature of ladder imagery, trying to understand why firmly concentrated power was attractive to historical people need not deter us from making our own evaluation as to whether ladder and ascent imagery, with its inevitable implication, for us, of "power over" is useful as a metaphor for social and political life in our time. Historical understanding and critical judgment are both essential to our project of critique and retrieval. It *is* illegitimate either to assume that historical people understood a word or idea in the same way moderns do or to apply the insights of historical people to our own situation without attention to the context of the nuclear world. The challenge is to scratch beneath the surface of verbal similarity in order to understand historical constructions of reality without neglecting the duty of critical analysis of traditional ideas and values in relation to our own historical location.

Let us examine some further implications of power embedded in the ladder metaphor. Christian life understood as a steady, if not speedy, ascent toward union with God, a climb up the rungs of a ladder, inevitably pictures some climbers on higher rungs than others. In ascent imagery, the external world is ordered hierarchically from material to spiritual, and those who climb take on the characteristics and the relative value of the rung on which they stand. Those further up the ladder, then, are not only more advanced but also can act as authorities for those nearer the bottom who are still heavily enmeshed in the material world. Pseudo-Dionysius gives a concise account of how spiritual power is distributed in a Christian community. Pseudo-Dionysius used the term "ecclesiastical hierarchy" to mean the whole clergy and congregation, the people of God, gathered at worship.[20] The treatise is not a manual for the instruction of lay people, but was written to a "fellow-elder" in response to the question: "What is the tradition of the ecclesiastical hierarchy and what is its purpose?"[21]

First, we must notice Pseudo-Dionysius's understanding of power; it is clearly stated in his treatise *The Divine Names*. Pseudo-Dionysius did not define God's power as "power over," but rather made it very clear that he conceived of God's power as primarily enabling power—the power of being—a power which infuses all of creation:

> God is power in that all power is initially contained within his own self. . . . He is the cause of all power. He gives being to all things through his power. . . . His transcendent power is inexpressible, unknowable, inconceivably great, and, as it flows over, it empowers whatever is weak and it preserves and directs the humblest of its echoes. . . . God's infinite power is distributed among all things and there is nothing in the world entirely bereft of power. . . . The benefits of this power reach out to humans, to animals, to plants, and indeed to all of nature.[22]

God's power, distributed among created beings, manifests itself in "intuition, reason, perception, life, and being."

God's enabling power is, however, distributed "according to merit," and some beings receive more than others. "Man," for example, receives more than animals:

> For man is, after all, intelligent and capable of looking toward the higher things. Sturdy and upright he is, by nature, a leader and a ruler, and even if, by comparison with the irrational animals he is least in the scale of the power of sense perception, still it is he who dominates all with the superior power of his intelligence, with the mastery deriving from rational understanding, and with the natural freedom and independence of his spirit.[23]

Even among "men," however, there is a great difference of power. God's power does not inform all of God's people equally. The "hierarch" who stands at the head of the church receives power directly from God; he is "divinely perfected and deified, and takes on "a likeness to God."[24] Through him, power is

> imparted to those below him according to their merit. . . . Subordinates, in turn, are to pursue their superiors and they also promote the advance of those below them, while these too, as they go forward, are led by others.[25]

Let us remind ourselves that Pseudo-Dionysius is still talking of enabling power, the power of being, but his tone has changed. He emphatically and repeatedly urges the necessity of secrecy, and the inaccessibility of the divine truth to those on the lowest rungs of the hierarchy, except as it is made available to them by the gracious generosity of those on higher rungs. The reason given for the necessity of an ecclesiastical hierarchy of clergy and people is that there must be a clear line of transmission of spiritual power from the hierarch downward to the lowest rank. Thus, even though the function of the entire hierarchy is to make accessible a flow of enabling power, the fixed ranks of a stable order are inevitable.

To modern people it is immediately apparent that Pseudo-Dionysius's "ecclesiastical hierarchy" contains a classic rationalization for the legitimacy of protected power postions for those in the upper echelons, the clergy that controls and dispenses the "sacred mysteries." Pseudo-Dionysius's authorial interest, focused by his language of "above" and "below," "superior" and "subordinate," "pursuit" and "advance," is on the relative positions within the hierarchy; the reader does not get a strong sense of the connectedness of the people of God in worship, but rather of a carefully graded participation in the language and ritual of the liturgy. In Pseudo-Dionysius's treatise to a fellow priest, full of injunctions to secrecy, it is difficult to fix one's eye on the ladder's uprights that hold together in being *all* of the ecclesiastical hierarchy.

We must now conclude by evaluating the usefulness of the metaphor of ascent for twentieth-century practice of Christianity. Having considered various features of the metaphor, we have already noticed that the reader's engagement with the metaphor permits the communication of multiple meanings.[26] Let us first summarize what the ascent metaphor and ladder imagery highlight about Christian life. Then we will consider what is obscured by the metaphor of Christian life as vigorous ascent. What is communicated by the metaphor as *vehicle,* which those who have advocated the use of the metaphor as conceptual scheme for a Christian life may have failed to notice?

First among the strengths of ascent as a metaphor for Christian life is its emphasis on vigorous engagement in selected practices by which a religious self—the self that listens and speaks to God—is created and cultivated. The metaphor of ascent incites a person to "take her life in her own hands," in the sense of taking responsibility for one's life. The contemporary psychologist Abraham Maslow has said, "A capacity is a need," a statement that historical authors of devotional manuals would have found both accurate and important. If human beings have a capacity to develop a concentrated interior life with cultivated rather than accidental continuity and growth, then that capacity is a *need* which, left unmet, can damage the whole fabric of one's life.

Moreover, the metaphor of ascent provides a strong countercultural alternative to passivity. In the entertainment culture of contemporary North America, there are few cultural inducements to understand one's life as an integrated project. This metaphor, like the metaphors of Christian life as pilgrimage and as imitation of Christ, formulates and presents the insight that Christian life is a vigorous engagement with the circumstances, opportunities, and difficulties of one's life. As a correction for female conditioning to passivity, for example, the ascent metaphor could be useful for encouraging women to recognize an inner authority that questions societal expectations.

Another feature of the ascent metaphor is emphasis on the dynamic quality of Christian life: "staying is nowhere."[27] As John Climacus put it: "If [the monk] does not force himself to mount higher, he will fall lower and lower."[28] Far from encouraging Christians to rest in enjoyment of passive acceptance of God's providence, the ascent metaphor urges the Christian to exert the utmost effort to mount the ladder. The energetic climber must not succumb to laziness, despair, torpor, lethargy, or inertia. John Climacus indicates the appropriate quality of involvement in the ascent; the ideal monk, he wrote, is one who "to the end of his life has not ceased daily to add fire to fire, fervour to fervour, zeal to zeal, love to love."[29] In addition to the attraction of achieving spiritual growth, the threat of falling inspires what often appears to be anxious pursuit of the spiritual goal. In their effort to stimulate energetic advance, authors of devotional manuals often used imagery that suggested very little trust in God's care and guidance. Before it is possible to assess whether this instruction, with its accent on intense, even anxious, engagement is fruitful for us or not, our communal historical context, as well as personal situations must be taken into account. In twentieth-century North America, it is possible that the incitement to activity contained in the metaphor could serve to correct expectations created by an entertainment culture. It might also balance tendencies to passive reliance on others for self-definition.

Moreover, Christian life pictured as ascent to God provides a model of life as an integrated continuity rather than as a "succession of unrelated emotional experiences."[30] Life's problems and difficulties, as well as pleasures and accomplishments, have a meaning within the scenario of ascent; each can play its part in urging or attracting—in pushing or pulling—the person to mount higher. In theory, wherever one is currently located on the ladder of ascent is the ideal place from which to begin—or to continue—to mount, since each rung is part of the whole momentum of ascending motion. Whatever his present situation, the Christian can assume that it contains opportunities for learning and spiritual growth.[31] This view of Christian life as a continual weaving of the circumstances of one's life into support and energy for ascent could be highly useful to twentieth-century people who often feel that life consists of a thousand threads, held in our hands.

Clearly, the metaphor of ascent still contains some valuable emphases for contemporary people. But what are its risks and dangers? There are several major implications of Christian life as ascent that make the metaphor problematic for lay people. As we have seen, it is primarily a metaphor for monastic life, and its advantages may still outweigh its dangers in a monastic setting; I will, however, not attempt to evaluate the metaphor in a monastic context, since my task here is to analyze and assess the instructions given to lay people for the pursuit of Christian life. In the context of a lay practice of Christianity, the metaphor's problems and dangers may outweigh its advantages. If, after discussing these dangers, it seems not only that it is *possible* to construe the metaphor of ascent in ways that are counterproductive in the twentieth century but also, as we noticed in Pseudo-Dionysius's account of an "ecclesiastical hierarchy," that it seems to have been repeatedly used to rationalize unexamined power relations, we will need to explore whether it is possible to preserve the metaphor's strengths in some other form than that of the ascent model.

The first problem of the metaphor need not be further discussed at length. By arranging the world of human experience on a ladder that reaches *from* the sensible world *to* the spiritual world, the metaphor cannot avoid an implicit, and often explicit, exaggeration of their separation and contrasting value. Although the ladder can be understood as a route, a map, rather than a scale of value, the implication of the far greater value of realities distant from the senses is inevitable.

The perceptible world often appears only as contrast or foil; although it is placed on the lowest, and most fundamental, stair, attention to the world of the senses is presented as a distraction from, rather than a clue to, its creator. The one who would contemplate spiritual things, Gregory of Nyssa wrote, must "withdraw himself from his customary intercourse with his own companion, that is, from his sense perceptions."[32] Ladder imagery necessarily entails a contrast between the sensible and the spiritual world; Augustine's description of sensible objects—trees and breezes, the sea and animals—as the most direct and immediate evidence of the creator, the place to *begin,* is not often maintained in devotional manuals. For example, the enormously popular sixteenth-century devotional manual, Erasmus's *Enchiridion,* tells the reader that, "compared to things unseen, the objects of the visible world present to the eyes nothing more than insubstantial copies of those realities."[33] Furthermore, the method that results from this evaluation of the visible world is one of transferring to the spiritual world *the same* attention and energy that one had "wasted" on the sensible world:

> If physical beauty charms you, why are you not burning all the more hotly for that beauty which lies within? Transfer your love to something permanent, something celestial, something incorruptible, and you will love more cooly this transitory and fleeting form of the body.[34]

In the nuclear world, this disparagement of the world of the senses is not merely unuseable; it is dangerous.

The second major problem of the ascent model of Christian life is its integration of an ontological hierarchy with an ecclesiastical hierarchy. Put simply: professional clergy and those in monastic orders have a greater share of God's power and authority, a greater share of being, reality, and value than lay people. Although this view remains unchallenged in many geographical areas, it is presently being increasingly questioned and rejected in centers of religious renewal and theological exploration, especially in North, South, and Central America.

Pluralism, both in relation to Christian tradition, and in relation to other religions, is increasingly evident in religious discourse. The first principle of pluralistic discussion is the acknowledgement that no one is in possession of an absolute perspective, a God's-eye view, from which to speak with dogmatic authority. Pluralism is not different emphases within an accepted system of ideas and values. Nor is it the *representation* of different life experiences and perspectives. Pluralism is the participation of different *people* in reality-defining discourse. It is the acknowledgment that all religious discourse consists of *interpretations* of religious authority—in Christianity, it may be scripture, tradition, the Spirit's leading, personal experience, or some combination of these. In a time when the particularity of all the perspectives from which these authorities are interpreted is being explored, not simply by a philosophical acknowledgment of the limitedness of all human understanding, but also by the engagement of women and minority people in articulating diverse interests and insights about Christian faith, the hierarchical implications of ascent and ladder imagery do not recommend this model of Christian life.

Some further difficulties associated with the ascent model of Christian life must be mentioned briefly. Incitement to strenuous effort may often be the precisely wrong advice for people for whom a sort of "works righteousness" is already a personality trait. In the past, the ascent model was also criticized by sixteenth-century Protestant reformers on grounds of its implicit neglect of attention to God's graceful and sustaining care for Christians. Implicit devaluation of lay people's practice of Christianity in relation to those whose entire lives are devoted to a combination of contemplation and service makes it problematic. The privileging of one Christian lifestyle over others is one of the historical results of ladder and ascent imagery. The uniqueness of each life and the learning it makes possible must not be sacrificed for a universalized scheme of upward advance in Christian life. Moreover, the idea of progress toward a goal that can be interpreted variously as momentary union with God in the present, or reception into heaven at death, is itself a problem in that it fails to insist on the beauty, goodness, and irreplaceable value of life on the earth in the present.

Finally, ladder and ascent imagery carries the assumption that the process of Christian life is roughly the same for everyone, namely, a gradual incremental learning to disengage oneself from attachment to human relationships, material possessions, success, sex—the world of sense objects. Stated in *this* way, as disengagement from *attachment,* the idea of detachment provides a valuable insight; as Augustine said, a slave cannot enjoy that to which he is enslaved. But injunctions to detachment, often stated with careful nuance in theological texts, were reduced in most devotional manuals to slurs on the *objects* of sense, rather than to critiques of the Christian's *relationship* to these objects. Again, the suggestion that objects of perception are themselves unreal or corrupt in relation to "higher things" is dangerous in the nuclear world, a world that we must learn to love and value enough to work to preserve.

Moreover, the universalization of stages or steps of ascent contains the assumption that a normative human being exists whose experience has become the rule for everyone. In the twentieth century, most people may have introjected a secularized version of the "stage theory" of ascent in which we focus on our intellectual and psychic needs and longings rather than on the natural world on which our bodies are dependent. To the extent that this is the case, we need to have our attention redirected to the daily, the "ordinary," for lack of a better word, to the beauty and worth of the natural world, human relationships, and the earth's provisions that we take for granted. Christians, who have always thought of Christian life as ascent to an ethereal and abstract realm, may need to reinterpret a responsible Christianity for our own time as a reinvestment of our attention, gratitude, and energetic protection in the transcendently valuable natural world.

If, as I have suggested, the model of ascent entails more potential for danger than help for twentieth-century Christians, can we identify ways to preserve the strengths of the metaphor in some other configuration of Christian life? The answer to this question will conclude the first part of this book.

But we cannot leave the topic of governing metaphors in the tradition of Christian devotional writing without acknowledging one of the most pervasive metaphors of all: Christian life as military combat. Military preparation, tactics, and fighting provided an almost inexhaustible field upon which to draw for descriptions of Christian practice. From Prudentius's *Psychomachia*,[35] an allegorical description of Christian life as warfare, and throughout Christian tradition, combat has been a primary rhetorical figure for Christian life (see fig. 5). Battle against strong and well-armed spiritual foes has provided the rationale for urgent calls to rigorous preparatory exercises, impeccable armor, and utmost effort. Christian life as warfare was a favorite metaphor for Calvin,[36] and John Bunyan wrote *The Holy War Made by Shaddai upon Diabolus*,[37] a less well-known devotional treatise than *The Pilgrim's Progress* but still popular. Erasmus's *Enchiridion*, written in 1501 to an actual soldier, also exploited the military metaphor as its primary figure for Christian life:

> In the first place, you should continually bear in mind that mortal life is nothing but a kind of perpetual warfare . . . and very much deceived are the general run of men, whose minds this montebank of a world captivates with alluring pleasures, who take unseasonable furloughs as if the fighting were already over and they were not living in a most hazardous peace.[38]

Erasmus's handbook, or soldier's field manual,[39] was written in order to provide its reader with "a kind of hand dagger," a "little blade"

> which you should never put aside, not even at the table or in bed, so that even if you must sojourn at times in the business of this world and find it cumbersome to carry around that whole armor, nevertheless you will not

Fig. 5. Christian Fights the Dragon, illustration from the first edition of *The Pilgrim's Progress*, 1678.

expose yourself at any time and have the waylayer pounce upon you completely unprepared.[40]

Who are the enemies in this "perpetual warfare"? "To the right and to the left, in van and in rear, this world assails us."[41] From external enemies, "the vilest demons," to the Christian soldier's own desire, projected as a figurative seductive "woman": "Keep in mind that 'woman' is man's sensual part: she is our Eve, through whom that wiliest of serpents lures our passions into deadly pleasures"—the list of enemies includes even "the most private recesses of our consciousness" in which the "ancient and earthy Adam," more intimate, domesticated, secret, and dangerous than any other enemy is alive and well.[42]

It is impossible to overemphasize the pervasiveness of the understanding of life as war in Christian tradition. Authors whose governing model of Christian life was ascent or pilgrimage frequently also wrote of these as involving warfare; even a summary of the influence of this metaphor on authors who wrote popular manuals of instruction in the practice of Christianity would take us far from our central task in this chapter. Nevertheless, it is important to notice as one of the constant features of popular devotional manuals this vision of the Christian's life in the world of human experience: his body and his consciousness, other people, and society, as potentially "mortall enemies."[43]

Considered from the perspective of the nuclear world, the problems of this construction of Christian life seem so obvious and overwhelming as to not require a great deal of discussion. The difficulties of the metaphor of ascent are made explicit and exacerbated by picturing Christian life as a battle to the death against a myriad of daily enemies. Although the metaphor of battle certainly provides a strong interpretation of the vigor and discernment necessary for Christian life, it overreaches its goal by requiring that one regard *all* that one encounters, both externally and interiorly as potentially—and usually actually—hostile and threatening. The religious self constructed by the use of this metaphor must be constantly "on guard." Any relaxation of vigilance could prove fatal to this beleaguered self; a constitutional paranoia must be the primary characteristic of the Christian soldier.

Issues surrounding the figuration of gender in the metaphor of Christian life as fight are so complex that I will only sketch them. The normative Christian is understood as male, engaged in one of the most exciting and demanding activities of historical men. In Christian societies, the metaphor of Christian life as warfare was part of male gender conditioning to aggressive and competitive behavior. Women and their bodies appear only as a metaphor for male lust, as we have seen in

Erasmus's *Enchiridion*. Women are not represented as human beings with subjectivity, but as threat to men's spiritual integrity,[44] as moral lesson,[45] and as daily temptation.[46] In this discourse between the male author and the male reader, Erasmus describes all sexual intercourse as "befouling ourselves in every hog wallow of lust."[47] Women have only two potential roles in this scenario: first, as obstacles to the male task of transcending the world. Urging the soldier to love his wife, "not in herself but in Christ," he added that "then in reality you love Christ in her, and so, at last, you love in a spiritual sense."[48] Second, Erasmus characterized the "other woman," the woman who excites male lust, as a "stinking tart."[49] The popularity of his *Enchiridion* may have come as a surprise to Erasmus, but its status as a best seller seems to indicate that Erasmus's views on women and sexuality and his use of "woman" as metaphor for lust was not questioned. Even if we do not try to determine the effect of this manual on actual relationships between sixteenth-century men and women, the universalization of a male perspective as well as the blatantly sexist imagery of the text disqualifies the *Enchiridion* and the instructions it advocates as useful in the twentieth century.

As in the case of the metaphor of ascent, we will need to ask whether the strengths of the imagery of Christian life as warfare, namely, its incitement to active engagement, can be preserved in some other model of Christian life. We will consider this question as we conclude this section.

Our discussion of some of the most frequently used metaphors for Christian life in the history of Christianity has revealed some highly problematic, even dangerous, features of these metaphors. The most rudimentary gender analysis, when applied to traditional devotional manuals, shows that women have been treated either as disembodied souls or as bodies, dangerous objects that incite male lust. The most popular manuals were written by men and, as we could have predicted, they display unexamined gender assumptions and attitudes. Women were the objects rather than the subjects of the practice of Christianity; most devotional manuals, even those specifically addressed to women, fail to reflect or to address women as subjects. The female religious self is cleanly split into spiritual soul, which may be cultivated and developed, and unredeemed body, dangerous to the woman herself, of course, but even more dangerous to men. Splitting women into body and spirit produced a corresponding split in men, whose understanding of women was narrowly channeled into the alternatives of loving her "in Christ" rather than "for herself" ("herself" defined as "because she provides you with sexual pleasure")[50] or as sexual object, the enjoyment of which, "for the sake of a trifling and filthy titilation of momentary pleasure, profanes the temple

Christ has consecrated with His own blood,"[51] namely, the male soul, "that high mind fashioned for the most beautiful things."[52] It is clear that in the most popular and influential devotional manuals of Christian tradition, women have not defined themselves, but have been assigned their roles in a male drama. Nevertheless, the inescapable law of unjust relationships is that both oppressor and oppressed suffer from the asymmetry of the relationship; the male subject, even though he had voice and determined the roles to be played, was flattened in a way that corresponded to the flattened and fragmented role he assigned the female object; he must speak as a subject defined by this female object.

A constant strain of devaluation of the sensible world in relation to a constructed spiritual world accompanied and corresponded to historical understandings of the nature and social roles of male and female. Although asymmetrical evaluation of the sensible and the spiritual could not be metaphysically justified in Christianity, its practical usefulness was a fact of experience. It simply "works" to inspire and energize spiritual labor by alienating a part of the person—the part that belongs to the transient physical universe—in order to cultivate another part of human capacity, participation in a spiritual world. It may be that only in the twentieth century can the full arrogance of this devaluation of the immediate, concrete, and vulnerable physical world be understood. Perhaps only the threat of losing, by nuclear holocaust or ecological crisis, the beauty and productivity of the sensible world, which Christians have for so long "despised," can prompt us to recognize and acknowledge the full extent of our dependence on this world.

The apparent univocity of Christian tradition on the subject of the consummately greater value of the spiritual than the sensual world of bodies, physical needs, and carnal temptations, however, should not finally obscure the profound revisionist activity that was always an ongoing aspect of the practice of Christianity. Because we have explored patterns *across* time, we have not highlighted the way devotional instructions functioned as corrections in their own time. The manuals we have discussed and the metaphors they employ became enormously popular because their contemporaries found them useful for addressing pressing needs and longings; they were popular and exciting—not too strong a word—because they translated Christian practice into an idiom that was accessible to the people for whom they were written.

It would take more time and space than we have to look in detail at how this conjunction of society and prescriptive manuals operated in each specific instance. No matter how cynical we may be about the way devotional manuals worked to maintain and reinforce powerful institutions and their representatives, however, the fact of their great popularity across centuries should remind us that, although our analysis should include notice of the role of gender, social, and institutional power that both prompted and resulted from devotional instructions, the power in question is much more subtle than it would be if it were merely the intentional propaganda of great institutions. The power represented by devotional manuals was the more important—more powerful—power of attraction. Each of the manuals we have discussed was able effectively to spell out to people a method for cultivating a countercultural self, a religious self free of social conditioning and capable of the most empowering activity they could imagine, relationship with God. We can, of course, identify some crippling flaws in the agenda of these manuals, but we should not, for that reason, ignore the longing for self-definition that motivated historical Christians' engagement with instructions for the practice of Christianity.

Historical Christians imagined themselves pilgrims on a long and arduous journey to the very gates of heaven; they imagined, and then enacted, what Christ might have said or done in the myriad encounters of their daily lives; they thought of themselves as climbing a mountain fraught with difficulty, but leading to home, a home replete with the comfort and joy they longed for and had never fully found. And they imagined themselves soldiers battling forces of evil and self-destruction that seemed perilously ubiquitous. Each of these metaphors, as construed in historical situations which we cannot fully reconstruct, have large and, in some cases, unaffordable liabilities in the nuclear world. Yet it requires only a modicum of imagination to envision historical situations in which each were useful.

A method for determining the usefulness, in the present, of the metaphors of Christian life, known and loved by centuries of Christian people, can be sketched, but the final discernment must be a personal and communal matter for the twentieth-century reader as it was for the sixth- or sixteenth-century reader of devotional manuals. It contains three questions or moments that can be distinguished for purposes of clarity, but must also, finally, be interwoven in the process of deciding on the appropriateness and productivity of traditional metaphors of Christian life. The first step asks about traditional interpretations of the metaphor: How is it described in historical devotional texts: What are its variations? What does the metaphor highlight? What are its strengths? And, what are its inherent risks or dangers?

The second step is one of application. A friend of Martin Luther's once quoted a scriptural text to him to prove a point he was trying to make. Luther, whose respect for the "Word of God" has never been doubted, replied to his friend, "Yes, I recognize that as the Word of God, but is it the Word of God to *me?*" The important step of asking whether any source of revelation or instruction is the "Word of God" to *me* at *this* moment cannot be evaded by citing an authority. Language, with its capacity to communicate conclusions detached from the contexts in which they originated and proved productive, creates the possibility that any axiom can be abused, any truth disastrously distorted by failing to consider its effect in relation to a particular situation at a particular moment. Luther's discernment—"Is it the Word of God *to me*"—is as important for twentieth-century Christians as it was for Luther.

The final, or perhaps, in practice, the first, critical moment is an analysis of the present personal, communal, or global situation within which one's decisions about what is useable are reached. This is a moment requiring humility because if one knows what an author thinks is wrong, she can evaluate the author's prescriptive advice more easily. To be willing to state one's analysis of what needs correction, then, is to acknowledge that analysis, as well as prescription, is interpretive and perspectival. We will return to this step in this book's conclusion. Our next topic is the most characteristic practices of Christian life, the exercises by which Christian life is embodied as well as learned imaginatively. The worth of a religious life depends ultimately not on what can be conceived but on what can be embodied.

## Part Two

# Practices of
# Christian Life

# Introduction to Part Two

*The point of spiritual labor is not to make you stiffer.*

*Robert Bly*

In Part I we explored several of the metaphors most frequently used by authors of devotional manuals to describe Christian life. We found it important to identify the explicit and implicit values that these metaphors entailed because they provided the conceptual scheme and the imagery by which Christians oriented themselves to their lives as Christians. The development, by Christian authors, of metaphors of imitation of Christ, ascent, pilgrimage, and fight revealed advocacy of some values that seemed problematic in various ways when we considered them in relation to the nuclear world. We also found some values that seemed not merely irrelevant, but dangerous if we were to imagine them in a contemporary practice of Christianity.

Even more fundamental to Christian life than the governing and value-laden metaphors within which Christians were encouraged to imagine a particular Christian life, however, are the religious practices by which the insight, or complex of insights, articulated by metaphors is realized in a person's life. The centrality of practices to the process of coming to understand has been obscured by the privileging of "insight" over the practical exercises that prepare and produce new understanding. For example, Martin Luther's realization that "The just shall live by faith" led him to speak so disparagingly of "works" that some of his followers claimed that "ungodly conduct" interfered not at all with their Christian faith. A hundred years after Luther, the Lutheran Johann Arndt wrote a manual, *True Christianity,* in order to refute a prevalent notion among Christians: "Many think that theology is a mere science, or rhetoric, whereas it is a living experience and practice."[1]

In the twentieth century, a similar secular privileging of intellectual and psychological understanding has led to a widespread assumption that change in behavior *follows,* rather than precedes, insight. Thus psychoanalysis and psychotherapies procede by creating, from a narration of the patient's experience, a new, more cohesive, more comprehensive, and more fruitful life story, a life story that permits the patient to reenvision and revise counterproductive or destructive patterns of thought and behavior.[2]

That the process of psychotherapy irreducibly involves, in contemporary secular dress, ancient religious practices of confession, repentance, contemplation, and commitment has not been a focus of attention. Rather, the objects of public attention and debate have been theories about psychological structures and the most effective methods by which patients can learn to recognize the patterns of their own experience. Twentieth-century disparagement of "going through the motions" is the result of Luther's understanding of "works" as following, rather than producing, intense religious feeling and understanding.

The emphasis placed on practices by historical Christian authors should not, however, be too sharply contrasted with their attention to "getting the mind right." Rather, it was the integration of thought and practice that defined the religious self. In contrast to twentieth-century consensus, most historical people thought it obvious that insight follows change; changed behavior—changed activities—*produce* insight. Enlightenment is the result of "doing the sacred acts," Pseudo-Dionysius wrote, in the *Ecclesiastical Hierarchy.*[3] The aim of religious practices was the production of a combination of understanding and strong experience that created a religious self and, ultimately, together with many people who have had the same experience and understanding, community. "Insight" was perhaps the ultimate goal, but the crucial need for a method of achieving the goal was met by the daily exercise of particular practices that cumulatively created the consciousness,[4] the psychic "place" at which the insight might be achieved. By the integration of a carefully performed program of dehabituating exercises, thoughts, visualizations, bodily postures, and verbal formulae, a state of consciousness was accomplished in which the desired insight seemed to appear spontaneously, that is, accompanied by an experience of effortless receptivity.

Monastic practices were based on the possibility of a coordination of effects—sexual abstinence, ascetic practices, diet—that, together with a communal rhetoric and mutual reinforcement, created experiential knowledge. Yet devotional manuals for lay people also recognized that the way to produce religious experience did not depend on ideas and beliefs so much as on "exercises."[5] We do not take seriously enough the constant monitory reminders in historical devotional manuals that practices are a sine qua non of understanding; twentieth-century interpreters tend to ignore the fact that practices were specifications for producing simultaneously a consciousness, an experience, and an understanding. Individual experiences, on the other hand, were preceded and confirmed by the interpretive rhetoric of a tradition and a community; they were enclosed—remote-controlled—in advance and in retrospect by the common language of the community.

Another way to describe the productive effect of a combination of "practices" and rhetoric is to say that, long before what we now call the "scientific method" was spelled out by Francis Bacon,[6] Christian authors were well aware of the possibility of the experimental reproduction of religious experience by reconstructing each of the conditions—a certain physical condition, certain beliefs, and certain exercises—that had created the experience for earlier candidates. From the same conditions and "steps," the same results can be obtained. After the religious experience has once been produced, its maintenance is relatively simple. Maintenance of the original experience consists first of the gradual articulation of a detailed reconstruction of reality, a reorganization and summary of all the "facts of experience" in a more satisfying hypothesis than that formerly held. In this rearticulation, alternative interpretations of experience are subordinated to a richer, more comprehensive and emotionally satisfying synthesis. Repentance, one of the most consistently advocated and vividly described Christian practices, for example, combined detailed introspection with tears of remorse. Tears were themselves condition and proof of psychic malleability. Repentance created a condition in which the person was vulnerable to suggestion, willing to exchange the patchwork of ordinary existence which by now appears pitifully shabby for the new religious interpretation of experience. Second, a regime that produces glimpses of the initial revolutionizing understanding is necessary to renew and refresh the practitioner.

Practices both prepare the conditions under which religious experiences are likely to occur and, subsequent to such experiences, provide a lifestyle that integrates and perpetuates them.[7] Hours spent in solitary prayer and meditation, tearful repentance, deprivation of food and sleep, routine physical work, exposure to cold, self-denying service to others—any combination of these and other practices was considered crucial to the cultivation of a religious self. It was understood that without the creation of a dehabituated body, a permeable psyche is not possible. The method described by Christian authors proceeds from dehabituation of the body to deconditioning of the psyche; as the condition of the body is altered by ascetic practices, the psyche loses its grip on former interpretive frameworks.

Devotional manuals have an especially intimate connection to the practices that shape a religious subject. They were, as Michel Foucault describes the self-help manuals of antiquity,

> texts written for the purposes of offering rules, opinions, and advice on how to behave as one should: "practical" texts, which are themselves objects of a practice in that they were designed to be read, learned, reflected upon, and

tested out, and they were intended to constitute the eventual framework of everyday conduct. These texts thus served as functional devices that would enable individuals to question their own conduct, to watch over and give shape to it, and to shape themselves as . . . subjects.[8]

In focusing on practices rather than on governing metaphors for Christian life in this section, our questions will shift slightly. We will still consider the range of interpretations that has been given and how particular practices have been understood theologically. We will also continue to examine the relationship of historical Christian practices and the values imbedded in them in relation to the nuclear world. But we will ask in addition what faculties or functions of human beings are engaged by particular practices. If Christian life is understood as the primary principle of organization by which the energies and priorities of a person or a community are organized, then the aspects of human beings that are engaged, cultivated, and trained by Christian practices are affirmed and honored; those not engaged are inevitably understood as less central or less significant to Christian life. For example, prayer was understood through Christian tradition as an important activity of Christian life: How was the practice of prayer understood? Was it understood as a dialogue between conversational partners, highlighting relationship? Did it involve prescribed bodily positions or postures, emphasizing the body's inclusion in Christian life? How were prayers directed? To an interior or an external recipient? Were petitions to be vocalized or silent? Should prayer occur at certain times of the day or week, or should it be woven through daily life without special attention to particular times or places? Was individual spontaneity in prayer important, or was "common prayer"—written prayers, joined in by a whole community—considered normative? Was the preferred medium of prayer words, visual images that focus contemplation, or imageless and wordless meditation? Were the senses engaged in prayer? What was the proper role of the intellect in prayer? What aspects of a person's life was prayer expected to affect?

The Christian practices we will explore in this section do not exhaust the range of useful disciplines of mind and body that historical Christian authors have advocated. Rather, we will examine what I understand as the most characteristic and continuously urged practices. Beginning with the most concrete—practices involving physical disciplines of various sorts—we will move to the more intangible practices of introspection, prayer, and the cultivation of mystical experience (see fig. 6). At the conclusion of the discussion of each practice, I will make some suggestions about the contemporary usefulness of that practice.

Fig. 6. Jesus Prays in the Wilderness, end 13th century. Ms. Italien 115. fol. 19. Bibliothèque Nationale, Paris.

# 5

## The Pleasure of No Pleasure: Asceticism

*We beg you, make us truly alive.*

*Serapion of Thmuis, fourth-century eucharistic prayer*

Asceticism is one of the currently least understood and most universally rejected features of historical Christianity. The word *asceticism* means simply discipline or training; in the fourth century, ascetics of the Egyptian desert were called "great athletes." Modern authors, whether secular or Christian, often use the general heading "asceticism" to designate what is actually a wide range of practices, goals, and rationales; they frequently do not attempt to discriminate between the gentle dehabituating practices advised by many historical authors and the harsh practices involving self-induced pain, which get far more attention. Clearly, asceticism does not appeal to modern people. It was frequently rationalized on an explicitly dualistic model of human being, and the more severe practices that damaged the body and sometimes caused premature death seem to us singularly dissonant in the religion of "the Word made flesh." In fact, as we will see, many historical authors objected to some ascetic practices on similar grounds. They cautioned against bodily abuse, while at the same time urging the frequent practice of dehabituating exercises, carefully chosen and individually tailored to address a particular person's compulsive behavior, addictions, or destructive thought patterns. Palladius, author of the *Lausiac History,* an account of fourth-century monastic asceticism, wrote:

Our holy and most ascetic master stated that the monk should always live as if he were to die on the morrow but at the same time he should treat his body as if he were to live on for many years to come. For, he said, by the first attitude he will be able to cut off every thought that comes from boredom and lethargy and thus become more fervent. . . . By the second device, he will preserve his body in good health.[1]

Recognition of the effectiveness of ascetic practices for the definition and cultivation of a religious self is not unique to Christianity; asceticism has been practiced across the world. There is nothing particular to Christianity in the recognition that practices of asceticism—from mild disciplines to body-damaging practices—change consciousness. Asceticism, although differently rationalized in different times and places, originated in the practical observation that an alteration of physical conditions produces a changed condition of the psyche. There is a direct and immediate connection, for example, between keeping one's stomach regularly nourished and maintaining the protection of a habitual psychological condition. Even a short fast makes the psyche accessible to observation, examination, and alteration. According to historical accounts, harsher practices can produce ecstatic states of consciousness.

In Christianity as in other religions, the practical effectiveness of asceticism for deconstructing the socially conditioned self and defining a religious self has been recognized. But in Christianity, an endemic problem exists in the contradiction between a rhetoric of disparagement of the body and theological descriptions of the permanent integrity of body and soul. Contempt for the body, a prominent feature of devotional manuals, is fundamentally inconsistent with the Christian doctrines of creation, the Incarnation of Christ, and the resurrection of the body. Throughout the history of Christianity, the problem of the relative value of body and soul has been written about a great deal, precisely because it *is* so difficult to define a rationalization of productive ascetic practice that does not seem to slight the goodness and integrity of physical existence.

Frequently Christian authors have slid down the slippery slope of dualism; the body has been rhetorically alienated from the "self" and understood as an object that the religious self must control at all costs, the target of stern discipline and even of abuse. As modern people have recognized, the distinction between "use" and "abuse" is frequently too subtle to provide trustworthy guidelines. Abuse of ascetic practices marks Christian tradition, as it does other religions whose metaphysical descriptions of human beings were more explicitly dualistic, in which human beings were envisioned as divided between a divine mind or spirit and a body contaminated by its materiality. "Abuse," defined as fascination with ascetic practice, not as a tool, but as an end in itself, has not been consistently overcome in Christianity, even by doctrines that should, in theory, provide a definitive affirmation of human bodies and the natural world. Ascetic practices are powerful, and therefore dangerous, tools; they are as capable of destruction as of help; yet they have always been considered an essential tool for Christian life.

My interest is not primarily in the theology supporting ascetic practices, however, but in the function of such exercises in defining a religious self. Ascetic practices rely on the intimate and strong connection of body and soul so that exercises that deconstruct the socialization and conditioning inscribed on the body by the "world" can produce a new organizing center or "self." For example, Augustine of Hippo, probably the most pervasively influential theologian of Christian tradition, explained the connection between fasting and desire for a relationship with God by connecting physical hunger and spiritual longing:

> When people are hungry, they stretch out toward something; while they are stretching, they are enlarged; while they are enlarged, they become capacious, and when they have become capacious enough, they will be filled in due time.[2]

Most Christian authors of the past have assumed a sort of erotic economy by which a direct exchange can be made from physical pleasures to spiritual pleasure, producing what one classical author called "the pleasure of no pleasure."[3] In ascetic practice, the body, conditioned in every culture to find gratification in objects specified by the culture, becomes the ally of the religious self, a tool for breaking mechanical attraction to the objects that gratify the social self and for reorienting desire and gratification. The *same* energy that originally organized the person's pursuit of sex, power, and possessions can be removed from the socially conditioned self and relocated in the religious self.

Proof of a person's attachment to objects in the world, Christian authors say repeatedly, is the difficulty and disorientation experienced by the person who tries to give up these objects.[4] The items most frequently sacrificed in Christian tradition have been food (temporarily) and sexual activity (temporarily or permanently). Renunciation of the greatest physical pleasures, because their pursuit firmly organizes a person's eros, or life energies, can release the greatest energy for the spiritual life. Christian authors until the sixteenth century were unanimous in finding chastity (variously defined) crucial to contemplation, the central and centering condition of the religious self.[5] Similarly, food, the earliest need and delight of every infant, was seen by Christian authors as tying, or "weighing down," the person to objects in the world. Unlike sex, Augustine complained, food cannot be given up once and for all, and its use thus requires constant vigilance and scrutiny.

Christian authors have understood ascetic practices as a shift of erotic attachment from sensible objects to a spiritual object. Their estimation of the greater beauty, reality, and value of spiritual objects over sensual objects has masked the fact that what was at stake was a relocation of the self. A consciously chosen self was created by the strategy of systematically dismantling the self automatically created by socialization. The real point of ascetic practices, then, was not to "give up" objects, but to reconstruct the self. Indeed, a "fringe benefit" of temporary renunciations—as historical authors also recognized, and sometimes cautioned against—is the sensory intensification that inevitably occurs as a result of deprivation. By deprivation, sensory habituation is deconstructed; the result is what Thomas Aquinas called "the renewal of the senses." Ascetic practices can also relieve sensory fatigue. Periods of silence, of sexual abstinence, of solitude, and of fasting readily demonstrate the extent to which the senses habituate and fatigue, becoming, in the course of ordinary living, "data-reduction agencies" rather than alert observers of the world of sounds, smells, sights, and touch.[6] Ascetic practices can break the bondage of the senses to the psyche's agenda, a form of habituation in which any stimulus that does not relate directly to physical and psychic protection is ignored. "The soul is the prison-house of the body," Foucault has written, inverting the Platonic maxim cited frequently by Christian authors.

Historically, however, ascetic practices have not been advocated for the purpose of renewing the senses. Rather, the greater value of spiritual over sensible objects has been argued, creating a practical dualism that has been much more influential than theological affirmations of human bodies and the natural world. "If the body is strong, the soul withers. If the body withers, the soul is strong," wrote one fourth-century ascetic teacher.[7]

Despite a body-rejecting rhetoric, ascetic practices were not undertaken primarily in order to deny the body or reject sensible objects. In *The Body in Pain,* Elaine Scarry has described ascetic practice as effectively augmenting the body's importance:

> The self-flagellation of the religious ascetic . . . is not (as is often asserted) an act of denying the body, eliminating its claims from attention, but a way of so emphasizing the body that the contents of the world are cancelled and the path is clear for the entrance of an unworldly, contentless force.[8]

The treatment of sexuality is another central feature in lay manuals of Christian devotion. In monastic manuals, of course, the one asceticism that was not considered temporary was celibacy. Lay manuals, although often derived from monastic manuals, could not forbid sexual activity. Yet

Christian authors seldom formulated the case for integrating an active sex life—even in marriage—with Christian life. Using the monastic model on which renunciation of the greatest pleasure had the greatest potential for freeing energy for the construction of a religious self, devotional manuals for lay people either ignored sexuality or implied that sexual activity belongs to the same category as eating or sleeping—regrettable physical necessities that should not be permitted to distract a person from spiritual pleasure. The pages of *The Pilgrim's Progress, The Imitation of Christ,* the *Introduction to the Devout Life,* or *The Way of the Pilgrim,* like other devotional manuals, give no directions concerning the role of sexuality in the formation of a religious self.[9]

The questions raised by this significant lacuna in devotional manuals are easier to pose than to answer: Was sexual activity seen as inevitably distracting or debilitating? Or were authors concerned about preoccupation with sex, a compulsiveness that could not be integrated, and thus must be renounced forever, as recovering alcoholics must abstain from alcohol? Augustine's description of his experience of sexual compulsiveness has defined a pattern for interpretation of sexuality in the Christian West. While involved in sexual relationships, Augustine says, he felt unfree, driven, compulsive. When a religious resolution occurred in his life, its first and decisive result was that it was a solution to his problems with sex: renunciation of all sexual activity, accompanied, he reports, by feelings of relief and freedom. Augustine's conversion was to celibacy; his famous preconversion prayer, "Give me chastity, but not yet,"[10] expresses both his recognition that sex was his particular problem area, and his awareness that, for him, an integrated sexuality was impossible.

Augustine did not urge his own resolution on anyone else. He did, however, describe his experience of relief and freedom in such a way that his readers could easily forget that he was talking about a resolution that emerged from, and responded to, his own particular situation, his own historically and geographically defined perspective. Augustine, when writing as a theologian, was careful to formulate a Christian anthropology that deliberately and insistently included the body in human personality. Because of his own experience, however, he was not able to describe the body's most intimate function, sexuality, as integral to human life. His description, in the last book of the *City of God,* of the resurrection of the body demonstrates and rationalizes the radical division he drew between human bodies and sexuality. In the frankly imaginary picture Augustine paints of the resurrection of the body, human bodies, male and female bodies, will participate in the perfection and completion of human beings. Human bodies, "risen and glorious," will be "the ultimate fulfillment" of whole persons. But although there will be sexes in the resurrection, since sexes are not an "imperfection," there will not be sex. For Augustine this is decisive. In the resurrection, he wrote, bodies will include sexual organs—in the interest of beauty, but not of "use." Augustine drew from this vision of perfection the inference that present sexual activity is not a foretaste of the reward, and so must therefore be a part of the state of punishment in which human beings presently live. This harsh evaluation of sexuality has been highly influential in Western Christianity.

There are some alternative suggestions in Christian tradition about sexual relationship, at least within marriage. (These will be discussed in greater detail in chapter 9, but I will sketch them briefly here.) Although sexuality has been tolerated or even approved of in heterosexual marriage, sexuality has never been understood as part of a practice of Christianity. Even though marriage was sometimes understood as a stimulating condition for spiritual growth, it was not sexual relationship itself that was seen as a form of learning and advance. Clement of Alexandria regarded marriage as a strenuous spiritual discipline; he saw the celibate life as luxurious by comparison with the demands of life in the world, the cares of a home, and the responsibilities of raising children.[11] And in the sixteenth century, Martin Luther advocated sexual activity on the grounds of its contribution to male health.[12] But Christian tradition does not provide an adequate exposition of sexual relationship as a format for self-knowledge, for learning to recognize and alter the glacial fears that isolate a person and prevent loving relationship, for discovering the shape and extent of personal and social conditioning, and for learning to relinquish the need for control rather than interdependence.

The difficulty we have in even imagining what a historical treatise on sexual relationship as a format for spiritual growth might say is indicative of the triumph of Augustine's treatment of sexuality in the Christian West. At the end of the fourth century, the British monk Jovinian was excommunicated and anathematized for saying that, for progress in Christian life, marriage was an equally viable lifestyle with celibacy. Both Augustine and Jerome wrote treatises against him, and their treatises remain, while Jovinian's writings were destroyed and disappeared. The ascetic excitement of the time partially accounts for the severity of his contemporaries' judgment against Jovinian, but his teaching was not only condemned and suppressed in his own time. His perspective has in fact been virtually absent from Christian tradition until the present century.[13]

Why has sexual relationship not been understood as a condition in which dramatic growth in self-understanding, ability to love, and spiritual growth is possible? An adequate answer to this question would need to explore a variety of explanations that can only be suggested here. Assumptions of male superiority in the patriarchal communities of the

Christian West have made it difficult for Christians to envision equal relationships. Moreover, since the most influential Christian authors were men, and the societies in which they spoke were male defined and dominated—that is, organized and governed by men—male perspectives on body and sexuality are necessarily and inevitably represented in their writings. The association of females with body and males with reason, though it was prior to and more widespread than Christian tradition, is also endemic to Christianity. The men who were the spiritual leaders in Christianity simultaneously alienated the vulnerable, dependent, plea-sure-seeking aspects of themselves, and projected these qualities onto actual women who were then seen to threaten their spiritual progress.

Contemporary feminist theologians, both those who still find Chris-tianity viable for modern women and those who identify themselves as "post-Christian," have been very critical of the central role of asceticism in Christianity. Their analysis rests on the traditional association of sex-uality—from the perspective of the male author—with woman, woman with body, body with sin, and sin with death. Sexual abstinence, within this complex of associations, entails rejection both of actual women, and of "woman" as symbol of sin. Rosemary Radford Ruether writes:

> Only by extricating the mind from matter by ascetic practices, aimed at severing the connections of mind and body, can one prepare for the salvific escape out of the realm of corruptibility to eternal spiritual life. All that sustains physical life—sex, eating, reproduction, even sleep—comes to be seen as sustaining the realm of "death," against which a mental realm of consciousness has been abstracted as the realm of "true life." Women, as representatives of sexual reproduction and motherhood, are the bearers of death, from which male spirit must flee to "light and life."[14]

Post-Christian feminist Mary Daly characterizes asceticism unam-biguously as a "sadomasochistic" phenomenon. Curiously, the infection of asceticism, she writes, is especially virulent in women, in whom pa-triarchal societies have "spawned self-loathing, a need for punishment, [and] hatred of other women."[15] Both Ruether's and Daly's critiques ignore the productive element in asceticism in order to make the point that male asceticism has usually scapegoated women as the source of sin—"original" and actual—and the bearers of temptation, illusion, and death. They understand traditional female asceticism as women's response to this evaluation of their "true selves," and their attempt to overcome the liabilities of being a woman in cultures designed by and for men.[16] Their analysis is substantiated by the writing of women ascetics who can be shown to have incorporated the gender conditioning and rhetoric of their societies. For example, in the fourteenth century the anchoress Julian of Norwich reveals her acceptance of the affiliation of women and death, even while she describes God as incorporating maternal qualities:

> Our great God, the supreme wisdom in all things, arrayed and prepared himself in this humble place, all ready in our poor flesh, himself to do the service and the office of motherhood in everything. The mother's service is nearest, readiest and surest. . . . No one ever could perform this office fully, except only for him. We know that all our mothers bear us for pain and for death. O, what is that? But our true Mother Jesus, he alone bears us for joy and for endless life. [17]

Clearly the social effect of asceticism and its embeddedness in gender relations in the Christian West makes asceticism problematic for contemporary women. It is difficult to see how any productive potential can be associated with a historical practice so loaded with misogyny—both male misogyny and the misogyny internalized by women as self-hatred. Surely asceticism provides an unambiguous example of a Christian practice that both *could* be directed against women and *was* directed against women in Christian communities and should therefore be rejected as without redemptive value for contemporary women and men.

Moreover, in the nuclear world, ideas and practices that even *seem* to reject or disparage bodies and the natural world are dangerous. We have seen that a wide range of interpretations of asceticism have existed in historical Christianity: from blatant disparagement of sensible things to insistence that it is not the enjoyment of sensible objects that debilitates spiritual life and threatens the cultivation of a religious self, but a compulsive attachment to them on the part of the Christian. Despite theological nuances, however, it was certainly the relative "worthlessness" of bodies, the world of social relationships, and the natural world that devotional manuals communicated and that contemporary popular caricature of Christianity still maintains.

But let us consider another possibility. If, as I claimed in the introduction to Part II, those aspects of human being engaged in particular Christian practices are implicitly affirmed and valued, is there a sense in which human bodies are affirmed in ascetic practices? Body is understood as affiliated with the religious self as the tool of its construction, while the "world" is rejected, both in its external and interior manifestations. Ascetic practices aim at separating the body from socialization since the body's "subjectivity" was created by socialization, by "the world"; the body has been nothing but the helpless victim of social conditioning. Socialization can be cumulatively untangled from body by ascetic practices, so that a chosen subjectivity is established as the religious self. The body becomes a field for deconstruction of the social self and reconstruction of a religious self. How are we to evaluate such a perplexing complex of simultaneous dependence on body and rejection of the body's "natural," that is, socially conditioned, response to pleasure and pain?

Since feminist theologians have given the most systematic critique of asceticism, let us consider it again with their concerns in mind. The cultivation of a centered and chosen self has been a goal of feminist theory and practice ever since feminists began to notice that women in patriarchal cultures are denied the power of self-definition. Ironically, at the same time that feminists identified women's need for individuation, the "individualism" of "autonomous Western man" has begun to be criticized as neither realistic nor desirable in Western culture. [18] Individualism has been identified as informing the ideology and practices that have led to the geopolitics of the nuclear world. Women, however, have not been conditioned to aggressiveness and illusions of autonomous individuality. Middle-class women's roles in North American culture have been defined as those in which relationship and responsibility for the well-being of others are emphasized—in contrast to, and in compensation for, male competitiveness and aggression. [19] Analyses of individualism as the dominant characteristic of "Western culture" have simply omitted women, whose conditioned self-images, attitudes, and roles have prevented adequate *individuation.* Certainly unusual women have learned to compete with men in businesses and universities, and most women have accepted some patriarchal values and resisted others. But for most women, embedded in family and social relationships that assumed and required their full-time attention and support, the central problem of consciousness-raising has been that of simultaneously learning new skills of self-definition and confronting obstacles in society that prevent women's self-definition. Does asceticism offer any tools for individuation for women and for other racial and social groups of people who have not been encouraged to define themselves?

Although asceticism, as a "technique of the self," in Foucault's phrase, has frequently been used effectively for the definition and cultivation of a religious self, it is a problematic tool for people who have been defined as those who must suffer by the societies in which they live. For women, whose affiliation with self-sacrificial support of others has been a cultural commonplace, traditional asceticisms seem counterproductive. If asceticism is for the purpose of deconstructing the socially conditioned subjectivity, it cannot serve this function if it effectively reinforces rather than dismantles cultural conditioning to femininity.

A feminist asceticism might rather take the form of the difficult disciplines of self-definition and self-assertion in situations in which one is tempted to revert to behavior calculated to please others at the expense of personal honesty and self-respect. The tangible and intangible rewards for adherence to patriarchal norms and values, for being a "good" woman, must be relinquished as ends in themselves before individuation and self-description can become a reality. A parallel asceticism for men in relation to feminist theory and practice might consist of renunciation of the assumption of a privileged voice to which centuries of authoritative male speech in the Christian West have accustomed them, a discipline of respectful *listening,* or even of absence,[20] when women need to speak together without male presence, while women work to articulate, understand, and change themselves and society.[21]

Asceticism, however, has been one of the most individually tailored practices of historical Christianity. In manuals for the use of lay people, there were no general rules or injunctions about ascetic practices beyond common fasts from particular foods during certain days of the week or periods of the liturgical year. It therefore seems unwise to try to predict which ascetic practices (if any) might be uniformly useful in addressing women's issues as well as the common problems of the nuclear world. From a global perspective, Americans who possess and use a greatly disproportionate amount of the world's wealth have a similarly disproportionate responsibility for the lack of food and other resources in the so-called Third World. Temporary or permanent renunciation of some of the consumer "goods" we find essential to our lives might begin to sensitize us, both to the conditions of hunger and want in which most of the world's inhabitants live and to our common conditioning as a society to expect and require consumer goods. A variety of asceticisms which have as their goal sensitivity to the lot of those in our society who are illiterate, or who live beneath the poverty level, of minority racial groups, homosexuals, or the aged could provide energy for informed action against the structures of injustice and oppression. An asceticism for our time must be far more concerned with engagement with, and political and social action in, the world than with withdrawal from the world in order to cultivate a religious self.

In spite of being able to reinterpret asceticism in ways that show the direct relevance of temporary disciplines to the social dilemmas and cultural blindnesses of the present, however, the question of whether practices that are explicitly and publicly labeled "asceticism" can be useful for contemporary Christians needs to be considered. Some people may be encouraged by thinking of themselves as actively engaged in redefining an ancient Christian practice that has often been abused and misunderstood. There are many others, however, and I include myself among them, for whom the word *asceticism* is itself the name of a pervasive internal misinterpretation of Christianity, a word that invites, if not entails, a dualistic disdain for bodies and the natural world. All the theological definition in the world will not either repair the human waste and loss that has occurred under the rubric "asceticism" or rehabilitate Christianity's public image in the eyes of contemporary secular people.[22] Rather, people who speak and write within Christian perspectives should turn our attention to interpretations of Christianity that emphasize love for the beauty and goodness of the created world, the equality of lifestyles in providing the circumstances within which a Christian loves God *by*—not instead of—loving other people, and concern over the part that the history of Christianity has played in the making of the nuclear world.

Language is not the private possession of theologians for interpretation and reinterpretation, although theologians have for centuries seemed to think that it was. The present public connotations of traditional theological words must be scrutinized—not merely the possibility of a new interpretation considered—before a word can be judged useable in the present. We can still explore the tradition in order to present a range of meanings and understandings that may, in their own time, have been useful and useable. But the effort of historical understanding must not preclude a responsible evaluation of the word—and its cluster of public meanings and associations—in the world in which we live. Although I have suggested that some practices we might understand as related to asceticism are useful and needed in the contemporary world, the word *asceticism* is, I think, no longer useful. Individual and communal practices of self-discipline based on self-knowledge must name themselves differently if Christianity is not to perpetuate its popular caricature as body denying and world rejecting. The question with which we will proceed to examine other traditional practices in the history of Christianity, then, is whether the still relevant and valuable functions of ascetic practice can be preserved and articulated under other rubrics in a contemporary Christian life.

# 6

## The Word Made Flesh: Worship and Sacraments

*For as the body is clad in the cloth, and the flesh in the skin, and the bones in the flesh, and the heart in the trunk, so are we, body and soul, clad and enclosed in the goodness of God.*

*Julian of Norwich[1]*

Devotional manuals, by definition, were written for people already affiliated with a worshiping community. Often the reader for whom the manual was written was known personally by the author, so that the general prescriptions are focused and tailored for a particular reader. In Francis de Sales's *Introduction to the Devout Life,* for example, the reader for whom the manual was written was a person who wanted to deepen and intensify her practice of Christianity, extending it beyond the basic requirements into voluntary practices that cultivate the religious self. Because manuals address readers who are eager to go beyond mandatory practices, most devotional manuals have little to say about the regular worship of Christian communities; most devotional manuals assume rather than develop the relevance of communal worship to Christian life.

There are, however, some issues surrounding worship that bear directly on the agenda of devotional manuals. Authors visualized the formation of a differently configured religious self according to the style of worship they assumed. Since worship is one of the most fundamental of religious duties, the orientation of worship—whether to words, images, or to silent, imageless contemplation—differently forms and focuses the religious self. Thus, although extensive theologies of worship were not usually to be found in devotional manuals, particular styles of worship are assumed, implied, or described in the course of discussing what the author considers the appropriate orientation of the religious self.

Although the many complex disputes over the proper style of worship in the long history of Christianity cannot be reconstructed here, by keeping our attention on the practical instructions of devotional manuals, we can understand better the role of different forms of worship in the definition of a religious self. In this chapter we will consider three choices concerning the most central feature of worship: the sacrament of the Eucharist, preaching, and interior worship without reliance on either words or images. The doctrinal formulation that provides the theological context for each author's view of what is central to worship will be our first topic. Then we will examine the nature of the religious self assumed and reinforced by each of these styles of worship, concluding with some suggestions about worship in relation to the present.

The three identifications of what is the central and most important feature of Christian worship are not exclusive; each implies and includes the others. If preaching is considered the central act of worship, for example, the sacraments and interior worship are also important, even if not as much emphasized as attendance to the "Word of God." Making one feature of worship central, then, did not entail exclusion of others. Our two Protestant examples, John Calvin and Johann Arndt, were proposed as corrections of contemporary worship that the authors considered wrongly conceived and practiced.

The final section of Francis de Sales's *Introduction to the Devout Life* is a series of instructions about the importance of the sacrament of the Eucharist and the need for careful and thorough preparation for participation in it. He understood the difficulty of maintaining intense and concentrated attention when communion was attended frequently, as he urged. How is a sense of overwhelming awe and all-consuming engagement possible if attendance at mass is a daily habit? How must one prepare one's heart and mind in order to guarantee such concentrated attention—as if one's life depended on it—to the sacrament? Because one's true "life," one's religious self, Francis de Sales wrote, *does* indeed depend on the spiritual nourishment of the Eucharist. Confession, penitence, and preparatory meditation, together with listening intently to the words of the mass and ingesting the eucharistic elements—these are the primary practices by which, according to Francis de Sales, the religious self is produced, cultivated, and fed.[2]

The doctrine that informed the practices Francis de Sales outlined was defined at the Fourth Lateran Council (1215). The doctrine of transubstantiation stated that the bread and wine of the Eucharist was converted into "the body and blood of Christ."[3] Only the appearances of bread and wine remain. A hymn attributed to Thomas Aquinas puts this strong interpretation of the Eucharist succinctly:

The Word made flesh by a word changes true bread
into flesh, and wine becomes the blood of Christ;
and if sense is deficient [in perceiving the change],
faith alone suffices to make the sincere heart
firm [in believing it].[4]

Centuries earlier, Augustine of Hippo had described the sacraments as
composed of a material and a spiritual element: the material object,
together with the word—the invocation of the Spirit—creates the sacrament.

The sacramental mysticism of Francis de Sales, like that of Thomas à
Kempis and many other authors before and after him, depended on the
doctrine of transubstantiation. The doctrine assumed an intimate interconnectedness of the physical and spiritual by which physical food can
nourish spiritual life. The implicit statement this doctrine makes about
the essential nature of human beings suggests that the boundaries of body
and soul are not absolute, but permeable. Because the eucharistic elements
combine spiritual and physical elements, they simultaneously provide
food for both aspects of human beings. Thus Thomas à Kempis, in *The
Imitation of Christ,* describes grace as "in" the body/bread and blood/wine
of the Eucharist, so that physical ingestion "brings salvation." Christ
"lives within" the Christian, physically as well as spiritually, "by this
sacrament."[5]

Understanding the Eucharistic sacrament as the substance and nourishment of the religious self suggests a further connection with physical
eating: frequent communion is not merely beneficial, but necessary for
spiritual life. Francis de Sales based his recommendation of frequent
communion on the theory that, literally, "you are what you eat." Physical
life was not merely *analogous* to spiritual life, but *connected* to it. Because of
the integrity of human being, feeding the body with Christ's body
maintains the soul in "life and health":

Just as hares in our mountains become white in
winter because they neither see nor eat anything
but snow, so, by adoring and eating beauty,
purity, and goodness itself in this divine
sacrament you will become wholly beautiful,
wholly good, and wholly pure.[6]

Francis de Sales's only description of the role of the "Word of God"
occurs in the second part of the *Introduction to the Devout Life.* I quote his
statement in full:

> Be devoted to the Word of God whether you hear it in familiar con-
> versations with friends or in sermons. Always listen to it with attention and
> reverence; make good use of it; take it into your heart like a precious balm.[7]

Notice that conversation with one's friends is as likely to communicate important messages to the Christian as is the preaching of the "Word." After this short statement on the spoken word, Francis de Sales went on to write about *reading*—not listening—for the rest of his short chapter on the role of language in the formation of a religious self. Clearly the lifelong process of the Christian's conversion has much more to do with attentive participation at the eucharistic sacrament than with hearing the "Word of God" in the words of a preacher.

John Calvin, himself a layperson—he was never ordained—was a second-generation Protestant reformer in Geneva. He evaluated very differently than Francis de Sales the relative importance of word and sacrament in worship. In his *Institutes of the Christian Religion,* each edition of which Calvin translated from Latin into French in order to make it accessible to literate laypersons, he described the "preaching of the gospel" as the central act of Christian worship. In contrast to Francis's description of the centrality of the eucharistic sacrament, Calvin called sacraments "another help" and an "antecedent promise."[8] By comparison with preaching, sacraments were an afterthought, a "kind of appendix" to the preaching of the gospel.[9] Indeed, the sacraments are a "visible word";[10] they place God's promises in "graphic bodily form," a concession to the weakness of the Christian's faith. A verbal communication is more readily comprehended by weak and easily distracted people if it is acted out:

> First, the Lord teaches and trains us by his word; next he confirms us by his
> sacraments; lastly, he illuminates our mind by the help of the Holy Spirit
> and opens up an entrance into our hearts for his word and sacraments,
> which would otherwise only strike our ears, and fall upon our sight, but by
> no means affect us inwardly. The sacraments only perform their office when
> accompanied by the Spirit, whose energy alone penetrates the heart, stirs
> up the affections, and procures access for the sacraments into our hearts.[11]

"It is not," he continued, "as if I thought there is a kind of secret efficacy perpetually inherent in them [the sacraments]. . . . The sacraments do not avail one iota without the energy of the Holy Spirit." The sacraments, in Calvin's view, do not *contain* grace, but "announce and manifest" grace.[12] The affiliation of the Holy Spirit and the word, in Calvin's description, parallels the identity of grace and the sacraments in

Francis de Sales's treatment. For Calvin, the centrality of preaching results from the Spirit's special affinity with verbal communication.

We must, however, be careful not to caricature Calvin's view of the importance, even if not centrality, of the sacraments. When his context is not a theological discussion of the relative significance of preaching and sacraments, but a discussion of the *practices* of baptism and the Lord's Supper, he wrote rather differently, describing the significance of sacraments in strong terms. Describing the Lord's Supper, he says that it is "as if Christ were placed in bodily presence before our view":[13]

> The rule which the pious ought always to observe is whenever they see the symbols instituted by the Lord to think and feel surely persuaded that the truth of the things signified is also present. For why does the Lord put the symbol of his body into your hands, but just to assure you that you truly partake of him? If this is true, let us feel as much assured that the visible sign is given us in seal of an invisible gift as that his body itself is given to us.[14]

Calvin's characterization of the Lord's Supper as life-giving is worded as strongly as is that of Francis de Sales and Thomas à Kempis: "everyone who communicates in his flesh and blood," Calvin wrote, "enjoys participation in life."[15] The Lord's Supper is "that sacred communion of flesh and blood by which Christ transfuses his life into ours."[16] The sacrament "invigorates and keeps alive the soul"; it "fosters, refreshes, strengthens, and exhilarates."[17]

Although different theological descriptions of the sacrament of the Eucharist, different evaluations of its centrality to worship, and even different names for this sacrament were used by Catholic and Protestant reformers, the *practice* of communion was described in similarly emphatic language. Communion was also understood, across the reformations of the sixteenth century,[18] as participation in Christ's life.

Johann Arndt, a second-generation Pietist and German Lutheran pastor at the end of the seventeenth century, reacted against a Protestant worship which he thought failed to relate to the Christian's inner life. Arndt described the religious self as an interior consciousness. His devotional manual *True Christianity* defined this consciousness, but he did not describe the external practices that might best stimulate and articulate it. "False worship," done "out of one's own meditation and self-established holiness and spirituality," contrasted with "proper worship," an interior event, consisting of "true knowledge of God, true knowledge of sin, and true knowledge of grace and forgiveness."[19] According to Arndt, neither sacraments nor "the Word" is primary in Christian worship, since the religious self was constituted neither by hearing and responding to the preached word nor by participation in the sacraments, but was entirely interior and invisible. From his chapter on worship, it is difficult to determine whether he assumed the reader's participation in a worshiping community or whether he found it peripheral to "true worship." Moreover, the religious self had no physical senses; neither did it require and involve the intellect, despite Arndt's labeling of worship as "true knowledge":

> This is knowledge of God. It consists in faith . . . and in a joyous, happy, and living trust, by which I discover *in myself*, in a strong and consoling way, God's power, how he holds me and bears me, and how I live, move, and have my being in him. I also feel *in myself* and discover his love and mercy. [20]

In this description of "true knowledge," Arndt identifies the religious self as essentially composed of a particular feeling or attitude, a feeling that was defined two hundred years later by Friedrich Schleiermacher, as a "feeling of absolute dependence."

We have seen that a religious self was differently imagined according to whether it was formed by a practice of attention to words, by sacramental participation, or by an interior recollectedness. Yet there are some common features in the assumptions and results of the three styles of worship. Worship is important because it generates a religious self in contrast to a socialized self, crusty with habit, heavy with opinions, without critical perspective on the culture that has formed and informed it. In the *Introduction to the Devout Life,* in the *Institutes of the Christian Religion,* and in *True Christianity,* the socialized self is repeatedly described as worthless when placed in the perspective of God's holiness, majesty, and beauty. The ordinary self is dramatically juxtaposed with the religious self in order to emphasize the need to reidentify and relocate the self. Because the religious self is created from the same energy that was formerly spent on the social self and its agenda, the self-importance of the socialized self must be reduced to nothing in order to achieve the new self-identification. Thus God and the social self are polarized in order to stimulate the creation of a religious self, a self defined by its relation of trust and confidence in God: "See, you are unutterably holy—I am the foulest of sinners. Yet how amazing—you stoop down to me when I am not fit to raise my eyes to you." [21]

Yet once a religious self has been defined, Thomas à Kempis wrote, God comes, "desires my company, invites me to [the eucharistic] feast"; the worshiper "becomes one with God in love."[22] In devotional manuals, descriptions of the religious self as constituted by verbal insight, by sacramental participation, or by a particular consciousness are less important than the common project of urging the possibility of a consciously chosen alternative to the socialized self and delineating the practices by which it is formed and strengthened.

Are traditional practices of Christian worship useful and useable in the nuclear world? Or are they a luxury that we no longer can afford? Is it important to create a self alternative to that constructed by complex social conditioning in a nuclear world—a world in which it is possible, as never before in the history of the world, to condition massive populations to social roles, expectations and attitudes, and to train a passive and voyeuristic reaction to violence and misery, and toleration of nuclear weapons? Put in this way, the question seems to answer itself. If the practice of worship is able to create a self alternative to, and critical of, the social self, however, it is important to scrutinze the new construction of self that results from various forms of worship.

A detailed inspection of the institutionalization of the various historical Christian identifications of the center of worship would reveal abuses of each of these forms of worship. Arndt's consciousness of total dependence on God, for example, may not be useful in a world in which human beings have the technological means of ending the world as we now know it. Perhaps twentieth-century Christians need to be more convinced of the need for action than for passive reliance on God to take care of the problems that human beings have created. Calvin's description of a word-oriented religious self may also be problematic in a society in which action in many arenas of public life is a greater need than refined linguistic skill. Similarly, the formation of a religious self around passionate attachment to the sacrament of the Eucharist can result in obliviousness to the world's problems, an escape from engagement.

Moreover, a sense of human worthlessness and nothingness in relation to God, a common theme of historical worship, is also not as useful to modern people as it once seemed to be. Many of us find it more difficult to achieve a sense of self-worth and empowerment than to experience low self-esteem. In fact, *which* historical people really experienced the psychic inflation—"pride"—the existence of which most manuals seem to assume? We have seen, in any case, that the "low self-esteem" advocated by historical devotional manuals was ambiguous, a strategy for a countercultural organization of the "true self."

Nevertheless, devotional manuals agree that a self capable of detachment from social conditioning is necessary for critical evaluation of "the world." The consolidation of that critical distance depends on the cumulative transfer of energy to a new center. Each of the three organizations of worship we discussed contributes an important insight into human life: language, ritual and the inclusion of the sensible world, and the cultivation of an inner life are each crucial to the formation of a religious self. The active organization and balancing of all of these can correct the abuses that might accompany each in isolation and become crucial to a process of responsible religious self-definition.

Worship can also be understood as creating and sustaining community in addition to creating a religious self in relation to God. Energy and support for active engagement with the myriad social, political, and personal problems of the nuclear world can be generated by communal worship. Since individuals are much more likely to be assailed by a sense of isolation and helplessness in the face of the nuclear world than tempted to submerge their identity in a community, worship can encourage and emphasize the necessity of cooperative work. Participation in a common liturgy—the word *liturgy* in Greek means work—is itself the beginning of, and impetus for, coooperative work in society. Communal worship is, in the twentieth century, one of the few exceptions to Rudolf Arnheim's perceptive observation, "Our experiences and ideas tend to be common but not deep, or deep but not common."[23] Both depth and commonality are central aspects of worship. The cultivation of a religious community is not antithetical to, but is necessarily entailed in the creation of a religious self. Change in individuals always requires the support, reinforcement, and encouragement of a formal or informal community. Devotional manuals, addressed as they usually were to individuals in order to achieve an intensely personal communication, did not explicitly emphasize, but assumed, the role of common worship in supporting the creation of individuals' religious identities. For this purpose, the particular style of worship is less important than commitment to regular participation in the worship of a Christian community. Devotional manuals are therefore not as rich a resource for reconstructing the passionate engagement with worship of Christian people of the past as are historical descriptions of the liturgies, architecture, and visual surroundings of worship.

Finally, worship in the nuclear world must be understood not only as an occasion for an exercise of the spirit or development of the soul but also as an orientation of physical life, the life of bodies in all their beauty and fragility. The liturgy and sacraments of Christian churches define and give religious meaning to potentially overwhelming physical experience, to birth, maturation, ecstasy, pain, joy, aging, and death. Through the media of language, music, visual images, gestures, movement, they insist on the inclusion of bodies and senses in celebration of being and gratitude for creation. As such, worship affirms the beauty and permanent value of human life, physical as well as spiritual life, in the face of the death-threatening forces that surround us in the last decades of the twentieth century.

# 7

## Gratitude and Responsibility: Service

*The trivial round, the common task,*
*Will furnish all we ought to ask;*
*Room to deny ourselves—a road*
*To bring us daily nearer God.*

*John Keble*[1]

The second topic of practical instructions we will explore is that of Christian service. Was Christian service considered essential or peripheral to the practice of Christianity in historical devotional manuals? What kinds of service were advocated? And, is the notion of Christian service relevant and useful for twentieth-century Christians? We will examine these questions by focusing on several popular devotional writings that represent a range of instructions given in particular historical situations.

Each set of instructions about Christian service was informed by theological assumptions, but it was also related to the author's analysis of the context in which he wrote, a context in which, inevitably, some practices were assumed to be necessary and essential while others were ignored. Each prescription for Christian service was the result of the author's diagnosis of what he thought was currently neglected and overlooked. Historical Christian authors were not usually aware that their instructions were contextual rather than universal. They assumed that their instructions were applicable to all people in every time and place and would, no doubt, have been offended if it were pointed out to them that the value of their instructions depended on the existence of particular social and religious conditions. Nevertheless, if we are to evaluate the appropriateness of historical instructions for our own practice of Christianity, we must first see how they functioned in their original circumstances. Let us consider some brief examples from the history of Christianity.

From the earliest Christian writings, service to others was advocated as essential to Christian life. Secular contemporaries of early Christians were amazed at Christians' insistence on caring for the needs of the poor, the sick, and the needy in the society around them, not only of people in their own families or congregations. In addition, they felt it their religious duty—parallel to their requirements for ritual assembly—to bury those who died without provision for their burial, a duty no secular Roman would recognize. In Roman culture corpses were ill-omened, and adherents of the religions of the Roman Empire were not permitted to attend religious rites for a prescribed period after being present at a deathbed or marching in a funeral procession. It is all the more striking, then, that Christians recognized in their Christian faith a mandate to care for the bodies, whether living or dead, of others.

Martin Luther, the German Protestant reformer, criticized a sixteenth-century religious practice that understood Christian "works" as necessary for personal salvation and Christian life. Luther's treatise *The Freedom of the Christian* represents his attempt accurately to describe the place of service to others in Christian life. It illustrates poignantly the difficulty that arises when equally true but apparently contradictory theological propositions are simultaneously asserted. Luther juxtaposed two statements: "A Christian is a perfectly free lord of all, subject to none"; and "A Christian is a perfectly dutiful subject to all, servant to all."[2] These statements, Luther realized, need somehow to be held in full strength, not diluted or mutually contaminated. The problem of asserting both is an intellectual one; in practice, however, each can exist in relation to the other as a mutually correcting balance. Many controversies have arisen in the history of Christianity because of the intellectual difficulty of holding contradictory statements in fruitful tension, both of which contain truths, either of which would be a distortion without the balancing presence of the other.

So Luther posed the two statements as paradox: a Christian is "perfectly free" *and* absolutely obliged to serve others. For Luther, good works *resulted from* justification by faith alone; they did not cooperate in justification. Good works were a necessary externalization of what had occurred in the secrecy and silence of "the bottom of the heart." "We do not reject good works," Luther wrote, "on the contrary, we cherish them and teach them as much as possible."[3] Yet a Christian's attention needs to be placed, not on his own strenuous effort to deserve salvation, but on God's promise to redeem. The first effect of faith, Luther wrote, is that it "destroys" the reliance of "work-saints" on their accumulated merit. But soon after Luther's dramatic realization ("the just shall live by faith alone") was broadcast across Europe, many people interpreted it as freedom *from* service to others. Luther repeatedly tried to explain that service to others followed, rather than contributed to, salvation:

> As our heavenly father has in Christ freely come to our aid, we ought also
> freely to help our neighbor through our body and its works, and each one
> should become, as it were, a Christ to each other that we may be Christs to
> one another and Christ may be the same in all, that is, that we may be truly
> Christians.[4]

Receiving from God, according to Martin Luther, is not passivity but
strenuous activity. Although his theology altered the status of good works,
he still considered Christian service the ultimate demonstration of the
reality of justification in the life of a Christian. His criterion for Christian
service was that it must flow spontaneously and effortlessly from "pleasure
and love," from gratitude to God for free justification.[5]

Luther's contemporary, the Spanish Roman Catholic reformer Juan de
Valdes, understood the place of service quite differently. In his devotional
manual *The Christian Alphabet,* written to a woman, a member of the
Spanish court, he urges, "effort, Signora, effort." Throughout the manual
he described the necessity of lifelong, vigorous effort in cooperation with
God for salvation. By contrast, Luther's alternative was framed in the
metaphor of marriage:

> And if they [the soul and Christ] are one flesh, and there is between them a
> true marriage—indeed the most perfect of all marriages, since human
> marriages are but one poor example of this true marriage—it follows that
> everything they have they hold in common. . . . Accordingly the believing
> soul can boast of and glory in whatever Christ has as though it were his
> own. . . . By the wedding ring of faith, Christ shares in the sins, death,
> and pains of hell which are his bride's, and . . . the believing soul by means
> of the pledge of its faith is free in Christ, its bridegroom, free from all sins,
> secure against death and hell, and is endowed with the eternal righteous-
> ness, life, and salvation of Christ, its bridegroom.[6]

The gender assumptions of Luther's society are evident in his model of the
soul's relationship with God: "this poor wicked harlot, the soul, marries
the divine and rich bridegroom, Christ," who redeems her from all evil
and adorns her with all goodness. However, a different feature of the
metaphor from that of gender roles interested Luther, namely, the empowering effect of the soul's marriage to Christ: the Christian that "clings
in faith to God's promises shares in all their power," and is "saturated and
intoxicated by them."[7] "Our faith in Christ," Luther concludes, "does not
free us from good works but from false opinions concerning works."[8] In
short, Luther, although he was perhaps the harshest critic in the history of
Christianity of what he considered wrongly conceived Christian service,
still maintained the centrality of service to Christian life.

We have noticed some of the "services" considered essential to Christian faith by Christians of the first centuries; let us look now at some other historical suggestions about practical Christian service. From New Testament times forward, Christian authors advocated forms of service that have begun, in the twentieth century, to be questioned. Care for the poor and the sick, charity to the needy, hospitality to strangers and visiting those in prison, although urged in the strongest terms in the Gospels and throughout the history of Christianity, are no longer done by most Christians. "Good works" that temporarily alleviate individual pain through "charity" seem to many Christians to be inadequate responses to the need of the world.

Moreover, forms of social and political engagement that seldom appear in historical texts seem highly important to many twentieth-century Christians. Have historical authors ever advocated the restructuring of societies so that poverty and institutionalized injustice and oppression could be lessened or eliminated? A few examples can be found, but it would be difficult to argue that responsibility for the public sphere was regarded historically as an important part of Christian service. At the end of the eighteenth century, John Wesley (d. 1791) argued for, and spent much of his time working to inaugurate, programs for changing the lot of the poor, rather than simply giving alms to those marginalized by society. After he retired from preaching, he continued to work long hours to collect money for programs to provide education, to fund business endeavors by which poor people might change their situation, and to write appeals to the government urging the establishment of various social reforms.

Similarly, John Woolman (d. 1772), the American Quaker who campaigned against slavery, urged that social activism be combined with daily commitment to just, honest, and truthful dealings with one's fellow human beings. As Woolman's "Plea for the Poor" makes clear, he was concerned for all people who, whatever their motivation, work too hard. He was even concerned that animals work too hard—a highly atypical worry in Christian tradition.[9] Woolman analyzed the culturally conditioned expectations that motivate overwork, including in his list of reasons for overwork the urge to amass unnecessary wealth, and war with its waste of the resources of human communities.

Undeniably, Wesley's agenda for Christian service as social reform and Woolman's analysis of society's demand for the labor of individuals were atypical in the history of Christianity. The social location of Christians may sometimes have accounted for the restriction of Christian service to the alleviation of immediate misery. Marginalized, poor, and powerless people must often do what they can, rather than attempting to establish more equitable laws and institutions, or more equality of opportunity. But the social class of some Christians must not be used to conceal the fact that maintenance of the social and political order, even in the face of glaring injustice, was advocated by scripture and urged by early Christian apologists; it has also been the policy of multitudes of wealthy and powerful Christians. Although reformative or revolutionary activity might, in some contexts, be understood as Christian service, it has seldom been understood as mandated by Christian faith. The norm of Christian service has been charity, the relief of immediate need, rather than critique and reform of societies.

Interpretations as to what form of service should be part of Christian practice have varied, but devotional manuals agree that service to others is integral and essential to Christian life. The late nineteenth century American Congregational minister Washington Gladden (1836–1918) wrote, in *The Christian Way:*

> Those Christians whose chief concern is their own spiritual condition, are a very poor sort of Christian. It is through a self-forgetful service that the highest culture is gained, through a faithful following of Him who came not to minister to himself, but to minister to others. . . . Too much genuine service there cannot be; but there may easily be too much parade of service; . . . service is the principal thing. [10]

The first theologically supported claim that the Christian gospel requires social reconstruction was that of Walter Rauschenbusch. His *Theology for the Social Gospel,* first published in 1917, represented a systematic reworking of theology in order to demonstrate that Christianity requires, not simply almsgiving, but social reform.

Rauschenbusch questioned the self-identification of theology with philosophical inquiry and proposed a new project for theology, namely, the construction of a theology "large enough to contain the social gospel and alive and productive enough not to hamper it." [11] Rauschenbusch insisted that "theoretically, the church is the great organization of unselfish service," even while he admitted that "actually, the church has always been profoundly concerned for its own power and authority." [12] Speaking in the context of the Protestant church in North America, Rauschenbusch recognized theology's ongoing need for "periodic rejuvenation," and diagnosed the main danger facing early twentieth-century Christianity not as "mutilation, but [as] senility." [13]

*A Theology for the Social Gospel* reworks traditional theological themes— God, Christ, church, sin, and salvation—in relation to contemporary social injustice. Rauschenbusch saw the salvation of individuals, for example, as essential but only a beginning of the agenda of the Christian gospel. Unless "getting religion" turns people "from self to God and to humanity," religion can become nothing but the sublimest form of self-intending: "We have the highest authority for the fact that men may grow worse by getting religion." Characterizing self-centered religion as mysticism, other-worldliness, and escapism, Rauschenbusch acknowledged: "There is no doubt that under favorable conditions it has produced beautiful results of unselfishness, humility, and undaunted courage. . . . [But] its danger is that it isolates."[14] Criticizing the traditional understanding of a saint as one who enjoys a personal relationship and communion with God, Rauschenbusch reinterpreted saintliness as producing social concern and responsibility:

> The saint of the future will not need a theocentric mysticism which enables him to realize God, but an anthropocentric mysticism which enables him to realize his fellowmen in God. The more we approach pure Christianity, the more will the Christian signify the man who loves mankind with a religious passion and excludes none.[15]

Christian service, for Rauschenbusch, primarily consisted of work in society to establish the "kingdom of God," or just social arrangements. Christians, he said, should work vigorously for a just social order now; they should not, as Christian authors have frequently advised, accept present inequality soothed by the expectation of perfect justice and equality in heaven:

> The kingdom of God is not confined within the limits of the Church and its activities. It embraces the whole of human life. It is the Christian transfiguration of the social order. The Church is one social institution alongside of the family, the industrial organization of society, and the state. The kingdom of God is in all these and realizes itself through them all.[16]

Why have Christian authors not emphasized the duty of working to establish just social arrangements as an essential part of Christian service? This must remain an unanswerable question. Reconstruction of the historical circumstances that have produced many twentieth-century Christians' sensitivity to issues of social equality and political justice would take us far afield from the present project. In fact, although many traditional authors speculated that the equality of all human beings would characterize eternal bliss, very few suggested that Christians should begin to work in the present toward just social arrangements. Like Augustine, most Christian authors understood present injustice as an inevitable and, for the present, irreversible result of the fallen condition of human beings.


Issues surrounding traditional ideas of Christian service seem to be so numerous and serious as to make the practice itself questionable. Yet the world has perhaps never before needed the labor of concerned people so desperately and on so many fronts. Let us explore some further problems with the notion of Christian service, and then ask whether there is some interpretation of Christian service that is relevant and useful for Christians who live in a nuclear world.

The first problem with traditional interpretations of Christian service is the notorious susceptibility of the phrase to indicate self-intending interference in the lives of others. Many historical Christians found ways to rationalize the most aggressive behavior under the rubric of "serving." Too many Christian rulers, from Charlemagne forward, concealed totalitarian disregard for the ruled by citing Augustine's formula that the one who rules household or kingdom must not do so out of "lust for domination," but out of loving concern for the "ruled."[17]

Ironically, the "self-denial" traditionally associated with Christian service has become, in contemporary usage, a pejorative term, implying the existence of thinly disguised motives of self-promotion. Modern people have become suspicious of such traditional formulae as "God first, others second, myself last." We recognize that in genuinely altruistic activity, the one who serves feels himself to be fully gratified and rewarded by the experience gained in the process of serving. Neither heavenly reward nor self-denial as an end in itself should motivate service to "humanity." Rather, contemporary people who work with prison inmates, in shelters for battered women, with abused children, and in soup kitchens insist that these jobs are immediately and richly rewarding, personally gratifying, and full of opportunities for self-knowledge and learning.

Traditionally, however, only service that was deliberately offered to God rather than to the recipients themselves was considered Christian service. But modern people have seen such severe abuses in the practice of this principle that, for many of us, the term "Christian service" is immediately disaffecting. It seems presumptuous, even contemptuous, to do something for another human being, not out of love and concern for that human being, but for the good of one's own soul, to amass future heavenly rewards, or, disinterestedly, to "serve God." If service is not performed as penance, as traditional devotional manuals frequently urge; if service is not "offered up," that is, done for Christ rather than for the person benefited, what makes service Christian? Perhaps it is Christian service only in the sense that one can specify how an activity relates to values associated with one's practice of Christianity.

In spite of frequent abuse of the *concept* of Christian service, the *practice* of a wide range of activities, based on sensitivity to the needs of others, cannot be abandoned. Perhaps, at the end of the twentieth century, the rhetoric of Christian service, loaded as it is with connotations of covert complacency, has become irredeemably counterproductive. The minimalist approach of relating one's service activities to values associated with Christianity may be the best rationale for "Christian service" today. Understood in this way, a Christian's impetus for service to others and to society is the result of the confidence and "self-esteem" of one who understands experientially the Christian claim that love is the origin and goal of human life, and that one's existence is itself the gift of a God who has no other defining characteristic than love.[18] Loving "service," from the perspective of this interpretation, is simply gratitude for being, acted out.

A second problem with traditional instructions relating to Christian service has to do with the universalization of exhortations to Christian service. Most devotional manuals assume that everyone needs equally to be reminded to be "mindful of the needs of others." Admonitions to selflessness may represent an important corrective for those who are inclined to aggressive competition with others. However, such admonitions work merely to reinforce the social conditioning of those who are already thoroughly trained to attend to the needs of others at the expense of their own needs, and at the cost of low self-esteem and resentment. Gender conditioning in Western Christian societies has usually confined women's familial and social roles to those that feature self-sacrificial care and nurture of others.[19] Although special circumstances may occasionally limit a particular man to a mothering role, it is much more likely that the gender conditioning of men will emphasize self-assertion and obliviousness to the feelings of others. Men's and women's socially conditioned "temptations" and sensitivities are not only dissimilar, but opposite in this respect.

Women's conditioning to disregard or remain unaware of their own needs has been as damaging to individual women and to society as has men's one-sided conditioning to competitive self-assertion. Competent and intelligent women have been frustrated by the limitation of their activities to the private sphere and the home. Their frustration has resulted not only in a host of unhappy women but also in families that experience various forms of lifelong suffering as a result of women's attempt to gain fulfillment from their husbands and children rather than from their own creativity and productivity in a larger arena than the home.

Devotional manuals were guilty of frequent proscriptions against women's uncircumscribed use of their talents and energy. Edwin Hubbell Chapin's 1848 manual, *Duties of Young Women,* for example, though not one of the best sellers of Christian tradition, takes a characteristic position in relation to women's use of their talents and energies. Far from counseling that women discern and cultivate their talents and skills, he defines women's "sphere" as the "HOME" (capitalization his), "in the beautiful offices of the daughter, the sister, the mother, and the wife."[20] Indeed, "woman's peculiar sway over us"[21] is threatened if she displays "a cold, masculine intellectuality,"[22] not recognizing that "her peculiar position, her own sphere, is with the affections, and wherever these affections have dominion."[23] In short, "no one who feels the true mission and dignity of her womanhood wishes to mingle . . . among the troubled elements of commercial, legislative, and political life."[24] Women's "peculiar" talent is rather to wear down the resistance of their husbands and children to Christian piety by patiently bearing every abuse they may encounter from them; this is the particular form of "Christian service" advocated for women by this manual.

Also, devotional manuals regularly neglect to specify for whom their instructions are designed, for whom their advice might correct what they are already well conditioned by their societies to do, feel, and think. Manuals written to an undefined reader inevitably assume the male as normative. If they do specify their ideal reader, as does the Reverend Edwin Chapin quoted above, rather than *correcting* the gender conditioning of "young women" by secular society, they reinforce and extend it by giving it the weight of religious duty and responsibility before God.

The advice of traditional devotional manuals addresses the temptations associated with male socialization, but Christian women have not received competent and sensitive advice for the correction of their gender-conditioned temptations. Correction of women's socialization must begin by analyzing the particular temptations of women, temptations I have already described as neglect of the development and exercise of talents, lack of a centered self or diffuseness, and dependence on others for self-esteem and fulfillment. That unusual women have occasionally managed to overcome these temptations—without the help of devotional manuals—is laudable, but it does not negate the fact that the social role served by devotional manuals was reinforcement rather than correction of secular gender conditioning. Even manuals specifically addressed to women missed the opportunity of alerting women to their tendency to dismiss God-given gifts that could not be exercised in "woman's sphere."

In 1848 Phoebe Palmer's devotional book *The Promise of the Father* quotes a poignant account from John Wesley's *Journal* of one young woman's reluctance to transgress gender roles by accepting a "calling" to Christian service. Wesley tells the following story of Sarah Mallet, age twenty-three:

> Some years since it was strongly impressed upon her mind that she ought to call sinners to repentance. This impression she vehemently resisted, believing herself quite unqualified, both by her sin and ignorance, till it was suggested, "If you do it not willingly, you shall do it whether you will or no." She fell into a fit, and, while utterly senseless, thought she was in the preaching house at Lowestoffe, where she prayed and preached for nearly an hour to a numerous congregation. She then opened her eyes and recovered her senses. In a year or two she had eighteen of these fits; in every one of which she imagined herself to be in one or another congregation. She then cried out, "Lord, I will obey thee; I will call sinners to repentance." She has done so occasionally from that time, and her fits returned no more.[25]

Phoebe Palmer commented on this quotation from Wesley:

> Probably the experience of this young woman, and the wonderful dealings of the Lord with her, greatly helped to enlarge the views of that great man, Mr. John Wesley, upon the subject of female preaching. It is very evident, from his letters and conduct towards her, that he believed her, as a preacher, to be doing what the Lord required at her hands.[26]

We have no record of the many young women whose urge to "call sinners to repentance" never took the dramatic form that this woman's did, and whose talents and skills were forced into socially acceptable forms. Surely one of the primary meanings of "Christian service," if the term is to be useful in the twentieth century, must be that it connotes a form of engagement in which a Christian may explore and exercise her or his talent and training in forms that may not conform to the secular socialization of their culture. For a few people of the past, like the woman described by Phoebe Palmer, Christian service was precisely the category that empowered them to transgress the gender conditioning of their cultures. But for many more, conventional religious instruction reinforced that of their societies, effectively preventing creative contributions to their communities.

In the twentieth century, Christianity no longer has the option of initiating a countercultural category within which women and men may develop their capabilities without attention to cultural expectations. Secular culture is further advanced than many Christian churches and denominations in establishing the equality of human beings. However, effective empowerment of human beings is a complex matter; mere legal permission does not provide the encouragement and energy necessary for the development of individual capacities and potential for service to society. The support of Christian people and congregations, then, is still crucial for developing and sustaining forms of Christian service that both expand people's horizons of possibility and contribute new insight, talent, and energy to the many problems of our world.

"Christian service" remains in the twentieth century, then, both a serviceable concept and a highly important practice, but the term itself remains problematic. It certainly needs to be given new meanings and interpreted in new ways. It should perhaps be seen less as "calling sinners to repentance" than as political and social activism. But if the term is presently so cluttered with negative meanings, how can Christians use it to describe to themselves why they feel it part of their practice of Christianity to act with vision and generosity in the nuclear world? And if the term is unuseable, must service in and to the world and other human beings be dissociated from religious practice? The separation of practical service from worship, prayer, meditation, or contemplation would result, either in Christians' failure to act in the public sphere, or in an increment of secularity in the lives of people who have undertaken to live as Christians. If, in fact, the energy and commitment that motivates service *is* the result of Christian commitment, it remains important to be able to specify, to oneself as well as to others, the connection of these activities to Christian faith.

We have seen that most of the traditional language associated with Christian service is no longer useful; terms like "self-denial" and "self-sacrifice" cannot describe the motivation of people who have learned that, inevitably, we *do* love our neighbors—not instead of or better than—but *as* ourselves. A language of self-development, self-discovery, and increasing self-knowledge seems to provide a much more accurate description of why Christians at the end of the twentieth century engage in peace activism or work in soup kitchens and shelters for battered women, why some of us commit two years of our lives to "missionary" ventures in which we teach Central American villagers to read and write or work as nurse-practitioners in a developing country. Shy as we rightly are of the traditional language of Christian service, and careful as we must be not to describe our motivation in words and phrases that do not convey what we intend, we still need to practice Christian service and to think of what we are doing as intimately connected to and fed by Christian faith. We can slowly, perhaps, alter the public connotations of "Christian service," but until that is accomplished—probably not in our lifetimes—we will have to relinquish a term that has come, in the curious permutation of language, to mean the opposite of Christian service. Rather, gratitude for being and the ability to specify how acts of service are related to values embedded in one's practice of Christianity will motivate and energize us.

# 8

# An Appetite for Prayer: Meditation and Contemplation

*My mother prayed on her knees at midday, at night, and first thing in the morning. Every day opened up to her to have God's will done in it. Every night she totted up what she'd done and said and thought, to see how it squared with Him. That kind of life is dreary, people think, but they're missing the point. For one thing, such a life can never be boring. And nothing can happen to you that you can't make use of. Even if you're racked by troubles, and sick and poor and ugly, you've got your soul to carry through life like a treasure on a platter. Going upstairs to pray after the noon meal, my mother would be full of energy and expectation, seriously smiling.*

*Alice Munro[1]*

According to Christian authors, prayer is the most central practice for the definition and exercise of a religious self. Although practices of prayer have taken a variety of forms, prayer, understood most broadly, is a habit of interior attentiveness, an activity that creates a formerly unknown self, a self neither imagined nor sought by secular culture. Our task in this chapter will be to examine, in representative devotional manuals, some practices of prayer, meditation, and contemplation. In conclusion I will suggest some guidelines for evaluating the usefulness of practices of prayer for Christian life in the nuclear world.

First, some definitions, and then we will examine each type of prayer in more detail:

*Prayer* was usually understood as a verbal exercise. Historical manuals describe many methods and many contents appropriate to prayer: intercession (praying for other people's needs); petition (praying for things); and thanksgiving (enumerating one's blessings in gratitude), as well as confession and adoration. Verbal prayers may be private or public, vocalized or silent. Prayer formulated by words has been described as the activity of "listening and speaking to God." All of these types of verbal prayer are derived from and based on the conversations that take place in intense and complex human relationships.

*Meditation,* or mental prayer, may be focused by a text or image that directs or stimulates the mind. Meditation has sometimes been described as a "free association," by which one weaves together one's own experience with the scriptural passage or visual image that focuses the meditation, allowing each to examine and challenge the other. Meditation is a play of the mind around stimuli; sometimes meditation is organized in stages by a process of moving from one stimulus to another.

*Contemplation* is defined by the *Westminster Dictionary of Christian Spirituality* as "the kind of prayer in which the mind does not function discursively, but is arrested in a simple attention and one-pointedness."[2] Contemplation is often initiated by verbal prayer or meditation which then becomes wordless, imageless attentiveness.

Having made these working distinctions, we must recognize that they are not absolute. Prayer is a generic word for communication with God; it includes meditation and contemplation, which always play a part in the interior attentiveness of prayer. It is, in fact, difficult and ultimately impossible to separate the three forms, but we can describe different practices in which one or the other predominates. Prayer is a huge topic, even when limited to description of the role of prayer in Christianity. And it has been written about voluminously. The huge body of historical writing about prayer suggests the importance and interest of the topic for historical people. Their sense of the brevity and precariousness of the body's life and their familiarity with physical pain, according to many historical descriptions, increased the pressure to cultivate a self or subjectivity that was seen as not coterminus with physical life. "Thoughts on Death" were a standard topic in devotional treatises on prayer, and the two, death and the need for prayer, were too repeatedly linked for us to ignore a connection that was so obvious to historical people.[3] John Donne (1573–1631), poet and preacher, described the scenario of human life and the need to develop a self in relationship to God—a self that could cross the boundary of death:

All our life is but a going out to the place of Execution, to death. Now was there ever any man seen to sleep in the Cart, between New-gate, and Tybourne? between the Prison, and the place of Execution, does any man sleep?[4]

One must pray because one must die, because prayer is the activity that focuses and strengthens a permanent subjectivity. There is, in most descriptions of prayer in Western Christianity, the suggestion, if not an explicit statement, that the function of prayer is cumulatively to draw one's subjectivity, or self, out of the frighteningly insubordinate body, the body which debilitates the self in pain and eventually deserts it altogether in death.

The definitions of prayer, meditation, and contemplation with which we began reflect this sense that a primary function of prayer is to differentiate, even to separate, the self from the body. The definitions seem divested of body, focused on mental activity. Yet some of the practices of prayer of Christian tradition have purposely included the body. Since these forms of prayer have been subordinated, if not entirely lost, in the West, while forms patterned after a verbal conversation are very familiar, we will focus, in this chapter, on instructions about kinds of prayer that engage the senses and integrate the body in the process of establishing a religious self.

*The Way of a Pilgrim,* an anonymous nineteenth-century manual on prayer from the Russian Orthodox Church, describes a mode of prayer whose goal is cumulatively to include the body in prayer, to "pray with the heart":

> Really to pray means to direct the mind and heart to constant remembrance of God, to walk in his divine presence, to arouse in oneself the love of God by means of meditation, and to say the name of Jesus in harmony with one's breathing and the beating of one's heart. One begins this process by vocally calling on the holy name of Jesus Christ at all times, in all places, and in all occupations, without interruption.[5]

Troubled by the scriptural injunction to "pray without ceasing," the pilgrim attempted to figure out how that can be done, and to do it. Adopting the simple prayer "Lord Jesus Christ, have mercy on me," he gradually progressed from rote recital of the prayer to engraving the prayer so firmly in his consciousness and body that it seemed involuntary. Beginning with repetition of the prayer three thousand times daily at the direction of his spiritual instructor, the pilgrim reports that the "Jesus prayer" eventually seemed to repeat itself involuntarily:

> After awhile I felt that the prayer was somehow entering the heart by itself. The words of the prayer seemed to be formulated according to the rhythm of the heartbeat. . . . I stopped vocalizing the prayer and began to listen attentively as my heart spoke.[6]

The lifestyle of perpetual pilgrimage was the form for the pilgrim's practice of prayer. He found that discomfort and pain were anesthetized by the prayer[7] and he discovered a "renewal of the senses" through looking at objects in the world through the lens of the Jesus prayer:

When I began to pray with the heart, everything around me became transformed and I saw it in a new and delightful way. The trees, the grass, the earth, the air, the light, and everything seemed to be saying to me that it exists to witness to God's love and that it prays and sings of God's glory. . . . I saw how it was possible to communicate with God's creation.[8]

The pilgrim writes of feelings of ecstasy, bliss, great desire, and intensity that accompanied the entrenchment of the Jesus prayer in his body—in breath, heartbeat, and senses. His advice to others who wished to experience prayer was simple, but difficult: "This is how one should proceed in prayer; for a pure and satisfying prayer one should choose simple but powerful words, and then repeat them frequently. In this way it is possible to get an appetite for prayer."[9] One must begin with one's own energy, but the process is experienced as one of moving into effortless cooperation with God's energy. According to the pilgrim, prayer becomes so powerful in one's life that one need not even consciously attempt to alter one's patterns of desire: "Pray, and do not try hard by your own power to overcome your passions. Prayer will destroy them in you."[10]

The pilgrim claims that the source of energy for prayer is "self-love." By an inversion of the ordinary pejorative meaning of "self-love," in which the socialized self is given unlimited license to seek the objects for which it has a conditioned taste, the "self-love" that prompts the life of prayer is one in which the religious self, or the subjectivity constructed by relationship with God, is "loved"—given license to seek the object of *its* passionate desire.

The root, the head and power of all passions and actions is self-love. . . . Every desire, every undertaking, every action has as its goal self-fulfillment and happiness. The natural tendency is to be preoccupied with self-fulfillment throughout one's whole life. But the spirit is not satisfied with anything sensual, and innate self-love never quiets down in its aspiration. Therefore, the desires are developed more and more, the longing for happiness grows, and fills the imagination and attunes the emotions to this. The outpouring of this desire inclines one toward prayer. . . . And so innate self-love, the chief element in life, is the basic reason which arouses people to prayer.[11]

By the practice of perpetual prayer, according to the author of *The Way of a Pilgrim,* one's life is effectively reshaped, one's desires redefined. Because human beings have an innate desire for an infinite object, no succession or accumulation of finite objects will satisfy infinite desire. It is only by strengthening one's relation to God, the infinite object of infinite desire, that satisfying and stabilizing "self-fulfillment" can occur.

The variety of different methods of prayer advised in devotional manuals reflects the creativity with which historical Christians sought and found the most personally effective ways to cultivate a religious self. Private prayer is better than public prayer, Washington Gladden wrote, because it permits greater intimacy and freedom; only in "secret prayer" can one's deepest needs, sorrows, and longings be formulated and expressed. One of the tricks of prayer counseled by Gladden is private but audible prayer: "The utterance of our wants helps us define them"; moreover, audible prayer is more likely to elicit the associated feelings: "for great is the reflex influence of the voice upon the feelings."[12] Martin Luther also advocated audible prayer:

> When I feel cold in heart or disinclined to pray I grab my book of Psalms and go to my room, or, if there's time, into church with the crowd and there, just as the children do, I say out loud the Ten Commandments and the Creed and if there's time a word or two from Christ or Paul or the Psalms.[13]

Jean Nicholas Grou (1731–1803), however, urged silent prayer, "in which we listen to Him and talk with Him, not with the lips, but in the heart."[14]

Another question relating to the practice of prayer that was variously answered in different devotional writings concerns the ideal time or times for prayer. Prescriptions range from the perpetual prayer advocated by the nineteenth-century "pilgrim" to certain fixed times—perhaps morning and night—to spontaneous prayer with no fixed times, to times that correspond to the frequency with which physical needs are attended to. For example, Francis de Sales wrote:

> Just as before the day's dinner you prepare a spiritual repast by means of meditation, so before supper you must prepare a light spiritual supper or collation. Set aside a free time a little before the hour for supper, prostrate yourself before God and place your soul before Jesus Christ crucified.[15]

The suggestion that a balance should be achieved between attending to the needs of the body and spiritual needs implies the desirability of an interweaving of physical and spiritual in human life in which the physical becomes a form for the care and feeding of the spiritual. Cotton Mather gave a different interpretation of the relationship of physical and spiritual needs. A passage from his diary for 1700 reads:

> I was once emptying the cistern of nature, and making water at the wall. At the same time, there came a dog, who did so too, before me. Thought I; "What mean and vile things are the children of men . . . How much do our natural necessities abase us, and place us . . . on the same level with the very dogs!"
>
> My thought proceeded. "Yet I will be a more noble creature; and at the very same time when my natural necessities debase me into the condition of the beast, my spirit shall (I say *at the very time!*) rise and soar . . .
>
> Accordingly I resolved that it should be my ordinary practice, whenever I step to answer the one or other necessity of nature to make it an opportunity of shaping in my mind some holy, noble, divine thought.[16]

In short, ingenuity and self-knowledge have always been required for the discernment of methods of prayer that maximally nourish a religious self! The avidness with which a reading public sought to learn these methods and "tricks" of prayer, evidenced by the large sales of devotional manuals, shows widespread agreement on the value of religious self-definition, if on nothing else.

In turning now to meditation, we will focus on several meditational practices—two visual and one verbal—that were popular at various times and places in the history of Christianity, but which are unknown to, or ignored by, most North American Christians. We have said that meditation employs a focusing device, either words, like the Jesus prayer, perhaps, or visual images. In fact, most historical Christians, and probably most contemporary Christians outside North America, meditate with the use of visual images. In Roman Catholic churches in Italy today it is common to see people praying with their eyes open, gazing at a painting, mosaic, or sculpture. Because many contemporary American Christians are accustomed to thinking of our religious selves as verbally constituted, it may be difficult for us to imagine meditation that is stimulated and challenged by a visual image. Yet some of the most striking conversions of historical people were prompted by visual engagement with a religious image. Saint Dominic, Saint Francis, and Saint Catherine of Siena, as well as many others, described their vivid experience of understanding something revolutionary about God, the world, and their lives while meditating on a crucifix.

Two forms of meditation using visual images were described and advocated by historical devotional manuals: the use of an actual religious image, and visualization—the mental reconstruction of a scene or religious figure. The most intense and vivid religious states were thought to

Fig. 7. Fra Angelico, *The Mocking of Christ,* 15th century. San Marco, Florence. Scala/
Art Resource, N.Y.

be accessible to the viewer who followed the instructions of numerous devotional manuals on how to use visual images to focus meditation and contemplation; visual images offer the viewer a democratic method of prayer. Some manuals even state that illiterate viewers have an advantage in that their minds are not cluttered and complicated by superfluous language. In addition to engaging the visual sense, instructions in the use of visual images for purposes of meditation frequently told readers to imitate in their own bodies the physical postures and gestures of the sacred figures of religious art.

Because educated modern people are accustomed to looking at examples of religious art from the past either as stylistically interesting or in order to identify the narrative content of the scene depicted, we tend to forget that most historical Christians were not at all interested in the former, and only peripherally interested in the latter.[17] Nor were religious scenes commissioned and painted in order to establish the artist's unique style or skill or to communicate a scriptural story.[18] Christians knew the narrative content of scriptural stories from sermons and religious dramas, as well as from popular devotional manuals—frequently read aloud in town squares.

What could not be activated as readily by verbal descriptions of Gospel stories was the emotional attachment of the viewer, a crucial factor for devotional engagement. The immediate accessibility of the painted scene to the eye of the viewer made it possible for the viewer to imagine herself *present* at the scene depicted. She was instructed by sermons and devotional manuals to reproduce in herself empathically the thoughts and emotions experienced by the original participants in the depicted story, to think and feel, for example, with the Virgin Mary as she holds on her lap the dead Christ in a Pietà scene, or to experience the Magdalen's histrionic grief as she embraces the cross, touching Christ's foot, or to feel her amazement and joy as she recognizes the risen Christ near the tomb where she has gone to embalm his body.

According to historical devotional manuals, visual images were not to be considered a preliminary or inferior form of prayer, a "crutch," even for the educated, but an honored and effective method. To scorn the use of visual images in prayer, John of Damascus wrote in the eighth century, was to come dangerously closer to doctrinal heresy, to seem to disdain the created world affirmed by Christ in his Incarnation:

> Perhaps you are sublime and able to transcend what is material, . . . but I, since I am a human being and bear a body, want to deal with holy things and behold them in a bodily manner.[19]

In the fourteenth century, the popular devotional manual *Meditations on the*

*Life of Christ* insisted that meditation using visual images is as important to the adept as to the beginner.[20] Even Ignatius Loyola, sixteenth-century founder of the Jesuit order, his biographer wrote, before he prayed, placed around his room the religious pictures that stimulated and informed his prayer.

In addition, instructions to viewers to place themselves *in* the sacred scene were extended by instructing them to assume the physical postures and gestures of the sacred figures. In a series of frescos in the monk's cells at the Dominican monastery of San Marco in Florence, depicting scenes from the life and passion of Christ, and painted in the fifteenth century by Fra Angelico,[21] the figure of a Dominican monk is included in each painting (see fig. 7). The contemporary figure in the painting, a monk dressed in the same way as the monk viewing the painting, modeled the specific reaction the viewer must reproduce. Placing his body in the same position, the meditating monk was helped to experience the feelings appropriate to the scene. This meditation then informed the sermon he was preparing. Similar to this monastic exercise, the *Meditations on the Life of Christ*[22] instructed the reader to meditate on the many illustrations accompanying the text—sometimes several on a single page—and to imitate the physical postures of the sacred figures who loved and followed the earthly Christ as a method for experiencing their emotions. *The Garden of Prayer,* a manual written in 1454 for young girls, goes further to claim that "specific states of mystical consciousness can be stimulated by deliberately assuming certain bodily postures."[23] By imitating a progression of bodily postures, accompanied by prayers, the viewer can exercise the full range of prayer, meditation, and contemplation. For example, humility is not only symbolized, but stimulated by a bow; compunction, by prostration; intercession and inspiration, by standing, with arms extended; ecstasy, by standing, hands joined and held directly overhead. The insight that a person's bodily stance affects her psychological state was well known to the authors and readers of historical devotional manuals.[24]

While paintings can inform and model appropriate religious feelings, historical people, before the invention of printing presses, did not have access to such images unless they were in church. The second kind of prayer that uses visual images as meditational devices, then, was mental reconstruction of an imagined scene. The best known example of the role of visualization in prayer is Ignatius Loyola's *Spiritual Exercises,* a sixteenth-century manual for the discernment of one's vocation. A thirty-day retreat, under the supervision of a spiritual director and based on the *Spiritual Exercises,* was required of every prospective Jesuit priest. As in the case of instructions in the use of actual visual images, visualizations, so effective in monastic settings, were also urged on lay people by devotional texts. *The Garden of Prayer* explains the usefulness of visualizations in prayer:

> The better to impress the story of the Passion on your mind, and to memorize each action of it more easily, it is helpful and necessary to fix the places and people in your mind: a city, for example, which will be the city of Jerusalem—taking for this purpose a city that is well known to you. . . . And then too you must shape in your mind some people, people well known to you, to represent for you the people involved in the Passion—the person of Jesus Himself, of the Virgin, St. Peter [etc.]. . . . When you have done all this, putting all your imagination into it, then go into your chamber. Alone and solitary, excluding every external thought from your mind, start thinking of the beginning of the Passion. . . . Moving slowly from episode to episode, meditate on each one, dwelling on each single stage and step of the story. And if at any point you feel a sensation of piety, stop: do not pass on as long as that sweet and devout sentiment lasts.[25]

Francis de Sales, in the *Introduction to the Devout Life,* also urged the use of visualizations:

> By such imaginative means we restrict our mind to the mystery on which we meditate so that it will not wander about. . . . Perhaps someone will tell you that it is better to represent such mysteries by the simple thoughts of faith and completely intellectual and spiritual conceptions, or else to consider them as taking place within your own soul. This method is too subtle for beginners.[26]

In addition to instructions in the use of visual images and visualizations for focusing and directing meditation, verbal methods of meditation were also described in many devotional manuals. Disciplined reading, derived from the monastic practice of *lectio divina,* was understood to be a valuable activity for concentrating attention in meditation. In *The Love of Learning and the Desire for God,* Jean Leclercq describes the practice of *lectio divina:*

> In the Middle Ages, as in antiquity, they read usually . . . with the lips, pronouncing what they saw, and with the ears, listening to the words pronounced, hearing what is called "the voice of the pages," . . . an activity which, like chant and writing, requires the participation of the whole body and the whole mind. Doctors of ancient times used to recommend reading to their patients as a physical exercise on an equal level with walking, running, or ball-playing.[27]

Reading, simultaneously a visual and auditory activity, was done slowly, pausing to "learn by heart" the lessons in the words:

> For the ancients, to read a text is to learn it "by heart" in the fullest sense of this expression, that is, with one's whole being: with the body, since the mouth pronounced it, the eyes saw it, and the ears heard it, with the memory which fixes it, with the intelligence which understands its meaning and with the will which desires to put it into practice.[28]

Similar instructions appeared in devotional treatises for laypersons. François Fénelon (1651–1715), archbishop of Cambrai and follower of the quietistic spirituality of Madame Guyon, wrote:

> As to the subject of your meditations, take such passages of the Gospel or of the *Imitation* of Jesus Christ as move you most. Read slowly, and when a passage touches you, use it as you would a sweetmeat, which you hold in your mouth till it melts. Let the meaning sink slowly into your heart, and do not pass on to something else until you feel that to be exhausted.[29]

Scripture was the reading matter most often advocated for meditation. Such dissimilar Christian authors as Isaac of Nineveh, Martin Luther, and Count von Zinzendorf all extoll the capacity of scripture, closely read and pondered, for shaping the religious self. Isaac wrote: "To drive away the wrong tendencies previously acquired by the soul, nothing is more helpful than immersing oneself in love of studying the divine scriptures, and understanding the depths of the thoughts they contain."[30]

In addition to scripture and various events from Christ's life and passion, the most frequent subjects for verbal as well as for visual meditations—both actual images and visualizations—were meditations on death. A long tradition of verbal and visual meditations on death existed in the Christian West, a tradition too variously articulated and pictured to discuss in detail here.[31] No historical society in the Christian West failed to produce devices for reminding people that their own deaths were both inevitable and imminent. From the practice of strolling in the underground burial chambers of the late Roman Empire to genres of art and artifacts—like the ubiquitous skull placed on the desks of scholars and on the dressing tables of beautiful women—historical Christians knew that thoughts of one's own death "wonderfully concentrated the mind" on spiritual matters (see fig. 8).

Reminders of death, moreover, were not seen as morbid or horrifying; rather, they were the first step toward managing death. Consciousness of one's own death provided the necessary stimulus for beginning and con-

Fig. 8. Georges de La Tour, *The Repentant Magdalen*, c. 1645. Giraudon/Art Resource, N.Y.

tinuing the long process of dissociating one's "self" or subjectivity from the moribund body. It is not accidental that, in the twentieth century, secularity—the rejection of a religious subject or self—and the attempt to eliminate reminders of death have advanced together. Although contemporary films and news media are full of images of violent death, the viewer's voyeuristic relationship to these images, together with habituation to violent images, precludes seeing the deaths of others as reminders of one's own death.

According to many devotional manuals, only the conscious and constant awareness of one's own inevitable death is sufficient to motivate the self to break its attachment to the body.[32] The difficulty of maintaining awareness of one's own death, however, comes from the fact that reminders of death are so numerous that human beings with rapidly fatiguing senses are habituated to them. Devotional manuals, as well as the popular arts of historical Christianity, thus try to revivify reminders of death. With this intent, Jeremy Taylor (1613–67), in *The Rule and Exercises of Holy Dying,* urged his readers to notice the daily increments of their progress toward death. Progress toward death could then become the impetus for forming a self that is not, like the body, biodegradable, a self whose strengthened connection to immortality made it capable of abandoning the dying body:

> Baldness is but a dressing to our funerals, the proper ornament of a person entered very far into the regions and possession of death: and we have many more of the same signification: gray hairs, rotten teeth, dim eyes, trembling joints, short memory, decayed appetite, . . . and while we think a thought, we die; and the clock strikes, and reckons on our portion of eternity; we form our words with the breath of our nostrils, we have the less to live upon for every word we speak.[33]

Were such frightening reminders in devotional manuals given merely in order to depress? Or were they intended—as devotional manuals explicitly insist—to provoke the reader to action, the action of cultivating a religious self? Dismaying as such rhetoric sounds to us today, in their original context, these "reminders," together with daily examples of older people who were already strenuously engaged in shaping a religious self, often achieved the desired effect. Authors of devotional manuals, in any case, relied on reminders of death to energize the practices of prayer they advocated. And it was these practices that created and strengthened a self no longer identified with the socially inscribed body—the mortal body.

About contemplation little, by definition, can be said. Strictly speaking, contemplation is a gift, the result of prayer and meditation that achieves prayer so concentrated that the person is absorbed in ecstasy.

Although contemplation was ultimately considered a gift, the literature of Christian devotion nevertheless urges that it be cultivated by various practices of prayer and meditation. Thomas Aquinas defined contemplation as "the simple act of gazing on the truth."[34] Without content, or rather, containing only imageless, ineffable content, contemplation is pure activity whose affective content, according to all accounts, is delight. Isaac of Nineveh, a seventh-century Nestorian bishop, wrote: "Sometimes from prayer a certain contemplation is born which makes prayer vanish from the lips. And he to whom this contemplation happens becomes as a corpse without soul, in ecstasy."[35]

One of the most immediate and noticeable effects of contemplation, according to devotional manuals, was unification of the individual personality and communal bonding among people who also participate in contemplation. Unification, either of individuals or of groups, we should notice, can be construed in several ways. In one understanding of unity, one role, function, or activity is declared normative or "highest," while others are tacitly discounted because they are not the "highest" activity. Frequently contemplation was described as creating this kind of a hierarchical organization or unity. Another understanding of unity, however, emphasizes the interdependence of all that shares in the unity. In this understanding, comparisons of "higher" and "lower" do not result in disparagement of some participants relative to others. Thomas Aquinas, for example, described contemplation as a rich integration of spiritual and physical senses: "In the present state of life human contemplation is impossible without sense imagery."[36] The distinction between a hierarchically arranged unity and one that highlights interdependence will be important for our consideration of the relevance and usefulness of contemplation in a pluralistic nuclear world.

If contemplation is not understood as engaging, and thus valorizing, an exclusively intellectual or mental aspect of human being, it will not disparage by comparison more active forms of Christian service as it often has in the past. If it need not be considered the "highest" or normative activity of a Christian, those most adept at contemplation will not be seen as the "best" Christians, while those whose Christianity compels them to work for such "worldly" goals as just social arrangements, political responsibility, or nuclear disarmament—to name only a few of the ways in which twentieth-century Christianity might be practiced—will not be regarded as having chosen "lesser goods."

Contemplation can be understood as gift—certainly a gift to be cultivated, but not a gift to be possessed, and definitely not a gift that entails status within Christian communities for its recipient. This understanding of contemplation can render it relevant and valuable in our world. New

Testament imagery of Christians as members of a single body whose diverse abilities and capacities are to be equally respected and valued has, in the hierarchically organized societies of the Christian West, rarely had the effect of creating a strong sense of interdependence in Christian communities. The postmodern world of pluralistic perspectives is, however, presently forcing twentieth-century Christians to understand diversity of perspectives and talents as a source of increased understanding and hope in a world that desperately needs multidimensional healing.

I have described practices of prayer as central to the creation and cultivation of a religious self, but this is not quite the language used by authors of devotional manuals. Their attention was not on the "formation of a particular mode of relationship with oneself," nor on the religious self as an alternative to the individual as conditioned by secular culture, but on the actualization of a connection with God already implicit in human beings. Yet the language of "the care of the self" would not have been foreign to them; they recognized both the psychological and social value of a consciously chosen and cultivated subjectivity, the increment of active self-definition to be gained by delineating a self whose desires and values were not passively shaped by socialization.

The creation of a religious subject is the radical result of the practices by which, cumulatively, a new relationship with oneself is defined. As a result of these practices, three interior "selfs" are differentiated: the socialized self, the religious self, and the parent self—the authoritative self-definer. The parent self stands behind the other selves, determining both their ideal structures and the methods for creating them. Christian authors often wrote of the care and feeding of the neonatal religious self in metaphors of infancy and childhood, demonstrating their awareness that in conversion a new organization of life had come into being and needed to be carefully and consistently nourished.[37] The frequent use of images of child rearing indicates that their attention was at least partially on this delicate new self and its care and training. Thus Teresa of Avila, in *The Way of Perfection*, wrote:

> Another excellent aid to recollection and vocal prayer is the reading of a good book, in the vernacular. And thus, either by means of coaxing the soul or by strategies, you can gradually accustom it to meditation without frightening it.[38]

Discipline, a necessary part of every child-rearing program, was understood as a necessary part of the cultivation of a new subjectivity. Instructions for the cultivation of the religious self were not, of course, spiritualized child-rearing manuals, but inevitably the image of the religious self as an infant evoked the intimate experience of childhood of Christian authors.[39] The full continuum of child-rearing methods appears in the advice of devotional manuals, from sadistic self-torture and bullying, to begging and promising, to loving patience. Some authors found that "strategies" worked better than threats, but there are also many authors whose vivid threats of eternal punishment reveal different and sterner tactics. Meditations on one's own death probably represent the middle range between threats of hell and damnation and the loving gentleness counseled by Teresa.

Francisco de Osuna, Spanish author of *The Third Spiritual Alphabet,* devoted a chapter of this manual to methods for the correction of one's own "soul." His advice is patience and gentleness; always "correct your soul with love and not in anger":

> A person will speak to his soul as kindly as to a student. And in overlooking past distractions, he can prevent future ones by taking away everything that is cause for distraction, and he should do this with the greatest possible love for there is nothing that encourages others to what we wish than our love for it. This exercise is not achieved by force but by skill.[40]

Patience is also required, and Francisco gives a rule of thumb to help the reader estimate how much patience is required: "If he has been exercising vice for one year, two years of practicing the opposite virtue are needed to remove the evil habit and clothe him with the habit of virtuous custom."[41] He commends sympathy for the discomfort caused by placing the self under the pressure of surveillance and pruning. Harshness, he concludes, is counterproductive:

> Recollected people in relation to their souls are like the hunter with the bird he captures alive to put in a cage. Outside of its enclosure, the bird rested quietly high in the trees, but once caged, it does not enjoy a moment's rest but hops from one part to another and hurts its head trying to escape. In almost the same way, when the devout person wishes to put his soul in the cage of recollection, he feels it more restless than before, and sees that he is losing all previous tranquility. . . . Some are so tormented by their fantasies that in their efforts to remedy them they drive too hard to cast them out and suffer headaches and bodily weakness and other similar difficulties. They try to correct in anger things that would be disciplined better by loving toleration.[42]

We have surveyed several methods of prayer recommended by historical devotional manuals. We must now examine the values implicit in practices of prayer, and evaluate the usefulness of prayer for contemporary

Christians. Throughout the chapter I have emphasized the function of prayer in creating a self by an interior attentiveness. Clearly, the decision to practice a form or forms of prayer represents "self"-definition at the expense of the culturally defined "self."

Every society creates individuals socialized to contribute to the maintenance of that society by desiring and pursuing the objects approved of and provided by the society. The individual's self-identification with this phenomenal self prevents the cultivation of a religious self; such self-identification is thus the first target of spiritual labor. In twentieth-century North America, for example, full-time commitment to pursuit of "the best of everything"—understood as consumer goods and services—leaves no time or energy for self-definition; rather, one is defined by what one owns. Anyone who has experienced the painful limitation involved in operating from such cultural models will recognize, in the historical practices by which the inevitability and finality of the socialized self were questioned and addressed, strategies for self-definition. For example, in *The Way of a Pilgrim* one can recognize in the nineteenth-century pilgrim's description of the effects of the Jesus prayer the definition of a strong center. This practice would surely need to be modified if it were to be useful to twentieth-century Christians, but it can also remind us of our own need for centeredness. Though the present entertainment culture is vastly different from that of the nineteenth-century Russian, it is still difficult to create a centered self. Methods of meditation involving a focus on empowering words or images could, for example, provide an alternative to the shaping of one's consciousness by contemporary communication media.

Clearly, it is possible to find useful insights and methods for a contemporary practice of Christianity in historical descriptions of prayer. We must now ask whether there are some implicit values in practices of prayer that seem questionable or even dangerous in the nuclear world. Three questionable attitudes associated with prayer occur in a number of historical devotional manuals and require our attention. First, as we have seen, prayer has frequently been understood as disembodied mental activity, a self-transcendence that ignores the material conditions of human life. Because the idea of prayer as disembodied has become a popular caricature of prayer, I have emphasized, in this chapter, several practices that explicitly recognize and articulate the body's role in prayer. In the twentieth century, a critical practice of prayer must be able to specify the relationship of body to the religious subject formed by prayer. Prayer need not be—though it frequently was—thought of as disembodied.

Second, historical manuals sometimes suggest that the decision to focus on the care and cultivation of a religious self must prevent the expenditure of energy in concern for other human beings. Stories of saints who strode over the prostrate bodies of loved ones begging them not to leave them for a life of contemplation abound and were treasured in the history of Christianity.[43] Miguel de Molinos (1640–97), in his *Spiritual Guide,* wrote:

> Interior solitude consists in the forgetting of the creatures, in disengaging oneself from them, in a perfect nakedness of all the affections, desires, thoughts, and one's own will. . . . Live as much as ever you can abstracted from the creatures, dedicate yourself wholly to your Creator.[44]

In twentieth-century North America, a society often characterized as individualistic and narcissistic, Christian practice must not become a new form of self-absorption. Yet the danger that prayer might become nothing more than sublime self-intending needs to be examined more closely. To characterize the 1980s as individualistic and narcissistic is to ignore and marginalize many people who do not share in the culture of competition, individualism, and narcissism, and whose life circumstances have not permitted or encouraged individuation, much less the development of an individualistic perspective. A mandatory concern for the needs of others has taken the place of self-definition. For people who were not offered the possibility of self-definition by their societies, prayer, as a method of formulating themselves as subjects, has been a frequent recourse. Historical women, for example, often had possibilities of self-definition by religious practices that they did not have in secular culture. Although we may deplore the fact that they were confined to religious roles, we can still recognize the provision of these tools for self-definition and applaud the creativity with which many women used them.

The final danger associated with prayer in devotional manuals is that a strongly centered prayer life can become an escape from public and private responsibility, consistently undermining one's sense of the compelling needs of the world. Although escapism is an undeniable strain in many devotional manuals, there are also some that insist that the primary function of prayer is to energize one for action, not to promote withdrawal and lassitude. There are authors, like Meister Eckhart, the fourteenth-century Dominican preacher and mystic, who said that even if a person were in the heights of mystical transport when a needy person came along, he should immediately turn away from prayer and help the person in need. Most devotional manuals have counseled a balance—difficult to achieve—of interior and exterior activity.

Advice given by devotional manuals took the form of the author's suggestions for the *correction* of contemporary practices; it was based on the author's analysis of what he, or people in his immediate environment, did too readily and with too much facility. This means, on the one hand, that no historical advice can be accepted without critical analysis and interpretation in the context of our personal and public situations. Thus, in the twentieth century, committed activists may need to develop an interior recollection that can save them from the outward flow of attention and energy that leads to fatigue and listlessness—burn-out; on the other hand, people who are inclined to avoid effort to serve and change the world need to discover the ultimate sterility of a subjectivity uninformed by engagement in the world. A fruitful practice of prayer is as likely to lead to loving service that makes vivid one's interdependence with other human beings, and to the self-knowledge to be gained in action and struggle, as it is to become the basis for a new self-relation and self-definition.

## Part Three

# Embodiment of
# Christian Life

# Introduction to Part Three

*If the body is to partake with the soul in the ineffable benefits of the world to come, it is certain that it must participate in them as far as possible now. . . . For the body also has an experience of divine things when the passionate forces of the soul are not put to death but transformed and sanctified.*

*Gregory Palamas*, Homilies

Several persistent attitudes and values appear embedded in devotional manuals throughout the history of Christianity. We will focus on attitudes and values that represent, for contemporary Christians, the most problematic aspects of historical Christianity. Clearly, twentieth-century values and interests have changed radically from those of historical Christian authors. Debates about the relative value of the active and the contemplative lifestyles, so prominent in historic manuals, for example, do not seem to trouble twentieth-century Christians; rather, most of the problems contemporary Christians find in historical Christianity relate to attitudes and values that have played a role in bringing Western societies to the brink of nuclear war. We have already discussed several of these problems as we examined the primary metaphors of Christian life and the practices which formed the countercultural religious self—problems that stem from a dualism that disparaged bodies, other people, and the natural world in favor of souls, God, and heaven.

The knotted clusters of attitudes and values to be examined in this section, then, are those which, along with the spirit/matter dualism of the tradition, perhaps represent the most dangerous contributions of Western Christianity. These are: teachings on the role of human relationships in Christian life and the relative value of happiness and suffering. Chapter 9 in this section will explore a range of traditional suggestions about the role of personal relationships—friendship, sexual relationship, marriage—in Christian practice. Chapter 10 will examine issues related to happiness and suffering—voluntary and involuntary suffering—Christian authors' advice about self-denial, detachment, and discipline. Our goal in these chapters will be twofold: on the one hand, to expose the danger of one strain of historical treatment on these subjects and, on the other, to determine whether there are some historical suggestions that can provide valuable corrections of contemporary values and practices and can therefore be usefully incorporated into Christian life a nuclear world.

# 9

## Loving the Neighbor in God: Personal Relationships

*First see whether you have learned to love yourself. . . . If you have not learned how to love yourself, I am afraid that you will cheat your neighbor as yourself.*

*Augustine* City of God *10.3.2*

Interpretations of the value of relationship in Christian life have differed enormously according to the lifestyle of the interpreter and the social context addressed. From the perspective of the individual who determines to create and cultivate a religious self, other human beings have been variously understood both as providing the most valuable challenge and support and as being the most threatening and potentially undermining representatives of socialization diametrically opposed to the religious self. We will look at two positive views of friendship, those of Aelred of Rievaulx and Augustine of Hippo, at one ambiguous account, Francis de Sales's, and at a variety of historical misgivings about friendship. Beginning with Aelred's description of the positive energy of friendship, we will go on to explore the dangers feared by several authors of devotional manuals, concluding with Augustine's influential and much misunderstood description of "loving the neighbor in God." We will explore accounts of community and society as extensions of friendship, and then go on to the forms of relationship that have proved more difficult for Christian authors to evaluate positively: sexual relationship and marriage.

Let us begin with self-relatedness, the basis of relationship with others. One of the most confusing features of devotional manuals' discussions of relationship is their ambiguous use of the term "self-love." Sometimes this term is one of opprobrium, indicating a self shaped by compulsive pursuit of the culturally defined objects of sex, power, and possession. In other contexts, "self-love" is used to name the intentions and practices by which one identifies and develops a religious self, the greatest self-actualization possible for human beings. We have already noticed the fluidity of the word *self* and the necessity of determining which self the author considers the "real" self before we can understand his instructions. An interesting correlation exists between positive regard for oneself and positive regard for others in devotional manuals; those that identify the "real self" as the self-before-God and counsel their readers to gratify and fulfill *this* self usually regard other human beings as potential sources of challenge and encouragement. Those who identify the "real self" as the sinful self are also suspicious of human relationships. For these latter, "self-love" is the enemy. The relation to oneself is thus decisive in determining how one will think about relationship with another human being as these relationships are extrapolated from one's self-relatedness.

The most positive evaluation of friendship to be found in the history of Christianity was formulated in a monastic context by Aelred of Rievaulx (1110–67). Aelred wrote: "I call them more beasts than men, who say that life should be led so that they need not console anyone nor occasion distress or sorrow to anyone, who take no pleasure in the good of another nor expect their failures to distress anyone, seeking to love no one nor be loved by anyone."[1] Aelred was not tilting against a "straw man"; we will shortly see that just such attitudes were commonplace in the monastic tradition he inherited. His case for the high value of friendship in the development of a religious self came primarily from the Platonic tradition in which friendship provided the best possible format for the cultivation of personal excellence; in Christian Platonism, male friends were urged to encourage each other to greater and greater self-actualization and spiritual achievement.[2] Aelred described friendship in glowing terms:

> What happiness, what security, what joy to have someone to whom you dare to speak on terms of equality as to another self; one to whom you need have no fear to confess your failings; one to whom you can unblushingly make known what progress you have made in the spiritual life; one to whom you can entrust all the secrets of your heart and before whom you can place all your plans! What, therefore, is more pleasant than so to unite to oneself the spirit of another, and of two to form one, that no boasting is thereafter to be feared, no suspicion to be dreaded, no correction of one by the other to cause pain, no praise on the part of one to bring a charge of flattery by the other. A friend is the medicine of life.[3]

"Among the stages leading to the highest," Aelred concluded, "friendship is the highest."[4]

Aelred wrote in the context of a monastic community, individuals vowed to the pursuit of what they called simply a "perfect life," the "life of the angels," without sexual or social complications. Strong friendships, he said, can help one to recognize God's love, and to experience directly and concretely God-who-is-love: "Friend, cleaving to friend in the spirit of Christ, is made with Christ but one heart and one soul, and so mounting aloft through degrees of love to friendship with Christ, he is made one spirit with him in one kiss."[5]

Aelred's erotic imagery evokes the Platonic model of friendship in which friends confront, comfort, reassure, and urge each other on in the practices that develop virtue. The friend is seen as "another self"; what one hopes for oneself, one endeavors to promote in the friend. Energy for growth and achievement in an incorporation of the Good comes from eros, a strong attraction that begins in physical attraction and, precisely *because* it is undifferentiated as to categories of spirituality and physicality, can work *with* physical attraction to produce, by extension, the intense longing by which the Good is actualized in a human life.[6] Eros, the energy of attraction, is not a property of body but of soul; the object to which the soul is attracted—whether physical or spiritual—defines and constitutes the soul's specific integrity. In Plato, there is no suggestion that eros should be (in a modern term) repressed; it should, however (again in a modern term) be sublimated, consciously extended to noncorporeal objects so that the full range of human possibility and self-actualization can be achieved, namely, an embodiment of the Good.

In the Christian interpretation of Platonic tradition, the ambiguity of eros was not acceptable. Like other Christian authors who understood friendship as mutual stimulation for spiritual growth, Aelred set a "definite limit" on "how far friendship ought to go."[7] This limit precluded sexual relationship.[8] In fact, "true friendship," for Aelred, as for other Christian authors, was defined by the absence of sexual interest, which was always understood as self-seeking. Sexual attraction, in fact, characterized the friendships of "the wicked." Friendship worthy of the name, Aelred wrote, can only "begin among the good, progress among the better, and be consummated among the perfect."[9] Moreover, "true friendship" excludes feelings of affection, which he calls "childish," at best a preface to friendship. In Aelred's analysis, the opposite of productive spiritual friendship is "affection"—what Francis de Sales calls "fond loves"[10]—because affection leads to "the desires of the flesh," desires which, in Christian authors, was seen as necessarily a "conflict of interests" and alien to the sort of friendship that brings advance in Christian life.

In pursuing Aelred's positive interpretation of the role of friendship among Christians, we have already discovered the "main danger" with friendship, according to Christian authors. In our discussion of sexual relationship, we will explore the ideal of virginity that informed their prohibition of sexuality in relationships that promote Christian growth. For now, let us remain with interpretations of friendship and its possibility and danger. Aelred describes friendship as a powerful, but volatile, force, an energy that can equally be used for damage or help; whether it will result in one or the other depends on isolating it carefully from "carnal affection." "Friendship is the most dangerous of all types of love," Francis de Sales wrote.[11] Unlike Aelred, who extolled the productive capacity of friendship, Francis was more alert to the dangers of friendship than to the potential for spiritual growth inherent in it. His warnings against these dangers are replete with harsh phrases like "animal allurement," "carnal pleasures," "lewd and sordid conduct." He assures the female reader for whom he wrote the *Introduction to the Devout Life* that physical desires play no part in Christian life and sketches a closed energy system in which human love can be "spent" either on the "foolish, useless and frivolous things" of the flesh *or* on love for God. Francis's distinction between "false friendships" and "holy friendships" turns on whether or not physical attraction is a part of the relationship.

A closer reading of Francis de Sales's discussion of friendship, however, reveals another concern, namely, the role of social conditioning in physical attraction. His discussion of "fond loves" does not focus as much on "wanton acts and impure deeds" as on culturally specific flirtation and courtship behavior. Flirtation distracts from "the devout life": "knowing, affected, and improper looks, sensual caresses, little sighs, complaints about not being loved, slight but studied and enticing postures, acts of gallantry, requests for kisses and other familiarities and indecent favors."[12] Although Francis describes these playful acts as the first stage in a progressive downhill rush into "carnal love"—one thing leads to another—they are also fruitlessly distracting from the integrity of Christian life. Moreover, in these courtship rituals, the other person is not so much loved for himself as used for the gratification of one's own ego.

Fear and distrust of friendship inspired many authors of devotional manuals to issue warnings that go far beyond Aelred's stipulation of purely spiritual friendship or Francis's objection to "fond" loves and frivolous flirtations. For some authors, it was not merely lurking sensuality or sexuality that made friendship problematic, but emotional engagement with another person at all. Thomas à Kempis, in *The Imitation of Christ,* wrote: "You are a fool if you find joy in any other than Jesus."[13] Often, the motivation of self-protection is given as the reason for not loving other human beings: "The man who has come to hate the world has escaped sorrow," wrote John of Damascus,[14] in a variation of Augustine's argument in the *Confessions,* that one should, in the final analysis, love only what one cannot lose, namely, God.[15] Despite Augustine's insistence that only loving the neighbor in God preserves the independent worth of the neighbor, the history of interpretation of his concept, evident especially in devotional manuals, tends to emphasize the danger of distraction from heavenly things inherent in love for earthly "creatures." Manuals that employ metaphors of Christian life as pilgrimage or ascent also, as we have seen, often regard the neighbor as potential obstacle rather than as a source of support for the pilgrimage or the ascent.

Nevertheless, Augustine's account of loving the neighbor in God, as set forth most clearly in *The Trinity,* is remarkable in its conclusion that love of neighbor *is* love of God (see fig. 9). Augustine did not have the same idea of relationship that many twentieth-century people do. Modern literature on relationship often emphasizes the value of relationship for overcoming isolation and creating bonds that bridge an experienced gap between human beings. This modern diagnosis, and prescription, however, already designates the sort of person who might profit from it and excludes those whose gender conditioning and life circumstances have precluded their individuation. Augustine's narration of his own life story demonstrates that his problem was primarily a need to individuate, not a need to overcome autonomous isolation. Augustine felt himself so connected to, so much a part of, those he loved that he found it difficult and painful even to differentiate himself from them. He had to move away from the city when his friend died, so unbearable was it for him to walk alone on those streets from which his friend had vanished. As an adult he had to sneak away from his mother and board a ship for Rome without her knowledge in order to leave her at all. And the woman with whom he lived in faithfulness for thirteen years was, in Augustine's vivid langauge, "torn from [his] flesh"[16] when they parted. In this context, "loving the neighbor in God" was Augustine's formula for breaking dependent relationships and acknowledging that those he loved did not exist to satisfy his needs and wishes but as "fellow pilgrims."

Augustine's description of friendship, then, illustrates the difficulty of understanding what historical people meant from reading what they said. Often, I suspect, a rhetoric that disparaged the significance of other people masked and attempted to overcome attachment and dependency, while modern rhetoric about the high value of relationship frequently conceals the fundamental narcissistic isolation of some twentieth-century people. We can, of course, feel more confident that we have understood historical authors if, as in Augustine's case, we have information about the life as well as the writings of the author. Since this information is seldom available in detail, however, we are often required to make some educated guesses from our knowledge of the author's lifestyle and institutional

Fig. 9. Jesus Covers the Disciples, end 13th century. Ms. Italien 115. fol. 28. Bibliothèque Nationale, Paris.

commitments about the problem or situation that has prompted the author's discussion. It is also important to keep in mind that, since much of the literature on friendship comes from authors committed to celibacy—even if it was addressed to lay people—the problems of the monastery have generated the author's discussion and have influenced his treatment of the topic. Treatments of sexual relationship and marriage were especially affected by monastic authors' frequent inability to imagine sexual experience that might contribute to, rather than debilitate, the cultivation of a religious self.

It is difficult to find, in the devotional literature of Western Christianity, any more positive interpretation of the role of sexual relationship and marriage in Christian life than a few scattered suggestions and fragments, often in condemned writings. Yet there is a considerable body of writings—whole treatises and treatments within treatises on other subjects—on virginity or celibacy.[17] If not always explicitly, at least implicitly by the amount of literary attention given to the subject, Christian authors were almost unanimous in declaring the greater value of abstention from sexual activity.[18] The most sweeping and enthusiastic claims for the greater appropriateness of celibacy for the development of a religious self can be found in this literature.[19] Virginity has been variously called the "cornerstone of the Church,"[20] a proof of the efficacy of the Christian gospel because it empowers women and men to achieve the impossible: sexual abstinence[21] and the "life of the angels."[22] Although the decisive Christianization of the Roman Empire at the end of the fourth century was accompanied by a wave of ascetic fervor, it is also true that apologists for virginity of both sexes had more time to write about the satisfactions of their chosen life than did people who were strenuously engaged in the demands made on them by the results of sexual relationship and marriage, bearing and caring for and rearing children. The literature of Christian celibacy was created by people who not only were committed to renunciation of sex but also, one may assume, frequently needed to remind themselves of the reasons for their commitment by writing about them.

One of the most important and effective arenas of human life which must be related to the cultivation of a religious self is sexuality.[23] Christian insistence on interpreting the Song of Songs of the Hebrew Bible as a description of the relationship of Christ and the church is symbolic of a firm sublimation of sexuality in Christianity. The Song of Songs, a collection of songs to be sung at wedding parties, celebrates the beauty and goodness of sexual love; it contains few suggestions for any other interpretations, and was understood as a love poem by many Jewish

interpreters.[24] Yet traditional Christian interpreters unanimously alle-
gorized the sexual passion praised in the Song of Songs as an extended
metaphor for mystical experience, ironically making it one of the most
important scriptural writings for sexual ascetics. Sexual love and "carnal"
love are contrasted with "spiritual love."[25] Rather than redeeming sexual
passion, the Song of Songs, in commentaries from Origen to Bernard of
Clairvaux and beyond, was hermeneutically tortured to sing the praises of
mystical rapture.

A complex theology of celibacy exists but will not be our primary
concern here. John Bugge's *Virginitas: An Essay in the History of a Medieval
Ideal* gives an excellent summary of the theology of virginity.[26] This
theology of sexual abstinence was not as influential in Christian tradition,
however, as the manuals in the practice of Christianity that were known
and loved by countless lay people. Devotional manuals, we have said, tend
to omit both sophisticated arguments and doctrinal warrants in order to
advocate the practices that create and exercise a religious self. Predictably,
then, we find in devotional manuals condensed versions of the reasons for
sexual abstinence, descriptions that often sacrifice the careful metaphysical
descriptions of the status of human bodies in Christianity in order to urge
the need for various practices. Positive suggestions about the value of sex
and marriage in the history of Christian tradition are to be found in
theological discussions rather than in devotional manuals.[27] Although
these suggestions were few and do not represent a majority opinion, to
sketch them will help us to see what Christian tradition has occasionally
managed in terms of a positive view of sex.

For reasons of clarity, we must simply state at the outset that any
attempt to find positive evaluations of sexual relationships in Christianity
will need to look only at descriptions of sex within marriage.[28] Even then,
it is, on closer examination, not sexual activity itself that the author finds
good, but marriage—the union of a man and woman that creates a new
social unit supportive of society. A dichotomy between marriage and
pleasure was assumed in many writings—marriage being good and pleasure bad. In marriage, sex was tolerated largely for purposes of the
continuity of the human race, although some authors can imagine a
companionship between husband and wife that is a good in itself. The
fourth-century ascetic Jerome once said that the husband who is "rather an
immoderate lover of his wife than a husband is simply an adulterer,"[29] and
this statement was repeated throughout the history of Christianity.[30] In
the fourth century, when marriage achieved sacramental status and was no
longer simply a secular and legal contract, the sacramental blessing was
added as a further good.[31] Clearly, it was never sexual intimacy or activity
itself that Christian authors valued and were grateful for.

The place of sexual relationship within marriage in the particular project of creating and maintaining Christian life has been mentioned by several Christian authors rather than systematically developed in a way that would parallel the extensive description of the benefit for the Christian of a life of celibacy. Clement of Alexandria understood marriage as an excellent test of one's progress in self-possession:

> True manhood is shown, not in the choice of a celibate life . . . but by him who has trained himself by the discharge of the duties of husband and father and by the supervision of a household . . . by him who in the midst of his solicitude for his family shows himself inseparable from the love of God and rises superior to every temptation which assails him through children and wife and servants and possessions . . . he who has no family is in most respects untried.[32]

Marriage envisioned as spiritual discipline may not be as romantic a picture as some twentieth-century people would like to find in the history of Christianity, but, for others, it presents a realistic picture of marriage. Clement's description, however, carries other connotations that spoil its positive presentation of marriage. He describes marriage from a male perspective as the opportunity of learning to "rise superior" to the irritations and temptations that come to him from his human and material possessions. There is no suggestion of marriage as a condition of mutual vulnerability in which one can learn to love another human being who, like oneself, struggles, suffers, learns, and enjoys.

The fourth-century British monk Jovinian also preached that marriage was a condition of life in which one could, equally with celibacy, grow in the knowledge and love of God. He spoke and wrote at a time when excitement over asceticism was at a peak, and his views of marriage were condemned by two of the most skillful Christian rhetoricians of the time, Augustine and Jerome. Jovinian was officially excommunicated, his teachings condemned, and his writings destroyed in the beginning of the fifth century, so that all we can reconstruct about his teaching appears in quotations—some of them extensive—in the rebuttals of his detractors. In Jerome's treatise *Against Jovinian,* we can piece together from Jerome's quotations of Jovinian a political and theological argument for the equality of persons in Christian churches no matter whether they are celibates or sexually active in marriage. Jerome accuses him of rejecting the notion that people are to be categorized, valued, and respected according to their sexual arrangements. Jerome describes four principles invoked by Jovinian: (1) whether Christians were married, widowed, or single made no difference to their attempt to achieve spiritual perfection; (2) repentance for sins removed both guilt and the effects of those sins; (3) Christians who fast are not superior to those who do not; and (4) life after death does not reflect the hierarchical values established in the earthly church; there is no differentiation of heavenly rewards.

Jovinian was, according to Jerome, against a hierarchical interpretation of the "diversity of gifts" among Christian people. In positing equality in difference, Jerome accuses Jovinian of removing all incentive for striving for "perfection." In response, Jerome reiterates the hierarchy of lifestyles that had come to be generally accepted in Christian churches as Christianity became the religion of the Roman state: virgins occupied the highest rung of the ladder, far above everyone else; then came married people in several grades, those who had been married once preceded those who had been married twice, three times, or to pagans; "fornicators" drew up the rear.

If we make a clear distinction between body and sexuality, it is not difficult to find, in Christian tradition, very positive statements about the goodness and beauty of human bodies;[33] if we proceed to separate marriage from sex, we can occasionally find appraisals of marriage as a condition in which spiritual growth is not only possible but also is positively stimulated. In the Protestant reformations of the sixteenth century, the reformers' rejection of ecclesiastical privilege and wealth led them to reject also the celibate lifestyle that provided the rationale for clerical privilege. Both Luther and Calvin married and extolled the benefits of marriage, though most of Luther's statements about marriage were marred by the polemical contexts in which they occurred.[34] It is not, however, our project to discuss theologians' evaluations of bodies or marriage, but to characterize, by using some representative examples, devotional manuals' evaluation of practices of sexual activity in relation to Christian life.

Theologians had a different agenda for their evaluations of body, marriage, and sexuality than did authors of devotional manuals. Characteristically theologians attempt to achieve a description of human life that is comprehensive—and therefore inclusive—and cohesive. They demonstrate the metaphysical, cosmological, and historical setting for human life within which all human capacities and functions have a place and a value. Devotional manuals, on the other hand, have more immediate goals. Their first interest must necessarily be to identify an energy source that can be tapped for the consistent and cumulative practices that form the religious self. For purposes of acquiring motivation and empowerment for Christian life, no formulation has proved so effective as identifying a scapegoat to represent that which requires the alternative formation of a religious self, and sex has usually been chosen to serve as that scapegoat.

Sex can serve to represent "the world, the flesh, and the devil" because the individual's desires are socially constructed and conditioned, not "natural" or biological. We will discuss the losses to an understanding of person-hood and Christian life that are entailed in scapegoating sex, but it is important that we recognize initially why Christian authors found it so useful to do so.

Erasmus's *Enchiridion* is illustrative of the strategy of isolating sex from body and from relationship in order to use it as rhetorical foil for Christian life. He describes both the body and marriage, when dissociated from the threatening undertow of sexual activity, as beautiful and good. When he speaks of body and marriage as associated with sexual activity, however, they share the stigma of sex. Body, though "sacred,"[35] when associated with sex is "the basest part of us upon which that crafty old serpent has foisted the law of sin through our inborn taint."[36] Marriage is similarly ambiguous, according to whether or not "carnal love" is central in it. Only if marriage can be cleansed of sexual pleasure can it be compatible with spiritual effort and growth:

> If you love [your wife] most deeply because in her you have seen the likeness of Christ, that is to say, goodness, modesty, sobriety, chastity, *and you love her now not in herself but in Christ,* then in reality you love Christ in her; and so, at last, you love in a spiritual sense.[37]

Like many other authors of devotional manuals, Erasmus contrasts "spiritual love" and "carnal love" in order to gather commitment for the creation and cultivation of a spiritual self. He finds the two utterly incompatible and mutually exclusive. Sexual pleasure is equated with "lust," the primary enemy of Christian life ("no enemy attacks us earlier, pricks us more sharply, covers more territory, or drags more people to ruin"[38]) in that it pursues sensible rather than spiritual objects:

> Think how foul, how base, how unworthy of any man is this pleasure which reduces us from an image of divinity to the level, not merely of animals, but even to that of swine, he goats, dogs, and the most brutish of brutes.[39]

"Man's" metaphysical status, it seems, is at stake when "Dame Lechery" has succeeded in attaching his neck to her halter.[40] Erasmus's "remedies for lust" apply indifferently to management of sexuality within or outside marriage. They involve "getting the mind right" by entertaining examples of other men, both those who have pursued self-indulgence dishonorably and disastrously," and those who have managed to live in "purity of mind and body." Erasmus counsels "stiffening your continence" by the "regulation of sleep and diet, temperance even in permissible pleasures, and being mindful of your own death, and meditating on the death of Christ."[41]

Erasmus's use of gender imagery suggests another problem that is connected to the pervasive devaluation of sexuality in devotional manuals: the identification, by male projection, of sexual temptation with women and the devaluation of women that accompanied this identification. Not surprisingly, devotional literature employed traditional figures or characterizations of maleness and femaleness at once reflective and supportive of cultural representations of gender. It is ironic that sensuality and seduction are ascribed to the very women who may have suffered most from male lust: the figure of the prostitute represented male lust, simultaneously temptation and threat to male spirituality. Erasmus quotes Proverbs 6 to emphasize the particular capacity of women—as "our Eve"[42]—to vitiate men's spiritual energy: "For the price of a harlot is scarcely a loaf of bread, but the woman ravishes the precious soul of man."[43] Erasmus was not original in the use of this figure, but was simply invoking a commonplace of devotional literature. Moreover, the figure of the prostitute in the male textual tradition sometimes represents all sexual relationships with women; it is difficult or impossible to determine, in the following quotation from Erasmus's *Enchiridion,* whether the author uses the language of prostitution literally or figuratively:

> And imagine to yourself just how ridiculous, how completely monstrous it is *to be in love:* to grow pale and thin, to shed tears, to fawn upon and play the cringing beggar to the most stinking tart . . . to endure a silly woman's dominating you, bawling you out, flying at you in rage, and then to make up with her and voluntarily offer yourself to a strumpet so she can play upon you, clip you, pluck you clean![44]

Mistrust of sex and female responsibility for sexual temptation together characterize the dominant representation of sexuality in Christian tradition. Women's bodies are for "use," that is, productivity, Augustine wrote; only in the resurrection of the body will women's bodies come to represent what male bodies have always represented: beauty, not use.[45] Women were created by a prescient creator, Thomas Aquinas said, solely for their role in reproduction; for any other purpose, a male friend would be preferable. Written from male, and frequently monastic, perspectives, even devotional manuals written explicitly for women do little to overcome the identification of women with sexual temptation.

Popularly accessible religious visual images supported this identification: any historical Christian before the present century, noticing on the facade of a cathedral a bas-relief showing a naked woman with pendulous breasts, would know that she represented Eve, the human lightning rod by which sin came to be grounded in the world, icon of the voracious and insatiable sexual "flesh." Depictions of Mary Magdalen demonstrate the same identification of woman, sin and sex; in paintings from the fifteenth-century forward, the Magdalen is nude or partially nude, her body representing simultaneously sexual sin and penitence. Literal and figurative communications are interwoven as "the flesh" is particularly represented by her breasts, exposed by hair which parts to reveal them. Insatiable in penitence as she formerly was in sexuality, Mary Magdalen represented both lust and repentance for seducing men.

This brief survey of attitudes toward personal relationships of various kinds as described in Christian devotional manuals has perhaps supported our impressions of Christian distrust for relationship more than it has helped us identify resources for envisioning more positive and loving forms of relationship. My purpose has been to expose the threadbare inadequacy of Christian tradition on these issues as well as to scan it for help in picturing Christian life in the nuclear world, but I have perhaps succeeded more in the first than the second. In order to achieve something like a collection of useful insights from what initially appears as an endemic fear of human attachments—especially, but not solely, sexual relationships—we will need to undertake a reconstruction of the assumptions that prompted Christian authors' evaluations of the role of human relationships in Christian life. Clearly, body, sexuality, and sexual relationships were interwoven and mutually implicated in a nexus of experiential problems. Even when theologians sometimes managed to distinguish them, for reasons that we have considered, authors of devotional manuals did not often attempt to—or succeed in doing so.

Christianity has largely deserved the bad press it has received in the twentieth century on issues of sexuality. I do not suggest that the female body was used as a rhetorical figure with which to advocate a management of sexuality that formed a central part of male cultivation of a religious self in order to "explain away" a deplorable consensus on the usefulness of this rhetorical strategy. Nor do I deny that such treatments of sexual relationship should alert contemporary readers to a pervasive and continuous misogyny in the Christian West. It is, however, important to recognize why Christian authors wrote as they did about women and women's bodies. We can only understand the usefulness of these textual strategies when they are placed in the context of the project of male self-definition and self-relatedness; in this context, sexual relationship was understood as danger and threat to the constructed self.

What assumptions about sexual activity underlie the unanimous rejection of sexual relationship as a condition in which to define and develop a religious self and Christian life? I have already suggested that one of these assumptions was a closed energy system in which spiritual love could be accomplished only to the extent that "carnal love" was extinguished. This formula implies, however, that we should interpret "carnal love," in the usage of Christian authors, as a term by which they implied, not sexual relationship as such, but the assumed effects of sexual relationship, effects that inevitably, they thought, included exploitation—disregard for the needs and wishes of the other and the use of the other for self-gratification.[46] Christian authors seem to have been unable to imagine gratifying sexual activity that was not, from the male perspective, simultaneously distracting and debilitating and an exploitation and violation of his partner. It is only honest to admit, however, that from the perspective of the project of the religious self, concern for the partner usually does not appear as a primary preoccupation of devotional texts. Nevertheless, it is important to our search for useable insights from the Christian West on the role of sexual relationship in a Christian life to note the assumptions that governed discussions of sex.

Twentieth-century constructions of the role of sexuality in human life have tended to emphasize a romantic view of sexual pleasure as subversive of society. At the beginning of this century, Freud described the creation of civilization as requiring sublimation of sexual pleasure. If sexual pleasure were to remain in its natural state, he said, it would exhaust itself in constant sexual activity, leaving no energy for cultural creation. On this view, the primary condition for the existence of civilization is the confinement of sexual activity to relationships that stabilize rather than threaten society. Even when this is managed successfully, however, sexual pleasure remains volatile, potentially insubordinate to the goals of society, naturally free, and only with the greatest difficulty subordinated to the requirements of culture.[47]

Michel Foucault has recently suggested another understanding of the role of sexual pleasure in society. In the volumes of his *History of Sexuality,* as in many articles[48] and interviews, he has described desire for sexual pleasure as itself socially constructed. It is not that a "natural" state of polymorphous desire preexists society's deployment of sexuality, but that the process of socialization within a particular culture *creates* a sexuality that serves social ends. Foucault's analysis offers an alternative to Freud's view of sexual pleasure as inherently subversive. If sexual pleasure is constructed by the socialization process, it can be understood less as the personal possession or birthright of individuals than as the location of their intimate connection with socially defined values, differentiated according to gender.

To become conscious of the social constitution of one's sexual pleasures is to construct a critical position in relation to society. One can begin to evaluate the assumptions, methods of pursuit and appropriation, and objects of sexual pleasures. On this view of sexual pleasure as serving rather than in fundamental opposition to society, one's own desire is understood as society subjectively reproduced, and analysis of that desire is a method by which social values may be recognized and critiqued,[49] not only as they appear subjectively but also in society.

Although historical devotional manuals demonstrate no awareness of the social construction of gender, they do unanimously insist that scrutiny of one's sexual pleasures at both the level of desire and of behavior is a central strategy of self-relatedness and religious practice. Clearly, many devotional manuals, like Erasmus's *Enchiridion,* understand sexual pleasure as threatening disruption of the fragile religious self and community rather than as the subjective reflection of society. Foucault's analysis, however, suggests the possibility that a surveillance of one's own sexuality, one's "socialized body,"[50] which devotional manuals present as an essentially antisocial activity, could serve not only private and idiosyncratic self-knowledge and self-definition but also can become the basis for a nuanced critical analysis of contemporary society. Moreover, rather than requiring a cultivated religious self that is isolated from other human beings and the social world, the project of understanding one's socialization requires community. Since the socialization of any individual, despite its particularities, is an orientation to socially defined attitudes and practices, it will be crucial to understand through conversation how one's own socialization relates to that of others. In the process of exploration, self-scrutiny comes to be understood as irreducibly communal and as a personal and social responsibility. This reconstruction of the process and effects of socialization, therefore, can be understood as at once something one does "for oneself," and a contribution one makes to society, a practice that cannot be characterized adequately by traditional descriptions of human beings as motivated *either* by "self-love" *or* by concern for others.

Our search for useable insights on the role of personal relationships in Christian life has tended to demonstrate not the richness of traditional resources, but their paucity. We have had to read between and behind the dominant rhetoric that understands other human beings as danger and threat to find positive interpretations of the effect of other human beings on spiritual growth. These interpretations do not spring easily from the most popular devotional texts. If, however, we find that the most public texts of Christian tradition do not make a persuasive case for the beauty and goodness of human relationships, must we not rather acknowledge than attempt to conceal this? The particular contribution of our own time might be to develop this neglected feature of Christian life on the basis of twentieth-century Christians' diverse, compelling, and converting experiences of friendship, sexual relationship, and marriage. Since it has not been adequately described by historical Christians, it is up to twentieth-century Christians to envision, articulate, and learn to experience an integrated sexuality, a sexual practice that contributes to the beauty and richness of human life without creating conflict with other valuable achievements.

# 10

# Dying Happily: Joy and Suffering

*It is only when one loves life and the world so much that without them
everything would be gone, that one can believe in the resurrection and a new
world.*

*Dietrich Bonhoeffer[1]*

The final issue emerging from devotional manuals that we will examine
is that of the relative value, for Christian life, of happiness and suffering.
Twentieth-century Christians frequently feel dismayed at the focus on
suffering in traditional Christianity, an insistence that it is suffering that
most efficiently breaks a Christian's attachments to other people and to the
good and beautiful things of this world. Suffering, more than anything
else, devotional manuals say, produces transcendence of the material
conditions of human life. Yet happiness, especially in the form of thanksgiving for life and salvation, also has its historical advocates. Christian
tradition has been ambivalent about the relative worth of happiness and
suffering, but even authors who thought of happiness as normative for
human beings seem suspicious of it in relation to Christian life. Strong
statements can be found concerning both the usefulness of suffering and
the importance of happiness, sometimes in the same devotional manuals.

The conditions of persecution in which the early Christian churches
originated and grew meant that Christians had to be prepared to suffer for
their faith at any moment. Until 312, when Constantine established the
legal right of Christians, like other sects within the Roman Empire, to
worship as they chose, persecution and martyrdom were intermittent but
persistent. Under these conditions it is not surprising that Christians felt
the need of finding ways to understand and accept suffering and of
converting danger and pain into advantage for Christian life. Ignatius of
Antioch, a late first-century Christian, while he was being taken by
military escort across the empire to be executed in Rome, wrote letters to
Christians in various places. These letters contain the rhetoric of an

ecstatic acceptance of martyrdom as a mode of imitation of, and unity with, Christ. Ignatius described himself as having a "passion for death," which he experiences as the "pangs of being born."[2] In vivid language that twists and inverts the ordinary meanings of words, he writes of his death as his way of "getting to God." Referring to his execution in a Roman arena, he wrote:

> Let me be fodder for wild beasts—that is how I can get to God. I am God's wheat and I am being ground by the teeth of wild beasts to make a pure loaf for Christ. . . . Then I shall be a real disciple of Jesus Christ when the world sees me no more. . . . But if I suffer, I shall be emancipated by Jesus Christ; and united with him, I shall rise to freedom.[3]

Ignatius's theology of martyrdom was repeated in many documents that record the trials and deaths of Christians. His conversion of the horror and pain of death into an approach to life was a method for handling an unalterable condition of Christian faith in the first Christian centuries. In the fourth century, however, the Christian churches came into a legal and political climate in which they were at first tolerated and later became the official religion of the Roman Empire; diverse understandings of the role of suffering for Christian life began to be articulated. In place of the possibility of sudden and violent martyrdom, Christians began to practice asceticism, which they called a "daily martyrdom." In place of the externally imposed sufferings of the persecutions, they imposed various physical, emotional, and mental disciplines on themselves. Many of them left their families and friends and went to solitary places in the Egyptian desert where they fasted, prayed, wept over their sins, and supported their simple existence by basket weaving or gardening. They chose and carefully cultivated a life designed around a relationship with God. They expected their austerities to dismantle their socialization and enable them to form a new self. In writings like *The Sayings of the Fathers*[4] and Evagrius Ponticus's *Praktikos and Chapters on Prayer,*[5] ascetics described the practices by which they created intense pressure on the formation of a religious self. These practices ranged from dehabituating exercises to harsher disciplines, some of which permanently damaged their bodies or caused premature death. Fasting, sleeplessness, restriction of water, nakedness, prayer, and even reading were mentioned as part of the "tools" of the great "athletes" of the ascetic life.

A century after the legitimation of Christianity as a licensed religion of the Roman Empire, a different attitude toward happiness and suffering was formulated by Augustine of Hippo. Augustine, deeply impressed by his own experience and its lessons, examined his early life to the time of his conversion in his autobiography, the *Confessions*. He was puzzled by a disjunction between every person's concerted efforts to be happy and the pain of human experience:

> Everyone, whatever his condition, desires to be happy. There is no one who does not desire this, and each one desires it with such earnestness that it is preferred to all other things; whoever, in fact, desires other things, desires them for this end alone . . . in whatever life one chooses . . . there is no one who does not wish to be happy.[6]

Why then, Augustine asked himself, did he find so little happiness in himself and in others? He described his life as a successful teacher of rhetoric as one of cumulative disillusionment:

> I panted for honors, for money, for marriage . . . I found bitterness and difficulty in following these desires. . . . How unhappy my soul was then! . . . I got no joy out of my learning. . . . I was eaten up by anxieties.[7]

Part of the pain of human life is, as Augustine saw, due to involuntary causes. In the *City of God* 22.21, he gave a lengthy list of the "pains that trouble all humankind." But it was the apparently voluntary way that human beings dismantle their own happiness as quickly and effectively as they build it that fascinated Augustine. He saw no other possible explanation than that of an ancient fall which had permanently debilitated and undermined human life. His famous advice was to alleviate unhappiness by learning to love only that which one cannot lose, God. Other human beings are to be loved "in God," and the good things of human life are to be "used" with gratitude, but they are not to be "enjoyed" as ends in themselves.

Augustine's axiom that only what is permanent is to be valued and pursued was repeated and extended in the devotional manuals of Christian tradition. Thomas à Kempis, in *The Imitation of Christ*, went beyond Augustine's sensitivity to real pessimism about life as human beings know it: "It is a wretched thing to have to live on earth," he wrote.[8] The only kind of "happiness" to be trusted under these conditions is the security that results from careful preparation for death:

> A man is not only happy but wise also, if he is trying, during his lifetime to be the sort of man he wants to be found at his death. We can be sure of dying happily if our lives show an utter disregard for the world, a fervent desire for progress in virtue, a love of discipline, the practice of penitence, denial of self, and acceptance of any adversity for the love of Christ.[9]

Valuing happiness, but despairing of achieving any permanent happiness in this life and devaluing "transitory" happiness as illusion and fraud, Christian authors felt a deep suspicion of present happiness, though they continued to consider it a goal to be achieved in a life after death. Extolling happiness, they nevertheless trusted suffering much more. Augustine is typical in finding no meaning in present human happiness except that it made one vulnerable to its loss; on the other hand, there was much to be learned, and merit to be gained from suffering. Although Augustine did not urge that Christians should seek or create suffering for themselves, he argued that when suffering appeared, the Christian must use it actively, must mine it for learning and growth, rather than tolerating it passively.

Yet happiness remained the ultimate goal of Christian life, even if it is impossible to achieve in this life, burdened as it is by life in the body. [10] Few authors can be found who, like Horace Bushnell, the nineteenth-century American Congregationalist, advocated practicing for heavenly happiness by learning present happiness:

> If you have been thinking of heaven only, as a happy place, looking for it as the reward of some dull, lifeless service, arguing it for all men, as the place where God will show his goodness by making blessed loathsome and base souls, cheat yourself no more by this folly. Consider only whether heaven be in you now. For heaven, as we have seen, is nothing but the joy of a perfectly harmonized being, filled with God and his love. [11]

Happiness, devotional manuals agreed, is elusive, often dangerous, and always distressingly transient. At best, some authors described happiness as a sort of peace or assurance, a confidence that, by declining to chase present happiness, one is securing permanent happiness. The theology of the fall of Adam and Eve and their banishment from the garden of earthly delights both explained and rationalized advice to seek heavenly delight. Reasons given for the difficulty and sorrow of human life vary, however. Sorrow, according to John Climacus, is caused by attachment, and "despising the world" is the antidote for sorrow. Sorrow is caused by attachment. Presumably, then, if one can manage to "despise" the world, one could be happy, but John Climacus forestalls this conclusion by insisting that penitence and mourning should be the perpetual activity of Christian life. In a variation on this interpretation of the cause of suffering, Henry Suso wrote that suffering is an indication that one's "sensual appetite" has not yet been eliminated. [12]

Other authors found comfort in thinking that suffering and sorrow are

Fig. 10. Giotto, *Crucifixion*, 14th century. Scrovegni Chapel, Padua. Marburg/Art Resource, N.Y.

given by God to test or challenge the Christian. John Wesley wrote, somewhat paradoxically:

> One of the greatest evidences of God's love to those that love him is to send them afflictions, with grace to bear them. Even in the greatest afflictions, we ought to testify to God that, in receiving them from his hand, we feel pleasure in the midst of pain, from being afflicted by him who loves us, and whom we love. [13]

It is easy to see that a conversion of pain into a privileged sense of God's special attention could be an effective strategy for managing "affliction." Like Wesley, Søren Kierkegaard insists that "to be loved by God and to love God is to suffer." [14]

Whatever the evaluation of the relative significance of happiness and suffering in Christian life, Christian authors wrote a great deal more about suffering and how to understand it than they did about happiness. Clearly suffering was both more compelling as a problem and more attractive as a tool than was happiness. The net effect of this attention to suffering is the impression, for readers of historical devotional manuals, that suffering, in the Christian tradition, was far more valued than temporary and transitory happiness. Implied in the view of present happiness as worthless or dangerous to Christian life was a disregard for the arena of present happiness, human bodies and the natural world.

Since suffering was understood as a condition in which maximal spiritual growth is possible, devotional manuals advocated a range of practices that, to varying degrees, seek and use suffering. Mild suffering that took the form of exercises involving introspection, self-denial, and self-discipline, were unanimously advocated by devotional manuals. But some went beyond these disciplines to a preoccupation with more severe suffering, both voluntary and involuntary, and its uses in Christian life. As in earlier chapters, I will conclude with some suggestions as to the problems and/or usefulness of various historical prescriptions regarding suffering.

Some of the primary "techniques of the self" [15] described in historical devotional manuals are practices of self-scrutiny. Again, we must note the ambiguity with which Christian authors use the word *self.* The "self" they begin with is the socialized self, turned inside out by the pursuit of culturally conditioned pleasures. An accurate look at this "self," according to devotional manuals, is a painful experience. In the account of his conversion in book 8 of the *Confessions,* Augustine describes this sighting of the socialized self in his characteristically vivid language:

But you, Lord, were turning me around so that I could see myself; you took me from behind my own back, which was where I had put myself during the time when I did not want to be observed by myself, and you set me in front of my own face so that I could see how foul a sight I was—crooked, filthy, spotted, and ulcerous. I saw, and I was horrified, and I had nowhere to go to escape from myself.[16]

Habit and self-deception shelter one from an accurate vision of the self. So methods that create the conditions under which "self"-knowledge is possible, and techniques for breaking down the psychological and emotional shelters that keep one from facing oneself become important. One of the primary agendas of devotional manuals was the definition of a graded process by which the reader could come to see himself accurately. The anonymous author of the fourteenth-century *Cloud of Unknowing* introduced his discussion of self-knowledge with a strident demand for the reader's attention. At the risk of offending the reader by his forceful address, the author wrote: "Pause for a moment, you wretched weakling, and take stock of yourself."[17]

Jeremy Taylor, the seventeenth-century Anglican bishop, gave a particularly vivid account of a procedure for achieving an accurate vision of oneself in his manual, *The Rule and Exercises of Holy Living*. Beginning with scrutiny of one's bodily condition, he leads the reader from one meditation to another. The goal of the series of meditations was a strong experience of "humility":[18]

Our body is weak and impure, sending out more uncleannesses from its several sinks than could be endured, if they were not necessary and natural: and we are forced to pass that through our mouths, which as soon as we see upon the ground, we loathe like rottenness and vomiting.[19]

Stripping the reader of all illusions of personal achievement and worth ("if it is bad, it is thine own . . . if it be good, thou hast received it from God"), Taylor led the reader to a "hearty and real evil or mean opinion of thyself."[20] Assuring him, "Thou canst not undervalue thyself . . . no contempt will seem unreasonable," Taylor advised a detailed process for making this self-knowledge experiential. One of the tricks he suggested for uncovering the "real self" is that the reader collect, in memory, the sins of a lifetime:

Look not upon them as scattered in the course of a long life; now an intemperate anger, then too full a meal; now idle talking, and another time, impatience; but unite them into one continued representation, and remember, that he whose life seems fair, by reason that his faults are scattered at large distances in the several parts of his life, yet if all his errors and follies were articled against him, the man would seem vicious and miserable: and possibly this exercise, really applied upon thy spirit, may be useful.[21]

Repentance is the next step, a step that follows quite spontaneously when the reader has seen himself without the blinders of his habitual regard for himself. The eighteenth-century Pietist August Hermann Franke agreed with Jeremy Taylor that it is not enough to resolve to do better in the future than in the past; one must "lay out properly [one's] earlier sinful way before God, [and] acknowledge it humbly and with repentance."[22] Devotional manuals identify the sign of true repentance as tears; the person who sees himself accurately necessarily weeps with contrition. Thus Catherine of Siena's *Dialogue* analyzes five kinds of tears and their usefulness in a Christian life.

Once the advisee has seen himself stripped of the usual rationalizing processes by which he has come to think of himself as a pretty good person, and has wept over his former ways, he must inaugurate and maintain a continuous "watch over himself." Devotional manuals provide lists of questions that aid the process of ongoing introspection: "Is there not some passion that has control over me? . . . Have I not neglected this commandment or that?"[23] He must "constantly examine and test himself, asking himself whether he mourns daily, as instructed in the Beatitudes, whether he is truly meek, and whether he hungers and thirsts for God's righteousness.[24] A regime of self-scrutiny must become a lifelong habit. Whenever the Christian finds pockets of unreformed inclinations, he must repent anew and attempt to maintain a closer and more continuous self-examination. Understanding that progress in Christian life is not easy and predictable, but must frequently be started again from the beginning, the Christian is encouraged not to despair:

To deny oneself in all things, to be subject to another's judgment, to mortify continually all inward passions, to annihilate oneself in all respects, to follow always that which is contrary to one's own will, appetite, and judgment, are things that few can do; many are those that teach them, but few are they that practice them.[25]

Admonitions to "self-denial" are woven throughout the instructions in the "techniques of the self" given by devotional manuals. Why are self-denial and self-discipline needed? Different rationales are offered: in book 3 of his *Institutes of the Christian Religion*, John Calvin discusses his reasons for saying that "the sum of the Christian life" is "the denial of ourselves."[26] For Calvin, it is not socialization to particular styles of the pursuit of sex, power, and possessions that is the problem. Rather, social conditioning is itself one expression of a much deeper problem with human nature. Human beings are "utterly incapable of any goodness" unless our "natural feelings are suppressed." Calvin fears that if self-denial is not practiced, "the foulest vices" are likely to be indulged.[27]

Calvin's reason for urging practices of self-denial—the unmitigated sinfulness of human nature as we know it—however, is perhaps the most forcefully stated, but it is not the only rationale for self-denial in historical Christianity. For the authors of most manuals, the premise of the spiritual direction they provide is that by a combination of human effort and God's help—a combination whose relative weights they are usually content to leave unspecified—people can and should progress in the Christian life. If people were "totally depraved," and could not cooperate at all toward the creation and cultivation of a religious self, it would be futile to write devotional manuals. Even in the Christian traditions that emphasize human beings' complete dependence on God's grace and their inability to earn that grace, devotional manuals, with all their assumptions that people can and must contribute to God's work in their lives, flourished.

Devotional manuals addressed themselves to individuals. Whether the denial of "self" was understood as a decision to reject every manifestation in oneself of a common sinful "nature," or whether social conditioning must be identified and changed within oneself, it was the individual who must undertake the work. Any twentieth-century woman or man who has seriously undertaken to understand and alter her or his social conditioning can recognize in these instructions the perennial attraction of an examined and chosen life.

Yet individual resistance to cultural conditioning is a limited and limiting project, as some contemporary women's collectives are finding. Without the insight and support of others, it is difficult to effect real change in oneself. Neither did manuals encourage that the individual who began with himself should go on to examine collective irresponsibility, unjust social arrangements, or political evils. They assume either that an individual must start with herself in order, eventually, to contribute to the public sphere, or that the creation of an individual religious self is an end in itself. We will need to examine further in the concluding chapter the focus on individuals that has characterized most of the popular self-help literature of the Christian tradition. For now it is sufficient to notice the unanimity with which Meister Eckhart's maxim, "Begin, therefore, with yourself, and forget yourself," was counseled in devotional manuals.

Although introspection and self-knowledge may produce severe emotional discomfort, they do not entail physical pain. In chapter 5 we explored some historical practices and rationales for the usefulness of physical pain. Ascetic practices were understood on one of two models in the history of Christianity. According to the first model, varying levels of physical discomfort and pain were known to create a condition of psychic vulnerability in which one could become conscious of aspects of oneself usually ignored or denied. On the second model, ascetic practices were understood to be the *result* of awareness of one's sinfulness, the externalization of something already subjectively recognized. In the first understanding, discomfort or pain is used for the insight it can produce; in the second, physical pain is an inevitable result of accurate self-knowledge; as such, it is not to be sought but accepted.

Sometimes it is difficult to tell from descriptions of physical pain which of the two understandings an author intended. Moreover, it is often difficult to interpret whether devotional manuals and personal accounts of historical people's experiences of physical pain describe voluntary or involuntary pain. Involuntary pain remains one of the more pressing of religious problems; understandably, in times of scant medical knowledge and little ability to control pain, historical texts reflect a preoccupation with pain. As we have seen, many historical Christians tried to accept inevitable pain by understanding it as productive of a greater self-knowledge and sense of dependence on God. In some accounts, it is impossible to tell whether the pain or illness described was self-inflicted, aggravated or induced by ascetic practices, or involuntary.

In the *Showings* of Dame Julian of Norwich, the fourteenth-century anchoress, it is difficult to know whether Julian produced the physical illness through which she understood God's infinite love, or whether she recognized in retrospect that the illness was an optimal condition for spiritual growth. She wrote that she had repeatedly requested from God, since she was very young, an illness that would bring her to the point of death. She wanted, it seems, to experience a sort of trial run of her own death:

> I wished that sickness to be so severe that it might seem mortal, so that I might in it receive all the rites which Holy Church has to give me, whilst I myself should think that I was dying, and everyone who saw me would think the same; for I wanted no comfort from any human, earthly life in that sickness. I wanted to have every kind of pain, bodily and spiritual, which I should have if I had died, every fear and temptation from devils, and every other kind of pain except the departure of the spirit.[28]

Julian's account of her illness at the age of thirty and the visions she received in it never indicate that she actively fostered disease by neglect or asceticism. The illness was apparently involuntary, but in writing about it, Julian realized that it had prepared her to understand something of the first importance about herself, God, and the universe. Through it she had seen that love permeates and organizes the universe, holding all living beings in life. The visions she had in the fifteen-day period of her illness provided the raw material for her contemplation for the rest of her long life. Her insistence that she had suffered voluntarily leads the reader to suspect that she had somehow caused the illness; it is more likely, however, that she accepted suffering in retrospect when she had understood its potential for growth. Julian's religious language gave her a way of formulating the important insight that all human pain is not waste and loss, but can yield new perspective and new confidence in God's providence.

Although many historical people, like Julian of Norwich, may have expressed their experience of involuntary suffering in similar religious language, there were clearly many others who created suffering for themselves by harsh ascetic practices that debilitated and damaged their bodies, sometimes causing premature death. The rhetoric of historical accounts of productive suffering must be examined carefully in order to determine whether the suffering they describe is voluntary or involuntary. The self-imposed suffering of some historical people must not be concealed or condoned, but neither should our judgment of self-imposed suffering blind us to the possibility that involuntary suffering, actively used as a condition for spiritual growth, may more accurately describe a historical text's agenda. A modern caricature of historical Christianity in which people fostered suffering and gloried in it needs to be reexamined.

Finally, however, it is difficult to deny that devotional manuals from the Christian West generally undervalued or discounted happiness. Even if one can identify historical reasons for this, it remains a regrettable and damaging feature of Christian tradition. High and constant levels of misery and pain certainly needed to be handled, and the awareness that illness and pain could be a fruitful condition for learning was no doubt exhilarating. But an attitude that overvalues pain and suffering and undervalues happiness is dangerous in a nuclear world, a world in which human beings have it in their power to create terminal suffering for whole populations. If suffering is understood as beneficial, people will be less motivated to work for the well-being of the human race and the planet that is our home. The critical religious project of the twentieth-century is not primarily that of finding ways to transcend individual suffering, but to mobilize and energize commitment to the preservation of the created world. As in the conclusion of the last chapter, we must find that, since historical Christians have not articulated a theology of happiness, it becomes the task of twentieth-century Christians to find ways to express the importance of happiness as gratitude for being and delight in the beauty of the created world.

# 11

# Conclusion:
# Pluralism and Main Danger
# in the Contemporary World

*Truly, we ought to labor most of our own time and take it most into account.*
*The future should not be overlooked, but what is present and urgent requires*
*our attention more. For we who live at the same time are bound together by*
*God with a stronger bond in order that, by consulting together, we may assist*
*each other as much as we can.*[1]

*Calvin* Commentary on Isaiah 39.8

*We are all linked together in a common chain.*

*Cicero*

As fragments of historical instruction in the practice of Christianity passed before us in the preceeding chapters, we have encountered two persistent themes across the variety of concerns evident in devotional manuals. Strategies for the definition and cultivation of a countercultural religious self have consistently rested on two fundamental and pervasive assumptions: that there exists a spiritual world whose permanence, beauty, and worth infinitely outweigh anything associated with the material conditions of human life, bodies, objects, and the natural world; and that individuals must resolve to identify and exercise the spiritual aspect of themselves, extricating their loyalties from other human beings, society, and "the world." Both of these assumptions represent dangers for the practice of Christianity in the nuclear world.

Let us summarize these principles that we found embedded in the most popular and accessible literature of the Christian traditions, in order to decide whether they can be reinterpreted in a way that would make them useful for late twentieth-century Christians. Perhaps the greatest difficulty

176

for us in a two-thousand-year tradition of instructions in the practice of Christianity is the continuity of agreement on the importance of "transcending" the physical conditions of human life.[2] No other devotional theme so clearly illustrates the claim I made in chapter 1 that Christian tradition is both rich in resources for a contemporary practice of Christianity and also, in some aspects, deeply problematic. Although in twentieth-century theological discourse the word *transcendence* connotes no more than self-awareness—consciousness of one's life—the human possibility of transcendence has usually been interpreted in historical Christianity as the belief that it is not only possible but highly desirable to despise, ignore, or use the material conditions of human life in such a way that the soul can spring free of those conditions to contemplate and enjoy God in a disembodied and timeless state. Enjoyment of God is, to be sure, imperfect and fleeting in this present life, but still powerful enough to wean our loves and our longings from the earth and other human beings to heavenly bliss. This interpretation of human transcendence has, I suspect, substantially contributed to creating the nuclear world, a world more literally "despised" than even the harshest medieval ascetic could have imagined.

Authors of instruction in the practice of Christianity frequently spoke of the soul as the "true self," the proper subject of human religiousness and the object of redemption. They seem to have been concerned about souls as the only aspect of human beings requiring and deserving religious attention. They designed "spiritualities" addressed to the soul, and construed the ideal spiritual life as a life minimally engaged in physicality, a celibate life. Clearly, in many—not all—historical theological texts and manuals in the practice of Christianity, transcendence referred to the potential independence of the soul from the body.

It is important to notice, however, that this interpretation of "self-transcendence" requires a context if we are accurately to understand its attraction for historical people. For a historian who works with ideas and practices of the past that are always distant, frequently alien, and sometimes vividly repugnant from her perspective, one of the most fruitful methodological questions in this: Can I imagine circumstances in which I might want to speak as this historical person spoke? If one can imagine such circumstances, the next step is to investigate whether, in fact, any such historical conditions are part of the immediate context of some statement or activity that we find puzzling. If we look at the interpretation of self-transcendence I have described with this question in mind, some historical reasons can be found to explain why the soul's transcendence over the body and the natural world was attractive in many times and places in the Christian centuries.

Most historical individuals and communities lived at high and constant levels of misery characterized by inadequate and insecure food supply, threat of death from war, childbearing, or from diseases and accidents we now consider minor, in societies without internal order, constantly vulnerable to attack, rape, and plunder. In such conditions, care for, and anxiety over, physical existence may have usurped such enormous amounts of time and energy that the possibility of developing a spiritual life was not at all evident. Thus religious leaders stated this possibility as adamantly, dramatically, and forcefully as possible. In this context, the more blatantly dualistic statements of Christian traditions—statements insisting that religious growth is directly proportionate to physical neglect and debilitation—become somewhat more understandable. If, in addition, people felt their constant vulnerability to death and their helplessness in the face of external danger with an immediacy from which North American society shelters itself, one can see that a rhetoric of body-denying, world-renouncing resolve may have helped to reconcile people to the harsh realities of their short lives. Resentment against a body so prone to unrelievable pain and sudden death does not even seem farfetched.

Although historical contextualization may help us understand why historical Christians talked about the soul's superiority over the body, however, this is not to explain away many destructive ramifications of the idea of self-transcendence. The transcendence of body by soul provided a model of dominance and subordination that was used to rationalize unjust social arrangements as well as plunder of the natural world. In addition, belief in the transcendence and greater value of the soul's rational powers over physical existence in the context of patriarchal societies in the Christian West has led a long series of Christian authors to insist that rationality exists most strongly in men, while women are associated with body, and body with sin, and sin with death. Rationality, the male prerogative, has been equated with power, and power with force, and force with dominance throughout society and, across societies, with war. The dominance of men over women in familial and social hierarchies was also advocated as analogous to the transcendent relationship of God over the world.

The dualism of body and mind, soul, or spirit in the Christian tradition is only one of the results of a pervasive habit of mind that understood people as well as ideas by distinguishing them and arranging them hierarchically. The dominant traditional argument for men's superiority over women is a good example of this habit of mind. A short version of this argument is sometimes explicit but more frequently is implicit in historical Christian theological and devotional texts. It goes as follows: biological difference constitutes difference in "nature"; women therefore have a different nature than men; different natures cannot occupy the same ontological category; therefore one of the sexes must be superior to the other. The defining characteristic of men is rationality, while the defining characteristic of women is physicality. Since rationality is more valuable than physicality, men possess a legitimate claim to superiority and therefore to normative "humanity."

The similarly "natural" dominance of human over plant and animal life has seemed even more obvious to Christian writers. Together with the scriptural injunction to conquer and subdue the earth, the superiority of humans has been understood as license for "man" to exploit the natural world and all "subhuman" living creatures. Today animals suffer the effects of human aggression even more dramatically than they have in the past. They are tortured for scientific experimentation, produced and cared for in order to be killed and used as food, and the natural habitats of wild animals are rapidly being destroyed. Many species are presently in danger of extinction. Human transcendence of the natural world has also been cited as a rationalization of irresponsible use of the earth's natural resources, now dangerously depleted.

But it is perhaps human beings—and some human beings more than others—who suffer the most direct results of human mismanagement of nature. It is an ironic feature of the present secular transformation of traditional Christian values that one of the continuities is a contemporary failure in North American culture, as well as in many other "developed" countries, adequately to value and care for human bodies. Even in North America, one of the wealthiest countries in the world, staggering numbers of people suffer from hunger and disease. Moreover, many financially secure North Americans fail to care adequately for their own bodies. The prevalence of such practices as alcoholism, drug dependence of all kinds, over- and under-eating, overwork, a killing life pace, and pollution of the environment demonstrates this. But failure adequately to value human bodies is evident in its most undisguised form in the nuclear world in which all living bodies exist in constant jeopardy.

In contrast to the neglect and disparagement of physical life advised by devotional manuals and translated into twentieth-century secular life, the cultural self-image of contemporary North American society is one of hedonism: belligerent enjoyment of physical delights and fanatical maintenance of the body beautiful. A reaction to the traditional Christian antipathy to the body, this affirmation of body at the expense of the development of a religious self may be a necessary stage in the reintegration of the physical part of human beings, consistently described in the most popular literature of the Christian West as nothing but a foil for the soul. Yet, ultimately, physical well-being and pleasure cannot bear the pressure under which they are placed when life is organized around achieving them. What has not yet been managed either by communities of Christians or by North American secular culture is an integration of all the capacities of human beings, a second naiveté, a centered and developed self fully invested in, and grateful for, its material conditions, body, senses, nature, and society.

Clearly, in a nuclear world it is dangerous and irresponsible to maintain traditional hierarchical notions of human functions and capacities in relation to one another, or human beings in relation to one another and to the natural world. Christianity in a nuclear age must reconstitute the traditional idea of self-transcendence that has contributed to disdain for the material conditions of life. Instead of interpreting human transcendence in the direction of its potential for body-denying, world-rejecting escapism, we must reinterpret transcendence, not only as individual self-awareness but also as recognition of the interdependence of all living beings. Christians must locate ideas and images—surely not an impossible task in the religion of the Incarnation, the Word made flesh—that help us, perhaps for the first time in the history of Christianity, fully to value, cherish, and treasure the natural world. We must reconstruct the idea of self-transcendence as an imperative to enter more deeply into the demanding religious disciples of physical existence, loving relationship, community, and worshipful expression of gratitude for the heavenly beauty of the earth. Only *this* kind of self-transcendence will give us the "sharp quick sense of life"[3] that will energize our passionate response to the problems of a nuclear world.

In spite of the difficulties and dangers of the dominant traditional idea of self-transcendence, twentieth-century people are, perhaps more than ever, in need of a concept that emphasizes the importance of a transcendence that overcomes the temptations of self-isolating individualism and narcissism. Neither of these attitudes, pervasive but unnamed as such in devotional manuals, can address the problems of the contemporary world. As never before, the quotation from Cicero that supplied the aphorism at the head of this chapter is not just metaphorically but concretely accurate; in a world in which we could all die together, we are literally linked together in a common chain.

Did the techniques of the self that we examined in devotional literature produce a new social relationship? Within the rhetoric of "self-denial" on the one hand, and the release of the religious self from attachments to other human beings on the other, a new weightlessness in social relations was claimed, a vivid sense in which each person stands in the same proximity to God and the same responsibility for his own choices, so that human authority and control of others are relativized. Rather than interpreting too literally the jargon of devotional literature—words like self-denial, despising the world, and remembering death—we found we needed to ask about the effects of such reconstructions of the relation of "oneself to oneself" and to others. When we noticed, in devotional manuals, the problematization of an area of life—other human beings, socialization, death, the body—we tried to understand what the author thought was to be gained by the deconstruction and reconstruction of these ultimately indispensible human involvements.

Yet the historical formulation of the human condition of connectedness, religious unity or uniformity, is no longer useful in the twentieth century. Devotional manuals agreed that there is *a* Christian life, or *the* Christian life, though they differed from each other in sketching what it might look like and feel like. Each of them proposed to define for their readers not Christian *lives*, a workable suggestion for a practice of Christianity among other workable suggestions, but *the* Christian life. Although the concrete pluralism of Christian traditions has been denied by a universalizing rhetoric, Christianity is, and historically has been, pluralistic in beliefs, creeds, and liturgical and devotional practices in different geographical settings as well as over the two thousand years of its existence. Yet the pluralism of Christianity has not been celebrated as one of its strengths. On the contrary, every effort has been made to compel uniformity of belief and practice and to eradicate pluralism, if necessary by executing tens of thousands of human beings who wanted nothing more than to be Christians according to their own convictions. Because Christian traditions have not accepted pluralism, differences among people within communities, individualism has resulted—the self-isolation of people who recognize few connections with, or responsibilities to, other human beings and society. In the last decade of the twentieth century, individualism can only be countered by pluralism, that is, by acceptance of, respect for, and delight in, the differences of perspective and concern among Christians.

Devotional manuals have been one of the methods by which Christian people were trained to a religious uniformity that concealed the injustices of the societies in which they lived. They seemed to address all Christian people equally by advocating the same practices, attitudes, and values to everyone. In fact, however, they effectively reinforced the social, class, and gender conditioning of many people by offering corrective devices addressed only to those who were trained—and supported by social and political institutions—to pride, aggression, and forgetfulness of the needs of others. While I do not question the fruitfulness, for some individuals, of a selective use of the advice given by devotional manuals, I suggest that the pluralism of twentieth-century religious discourse has revealed a fundamental contradiction in the assumption that the same practices and ideas can correct the socially constructed temptations of all Christians.

Only the most general of the conditions in which communities and societies exist can define characteristics for which all or most people need corrective exercises. In North America in the late twentieth century, such conditions consist of an entertainment culture, inequitable distribution of wealth, and the nuclear threat. The contours of a particular life in which one undertakes to live as a Christian cannot, however, be characterized and generalized. Thus the daily practices by which one can dismantle habituations, retain alertness to personal and communal danger, and maintain an active and loving engagement with others cannot come from universal prescriptions.

Perhaps the primary service that suggestions for designing a Christian life can offer is the clear delineation of a method for analysis and correction of the reader's present situation. I have urged, for example, that historical advice on the practice of Christianity be evaluated in relation to twentieth-century North American media culture and to the complex global condition in which nuclear weapons threaten the well-being and life of every human being. Rather than carrying prescriptive suggestions to a more individual and intimate level, however, I have suggested questions that the reader might use in order to achieve the self-knowledge and discernment that is necessarily preliminary to the identification of corrective exercises. For example, examination of one's class and gender conditioning in the context of an honest and supportive community has been suggested throughout as a crucial preliminary exercise for identifying useful corrective practices.

Curiously, the individualism of the Christian traditions can be corrected only by individual responsibility for the creation and maintenance of communities of concern and action. The agenda of devotional manuals—undifferentiated inspiration, strategies, and practices—cannot meet the needs of the nuclear world. Rather, a different literature of Christian devotion is needed in the present. Spiritual autobiography might, for example, provide inspiration and concrete suggestions for a religious life while contextualizing those suggestions firmly in a particular life. Readers could then evaluate the usefulness for themselves of the author's insights in the light of differences or similarities between author's and reader's situations.

Christian traditions' emphasis on the individual must also, in the twentieth century, be addressed not only by commitment to face-to-face communities but also by transcending the privatism of traditional descriptions of Christian life. The world desperately needs Christians who consider it a central part of their religious duty to participate in social action,

that feel responsibility, not only for the development of a private re-
ligiosity but also for the public sphere. In our time the cultivation of a
religious self is more crucial than ever, but the model can no longer be
either that of isolated individuals "fleeing from the wrath to come," or
that of uniformity of belief and practice. Can people who do not necessarily agree on all matters of belief and practice act together? Can people
who do not feel a strong claim to a universal imperative gather energy for
social action?

Michel Foucault practiced commitment to action without claiming
universal rightness. He was frequently asked to explain how he could act if
he were unconvinced that his action was the result of nonnegotiable
principles. "The ethico-political choice each of us has to make every day,"
he said in an interview, "is to determine what is the main danger and to
focus our efforts there."[4] This principle of personal responsibility without
categorical pretensions is a promising one for twentieth-century Christians. Everyone does not have to agree on what the "main danger" is if we
can agree that this danger is not a single danger. Each person can focus her
effort on what she identifies as the main danger, reassured and strengthened by the awareness that others are focusing their efforts on other
dangers they take to be the most pressing. To act as a historical subject is
to take the risk and responsibility of deciding on the focus of my efforts
without requiring that they be supported and reinforced by the efforts of
others. It is, finally, to be grateful that I need not consider my efforts
normative for everyone, but that others are correcting the one-sidedness of
my vision by addressing dangers that my experience has not prepared me
to detect.

The most recent form in which medieval Christianity's intolerance of
difference still influences Christianity is the Enlightenment project, the
rational negotiation of difference. In recent decades, this project has been
decisively undermined by authors who, from a variety of perspectives,
have shown that human knowledge is always both informed and limited
by the perspective of the person who holds it.[5] Nevertheless, the rational
negotiation of disagreement is still the method of many academic and
public discussions. The transcending of real differences among Christians—what Christians believe and what they value—should not be the
goal of religious discourse. Rather, dialogue in which particularity and
difference is respected is an opportunity for repair of the limited vision of
each.

The literature of Christian devotion has been influential in the creation
of the contemporary world: preoccupation with death, transcendence of
bodies and the natural world, universal prescriptions that ignore differences of gender conditioning, social location, and perspective—all of

these attitudes were translated by devotional literature into practices that wove them into the lives of individuals and societies in the Christian West. Instead of providing alternatives to social conditioning, devotional literature was an effective means for the reproduction of social arrangements in the Christian West. Exposing and acknowledging the limitations of devotional literature, however, does not negate its vision of the possibility of a human life, thoughtfully chosen, actively trained by daily exercise, and bodied forth with gratitude and responsibility. The practical project of devotional manuals was to designate the energy and to provide methods for the construction of a critical perspective on one's society—as society appears subjectively as well as in the public sphere. That project has never been so crucial.

# Notes

1. Quoted in Herbert L. Dreyfus and Paul Rabinow, *Michel Foucault: Beyond Structuralism and Hermeneutics* (Chicago: University of Chicago Press, 1982), p. 187.

2. *Apology* 38A (Loeb Classical Library trans. Harold North Fowler [Cambridge: Harvard University Press, 1977], p. 133).

3. Michel Foucault, *The Care of the Self* (New York: Pantheon, 1986), p. 45.

4. For identifying the complex of Christian ideas, images, and activities, I prefer the traditional terms "Christian life," "practice of Christianity," or even "Christian piety" rather than the modern term "spirituality." There are several reasons for this: "spirituality" seems to suggest a cultivation of mind or, in traditional language, "souls" in contrast to bodies, practices, and biological life in the natural world, an emphasis that is itself an aspect of Christian tradition that we will need to examine and evaluate.

Although Paul Tillich, in volume 1 of his *Systematic Theology* (Chicago: University of Chicago Press, 1951), writes: "Spirit does not stand in contrast to body. Life as spirit transcends the duality of body and mind" (p. 250), he despairs, in volume 3 (1963), of "rescuing the adjective 'spiritual' " from the "semantic confusion" of its many denotations and connotations (pp. 222–23). The noun *spirituality,* as Tillich points out, is even more encumbered with tangled meanings, the most problematic of which imply the possibility of a religious life in which one's body, physical life and what one *does,* is "transcended" or ignored as irrelevant.

5. Saul Bellow, *Humboldt's Gift* (New York: Penguin, 1975), p. 301.

6. See, for example, Hendrik Kraemer, *A Theology of the Laity* (Philadelphia: Westminster Press, 1958); also, Yves M. J. Congar, O. P., *Lay People in the Church* (Westminster, MD: Newman Press, 1965); cf. Ernst Curtius's statement, "Much of what we call Christianity is purely and simply monastic," in *European Literature and the Latin Middle Ages,* trans. Willard Trask (London: Routledge and Kegan Paul, 1979), p. 515.

7. See my *Image as Insight: Visual Understanding in Western Christianity and Secular Culture* (Boston: Beacon, 1985) for a treatment of the importance of religious images in the history of the Christian West.

8. George Lakoff, *Fire, Women, and Dangerous Things* (Chicago: University of Chicago Press: 1987), writes: "Ordinary people without any technical expertise have theories, either implicit or explicit, about every important aspect of their lives" (p. 118).

9. Symeon the New Theologian, *The Discourses* (New York: Paulist, Classics of Western Spirituality, 1980), p. 231.

10. For example, Augustine, in discussing Isaiah's description of the threat of God's judgment on sinners in *City of God* 20.21, wrote: "It is obvious that . . . translators used 'men' to convey the same meaning as 'human beings.' For no one is likely to assert that women who transgress will not incur the same punishment! The fact is that both sexes are included under the important sex, especially as that was the sex from which woman was created." A slightly more generous impulse for insistence that male language functions generically occurs in *City of God* 12.18. Here Augustine quotes Psalm 1:1, "Blessed is the man who fears the Lord," commenting that the verse "obviously includes the women who

fear him"; quoted from the *City of God,* ed. David Knowles, trans. Henry Bettenson (Middlesex, England: Penguin, 1972).

11. Valerie Saiving, "The Human Situation: A Feminine View," in *Womanspirit Rising,* ed. Carol P. Christ and Judith Plaskow (San Francisco: Harper & Row, 1979), p. 27.

12. For an excellent detailed discussion of how female socialization and conditioning to femininity operate by fetishizing and sexualizing parts of the body as well as postures, gestures, and behavior, see *Female Sexualization,* ed. Frigga Haug (London: Verso, 1987).

13. Margaret Mead wrote: "We know of no culture that has said that there is no difference between men and women except in the way they contribute to the creation of the next generation; that otherwise, in all respects, they are just human beings with varying gifts, no one of which can be exclusively assigned to either sex" (quoted by Saiving, "Human Situation," p. 29).

14. *Beowulf,* trans. David Wright (Baltimore, MD: Penguin, 1957), chap. 21.

15. Yes, the monster is female; the story begs for a psychoanalytic interpretation, but I will resist this temptation to transgress the limits of my capacity as a historical theologian.

## Introduction to Part One

1. Roger R. Rollin, "The Hero as Popular Culture," in *The Hero in Transition,* ed. Ray B. Browne and Marshall W. Fishwick (Bowling Green, OH: Bowling Green University Popular Press, 1983), p. 43.

2. Sallie McFague, *Metaphorical Theology* (Philadelphia: Fortress, 1983), p. 37.

## Chapter 2   An Image of the Image

1. Athanasius, *On the Incarnation,* in *Christology of the Later Fathers,* ed. Edward Hardy (Philadelphia: Westminster Press, Library of Christian Classics, 1974), p. 68.

2. Gregory of Nyssa, *On Perfection,* Fathers of the Church, vol. 58, trans. Virginia Woods Callahan (Washington, DC: Catholic University of America Press, 1967), p. 110.

3. Thomas à Kempis, *The Imitation of Christ,* trans. Betty I. Knott (London: Collins, 1963), p. 126.

4. I do not use the word *rhetoric* in a pejorative sense; I indicate by it simply the style and emotional quality of an author's effort to persuade.

5. *The Imitation,* p. 70.

6. See my discussion of dualism, chap. 1, n. 4.

7. *The Imitation,* p. 64.

8. Ibid., p. 58.

9. *On Perfection,* p. 99.

10. Ibid., p. 105.

11. Ibid., p. 107.

12. Ibid., p. 109.

13. Plato *Timaeus* 88b.

14. G. W. H. Lampe, *A Patristic Greek Lexicon* (Oxford: Clarendon Press, 1961), pp. 170ff.

15. *On Perfection,* p. 121.

16. Plato *Symposium* 210a; also *Phaedrus* 251a; in *The Collected Dialogues of Plato,* ed. Edith Hamilton and Huntington Cairns (Princeton: Bollingen, 1961).

17. *Acts of St. Francis and His Companions,* in *St. Francis of Assisi: Writings and Early Biographies,* ed. Marion A. Habig (Chicago: Franciscan Herald Press, 1983).

18. Thomas of Celano, *First Life,* in *St. Francis of Assisi,* p. 329.

19. *The Little Flowers of St. Francis,* ed. Raphael Brown (New York: Doubleday Image, 1958), pp. 192–93.

20. *Meditations on the Life of Christ: An Illustrated Manuscript of the Fourteenth Century,* ed. Isa Ragusa and Rosalie B. Green (Princeton, NJ: Princeton University Press, 1961), p. 5.

21. Durandus of Mende *Rationale divinorum officiorum* 3.4.

22. Michael Baxandall, *Painting and Experience in Fifteenth-Century Italy* (Oxford: Oxford University Press, 1972), p. 45.

23. In the manuscript edited by Ragusa and Green, however, the sequence of pictures ends during the accounts of Christ's ministry.

24. *Meditations,* plate 120; pp. 137–39.

25. Ibid., p. 309.

26. *The Imitation,* p. 82.

27. Meister Eckhart, "Talks," in *Meister Eckhart: A Modern Translation* (New York: Harper & Row, 1941), p. 5.

28. *On Perfection,* p. 103.

29. Michel Foucault, *The Care of the Self* (New York: Pantheon, 1986), pp. 50–1.

30. See my *Fullness of Life: Historical Foundations for a New Asceticism* (Philadelphia: Westminster Press, 1981) for a discussion of the care with which many historical authors discussed the role of human bodies in Christian life.

31. *The Sayings of the Fathers,* in *Western Asceticism* (Philadelphia: Westminster Press, 1958), p. 109.

32. *Little Flowers,* pp. 183–84.

33. *The Imitation,* p. 105.

34. Ibid., p. 104.

35. Augustine *In Ps.* 127.8, 9.

36. Augustine *Enchiridion* 117 (trans. Henry Paolucci [Chicago: Henry Regnery, 1961], p. 135).

37. Juan de Valdes, *The Christian Alphabet,* in *Spiritual and Anabaptist Writers,* ed. George H. Williams and Angel M. Mergal (Philadelphia: Westminster Press, Library of Christian Classics, 1957).

38. Augustine *Confessions* 13.9 (trans. Rex Warner [New York: New American Library, 1963]).

39. *The Imitation,* pp. 77–78.

40. *Meditations,* p. 172.

41. *The Imitation,* p. 72.

42. Ibid., p. 73.

43. See the account of the twelfth-century debate over whether women were created in God's image in Barbara Newman, *Sister of Wisdom: St. Hildegard's Theology of the Feminine* (Berkeley: University of California Press, 1987), pp. 91ff.

44. Augustine *On the Trinity* 12. 7 (trans. Stephen McKenna, Fathers of the Church, vol. 45); see also the carefully nuanced discussion by Mary Anne Horowitz, "The Image of God in Man—Is Woman Included?" *Harvard Theological Review* 72, no. 3/4 (July–October 1979): 175–206.

45. Heinrich Kramer and James Sprenger, *The Malleus Maleficarum,* trans. Montague Summers (New York: Dover, 1971), p. 47.

46. Thomas Aquinas *Summa Theologica* 3a, q. 31, art. 4 (Blackfriars ed. [New York: McGraw-Hill, 1969]).

47. See my previous discussions of the role of images of the Virgin in medieval communities in *Image as Insight: Visual Understanding in Western Christianity and Secular Culture* (Boston: Beacon, 1985), esp. chap. 4, "Images of Women in Fourteenth-Century Tuscan Painting"; and "The Virgin's One Bare Breast: Female Nudity and Religious Meaning in Tuscan Early Renaissance Culture," in *The Female Body in Western Culture,* ed. Susan R. Suleiman (Cambridge: Harvard University Press, 1986).

48. Rosemary Radford Ruether, *Sexism and God-Talk* (Boston: Beacon, 1983), chap. 5, "Christology: Can a Male Savior Save Women?" pp. 116–38.

49. Judith Plaskow, *Sex, Sin, and Grace: Women's Experience and the Theologies of Reinhold Niebuhr and Paul Tillich* (Washington, DC: University Press of America, 1980).

50. Giovanni Boccaccio, *The Decameron,* trans. Mark Musa and Peter Bondanella (New York: New American Library, 1982), pp. 16–17.

51. *In Jo. Epist.* 7.8.


## Chapter 3    A Society of Aliens

1. Augustine *In Ps.* 137.1.

2. Augustine *City of God* 19.14, 17 (ed. David Knowles, trans. Henry Bettenson [Middlesex, England: Penguin, 1972]).

3. Jerome *Ep.* 108.9 (trans. in *A Select Library of Nicene and Post-Nicene Fathers,* second series, vol. 6 [New York: Christian Literature Company, 1893]).

4. For a refutation of the claim that Egeria was a Spanish nun, see Hagith Sivan, "Who Was Egeria? Piety and Pilgrimage in the Age of Gratian," *Harvard Theological Review* 81, no. 1 (forthcoming, 1988).

5. *Egeria's Travels,* trans. John Wilkinson (London: S.P.C.K., 1971); see also E. D. Hunt, *Holyland Pilgrimage in the Later Roman Empire AD 312–46* (Oxford: Oxford University Press, 1982).

6. Hans-Georg Gadamer's definition of "presence" is helpful for reconstructing Egeria's experience of the "holy places": "It is only in a derived sense that presence at something means also a kind of subjective attitude, that of attention to something"; rather, presence is defined by the engagement of the senses. See *Truth and Method* (New York: Seabury, 1975), p. 111.

7. *Egeria's Travels,* pp. 122–23. In the eleventh century, Richard St.-Vanne had a similar experience to that of Egeria on pilgrimage to the Holy Land. His biographer wrote: "It is not for me to describe the anguished tears which he shed when at last he reached those venerable places. When he saw the pillar of Pilate in the Praetorium he witnessed in his mind's eye the binding and scourging of the Savior. He thought of the spitting, the smiting, the mocking, and the crown of thorns. Then, on the place of Calvary, he passed through his mind an image of the Saviour crucified, pierced with a lance, reviled and mocked by all around him, crying out with a loud voice, and yielding up his spirit. And meditating on these scenes, he could no longer hold back his tears, and surrendered to the agony he felt." Quoted in Jonathan Sumption, *Pilgrimage* (London: Faber and Faber, 1975), p. 92.

8. Sumption, *Pilgrimage,* p. 105.

9. A twelfth-century sermon, preached on one of the two feasts of St. James to pilgrims to the "Great Pilgrimage" destination, St. James, Compostela, instructs: "The pilgrim must bring with him no money at all, except perhaps to distribute it to poor along

the road. Those who sell their property before leaving must give every penny of it to the poor, for if they spend it on their own journey they are departing from the path of the Lord. In times past the faithful had but one heart and one soul, and they held all property in common, owning nothing on their own; just so the pilgrims of today must hold everything in common and travel together with one heart and one soul. To do otherwise would be disgraceful and outrageous . . . the pilgrim who dies on the road with money in his pocket is permanently excluded from the kingdom of heaven." Quoted in Sumption, *Pilgrimage,* p. 124.

10. Ibid., p. 182.

11. *The Book of Margery Kempe,* ed. W. Butler-Bowdon (New York: Devin-Adair, 1944), chap. 28, pp. 56ff.

12. Gregory of Nyssa, *On Pilgrimage,* in *A Select Library of Nicene and Post-Nicene Fathers,* second series, vol. 5 (New York: Christian Literature Co., 1893), p. 383.

13. Berthold of Ratisbon, quoted in Vera and Helmust Hell, *The Great Pilgrimage of the Middle Ages: The Road to St. James, Compostela* (New York: Clarkson N. Potter, Inc., 1966), p. 27.

14. *The Westminster Dictionary of Christian Spirituality,* ed. Gordon S. Wakefield (Philadelphia: Westminster Press, 1983), p. 63.

15. John Bunyan, *Grace Abounding to the Chief of Sinners* (Grand Rapids, MI: Baker Books, 1978), p. 9.

16. Ibid., p. 10.

17. Ibid., p. 22; see also Dayton Haskin, "*The Pilgrim's Progress* in the Context of Bunyan's Dialogue with the Radicals," *Harvard Theological Review* 77, no. 1 (January 1984): 73–94.

18. John Bunyan, *The Pilgrim's Progress* (Glasgow: Collins, 1979), p. 30.

19. Ibid., p. 50.

20. Ibid., p. 174.

21. Ibid., pp. 48–49.

22. Ibid., p. 210.

23. Jonathan Edwards, "The Christian Pilgrim," *The Works of President Edwards,* ed. S. B. Dwight, vol. 2 (Boston: J. B. Jewett, 1854), pp. 135–46.

24. Augustine *Sermon* 97.4.4.

25. Edwards, p. 137.

26. *Pilgrim's Progress,* p. 27.

27. Edwards, p. 147.

28. Augustine *In Ps.* 136.5.

29. See, for example, Thomas à Kempis, *The Imitation of Christ,* trans. Betty I. Knott (London: Collins, 1963): "When you reach a state in which troubles become sweet and satisfying to you for Christ's sake, then you may think that all is well with you because you have found a paradise on earth. As long as you find suffering a burden and try to escape it, things will go badly with you, and you will always be running away from trouble; but if you once accept that suffering . . . your state will soon improve, and you will find peace" (p. 107).

30. For a discussion of the effect of child rearing on adult personality, see Alice Miller, *For Your Own Good* (New York: Farrar, Straus & Giroux, 1984).

31. *Pilgrim's Progress,* p. 174; see also Elizabeth Rowe, "Roll faster on, ye lingering minutes: the nearer my joys the more impatient I am to seize them: after these painful agonies, how greedily shall I drink in immortal ease and pleasure " ("A Joyful View of

Approaching Death," in *An Anthology of Devotional Literature,* ed. Thomas Kepler [Grand Rapids, MI: Baker Book House, 1947], p. 471).

32. Edwards, p. 118.

33. Philippe Ariès, *Western Attitudes Toward Death,* trans. Patricia M. Ranum (Baltimore, MD: Johns Hopkins University Press, 1974), p. 28.

34. Edwards, p. 148.

35. Edwards, p. 141.

36. *Pilgrim's Progress,* p. 155.

37. Augustine *In Ps.* 55.4.

38. We should note, however, that Augustine did not promote the usual correlate of this position: denial or glorification of death. To his own rhetorical question, "Is death, which separates soul and body, really a good thing for the good?" he answers, "The death of the body, the separation of the soul from the body is not good for anyone . . . it is a harsh and unnatural experience" (*City of God* 13.6).

39. Johann Arndt, *True Christianity,* trans. Peter Erb (New York: Paulist, 1979), p. 67.

40. Augustine *Sermon* 306.3.

41. *City of God* 22.21.

42. Arndt, p. 108.

43. Thomas Hobbes, *Leviathan,* chap. 18.

44. For detailed studies of environmental exploitation and the rationales that supported it, see William Cronin, *Changes in the Land* (New York: Hill and Wang, 1983); Carolyn Merchant, *The Death of Nature* (New York: Harper & Row, 1980); Keith Thomas, *Man and the Natural World* (New York: Pantheon, 1983).

45. Rainer Maria Rilke, *Letters to a Young Poet,* trans. M. D. Herter Norton (New York: W. W. Norton, 1934), p. 69.

46. Augustine *Enn. in Psalm* 121.

47. For example, Edwards: "The bulk of mankind are hastening onward in the broad way to destruction" (pp. 144–45).

48. Edwards, p. 149.

49. Augustine *On Christine Doctrine* 1.23 (trans. D. W. Robertson, Jr. [Indianapolis, IN: Bobbs-Merrill, 1958], p. 18).

50. Ibid., p. 19.

51. Ibid.

52. Augustine *Soliloquies* 1.1.

53. *On the Trinity* 8. 8.12.

54. Arndt, *True Christianity,* pp. 126–27, 130.

## Chapter 4   Staying Is Nowhere

1. Augustine *Epistula* 155.

2. John Bunyan, *The Pilgrim's Progress* (Glasgow: Collins, 1979), p. 170.

3. St. John Climacus, *The Ladder of Divine Ascent* (Boston: Holy Transfiguration Monastery, 1978), Prologue, p. xlv.

4. Ibid., p. 13.

5. Practices associated with advance in Christian life will be discussed in the next section; for a discussion of differences between lay and monastic theology in the Middle Ages, see Dennis D. Martin, "Popular and Monastic Pastoral Issues in the Middle Ages," *Church History* 56, no. 3 (September 1987): 320–32.

6. Gregory of Nyssa, *The Life of Moses,* trans. Abraham J. Malherbe and Everett Ferguson (New York: Paulist, 1978), pp. 55–6.

7. Benedict of Nursia, *Rule,* in *Western Asceticism,* ed. Owen Chadwick (Philadelphia: Westminster Press, 1958), Prologue, pp. 291f.

8. Gregory of Nyssa, *Life of Moses,* p. 135.

9. *Pseudo-Dionysius: The Complete Works,* trans. Colm Luibheid (New York: Paulist, 1987), p. 138.

10. John Rupert Martin, *The Illustrations of the Heavenly Ladder of John Climacus* (Princeton: Princeton University Press, 1954).

11. John Climacus, *Ladder,* p. 11.

12. *Pseudo-Dionysius,* p. 146.

13. Bonaventure, *The Mind's Road to God,* trans. George Boas (Indianapolis, IN: Bobbs-Merrill, 1953), p. 8.

14. Since I have explored a range of hierarchical interpretations elsewhere, I will cite, rather than reproduce those discussions: see *Fullness of Life: Historical Foundations for New Asceticism* (Philadelphia: Westminster Press, 1979), pp. 94ff and 117ff; and *Image as Insight: Visual Understanding in Western Christianity and Secular Culture* (Boston: Beacon, 1985), pp. 104ff.

15. Augustine *Confessions* 10.6; italics mine.

16. Bonaventure, *The Mind's Road to God,* p. 10.

17. John Climacus, *Ladder,* p. 10.

18. *The Celestial Hierarchy,* in *Pseudo-Dionysius,* p. 154.

19. For a discussion of Machiavelli's understanding of power, see Hanna Fenichel Pitkin, *Fortune Is a Woman, Gender and Politics in the Thought of Niccolo Machiavelli* (Berkeley: University of California Press, 1984).

20. See editorial note no. 2, in *Pseudo-Dionysius,* p. 195.

21. *The Ecclesiastical Hierarchy,* in *Pseudo-Dionysius,* pp. 195ff.

22. *The Divine Names,* in *Pseudo-Dionysius,* pp. 110–11.

23. *The Celestial Hierarchy,* in *Pseudo-Dionysius,* pp. 184–85.

24. *The Ecclesiastical Hierarchy,* in *Pseudo-Dionysius,* p. 201; see also p. 197: "If you talk of 'hierarchy' you are referring in effect to the arrangement of all the sacred realities. Talk of 'hierarch' and one is referring to a holy and inspired man, someone who understands all sacred knowledge, someone in whom an entire hierarchy is completely perfected and known."

25. Ibid., p. 196.

26. Helena Michie, *The Flesh Made Word: Female Figures and Women's Bodies* (New York: Oxford University Press, 1987), p. 86.

27. Rainer Maria Rilke, *Duino Elegies,* trans. J. B. Leishman and Stephen Spender (New York: W. W. Norton, 1939), p. 23; the original reads: *Denn Bleiben ist nirgends.*

28. "A Sermon of Metropolitan Philaret," in Martin, *Illustrations,* p. xxxi.

29. Ibid.

30. Aristotle *Nichomachean Ethics* 1. 3 (trans. J. A. K. Thomson [Baltimore, MD: Penguin, 1953], p. 26).

31. I am indebted to Father Richard Valantasis, chaplain to the Sisters of St. Margaret, Lewisburg Square, Boston, for the interpretations of ascent described in this paragraph.

32. Gregory of Nyssa, *The Life of Moses,* p. 93; Gregory's sexual image here is startling, especially as he has already defined as male "sober and provident rational thoughts," and as female, sense perception (pp. 56ff). This intrusion of gender imagery in a mystical treatise, however, will not detain us in this context.

33. *The Enchiridion of Erasmus,* trans. Raymond Himelick (Bloomington, IN: Indiana University Press, 1963), pp. 101–2.

34. Ibid., p. 104.

35. Prudentius, *Psychomachia,* Loeb Classical Library, trans. H. J. Thomson (Cambridge: Harvard University Press, 1949).

36. John Calvin, *Institutes of the Christian Religion,* ed. John T. McNeill (Philadelphia: Westminster Press, Library of Christian Classics, 1967), 1:173–78, 2:913–14, for example; see also Michael Walzer, *The Revolution of the Saints* (New York: Atheneum, 1976), pp. 63–4, for a discussion of warfare as pervasive in Calvin's writing.

37. John Bunyan, *The Holy War Made by Shaddai upon Diabolus,* ed. Roger Sharrock and James F. Forest (Oxford: Clarendon Press, 1980).

38. The *Enchiridion militis Christiana,* literally "Handbook of the Christian Soldier," was a best seller in the Renaissance; "first published in 1503, it had more than thirty editions in the next twenty years—in French, Dutch, Spanish, and English, as well as in the original Latin—and dozens more by the end of the century" (Raymond Himelick, "Introduction" to *The Enchiridion of Erasmus* [Bloomington, IN: Indiana University Press, 1963], p. 38).

39. Ibid., pp. 11–12.

40. Ibid., p. 58.

41. Ibid., p. 38.

42. Ibid., p. 39.

43. The popular devotional work by the Puritan minister, John Downame, *The Christian Warfare* (1604), instructed Christians to picture themselves as engaged in deadly daily struggle: "Hee travaileth . . . like a souldier through the thickest of his mortall enemies, who daily encounter him, and with their continuall assaults on all sides labour to hinder him in his Christian march" (London, 1634), p. 22.

44. *Enchiridion of Erasmus,* pp. 39, 75, 159–60.

45. Ibid., p. 87.

46. Ibid., p. 179.

47. Ibid., p. 160.

48. Ibid., p. 83.

49. Ibid., p. 179; in the original: *scorto putidissimo* (Erasmus von Rotterdam, *Enchiridion militis Christiani,* ed. Welzig Werner [Darmstadt: Wissenschlaftliche Buchgesellschaft, 1968], p. 334).

50. *Enchiridion of Erasmus,* p. 83.

51. Ibid., p. 178.

52. Ibid., p. 179.

## Introduction to Part Two

1. Johann Arndt, *True Christianity,* trans. Peter Erb (New York: Paulist, 1979), p. 21.

2. Jürgen Habermas, *Knowledge and Human Interest,* trans. Jeremy J. Shapiro (Boston: Beacon, 1971).

3. Pseudo-Dionysius, *Pseudo Dionysius: The Complete Works,* trans. Colm Luibheid (New York: Paulist, 1987), p. 200.

4. Luther's *conscientia.* See my article " 'The Rope Breaks When It Is Tightest': Luther on the Body, Consciousness, and the Word," *Harvard Theological Review* 77, no. 3/4 (1984): 239–58.

5. The primacy and effectiveness of "going through the motions" without constant

evaluation of whether one is experiencing the right feelings or thinking the right thoughts seems to be more characteristic of contemporary self-help manuals than of the literature of Christian spirituality in the twentieth century. For example, Joan Borysenko's *Minding the Body, Mending the Mind* (Reading, MS: Addison-Wesley, 1987), emphasizes the importance of continuing to practice an exercise of breathing and meditation *whether or not* it seems to be effective: "Remember that practice is indispensable to progress at anything. . . . The session itself is the goal. In the true sense, the process is the product" (p. 45).

6. For Francis Bacon's scientific method, see especially *The New Atlantis,* published in 1627, in *Works,* 14 vols., ed. James Spedding, Robert Leslie Ellis, Douglas Devon Heath (London: Longmans Green, 1870), vol. 3; see also Carolyn Merchant's discussion of Bacon's scientific method in *The Death of Nature* (San Francisco: Harper & Row, 1980).

7. In Augustine's formulation, *incipit configuari veritate,* the soul takes the shape of truth; *On Christian Doctrine* 1.20.19 (trans. D. W. Robertson, Jr. [Indianapolis, IN: Bobbs-Merrill, 1958]).

8. Michel Foucault, *The Use of Pleasure* (New York: Pantheon, 1985), pp. 12–13.

## Chapter 5   The Pleasure of No Pleasure

1. Palladius, *The Paradise of the Holy Fathers, The Lausaic History of Palladius,* ed. J. Armitage Robinson (London: Chatto and Windus, 1907), 6:239–40; cf. St. Syncletice, a fourth-century female desert teacher: "The devil sometimes sends a severe fast, too prolonged—the devil's disciples do this as well as holy men. How do we distinguish the fasting of our God and King from the fasting of that tyrant the devil? Clearly by its moderation. Throughout your life, then, you ought to keep an unvarying rule of fasting. . . . Everything which is extreme is destructive. . . . Our body is like armour, our soul like the warrior. Take care of both, and you will be ready for what comes" (*The Sayings of the Fathers,* in *Western Asceticism* [Philadelphia: Westminster Press, Library of Christian Classics, 1981], pp. 120–21).

2. Augustine *De utilitate jejunii* 1.

3. We should also notice the specific erotic element in asceticism itself. In *Middlemarch* George Eliot makes Celia comment that the heroine, Dorothea, "likes giving up," a comment anticipated many centuries before by Diogenes Laertius's more philosophical statement: "Even the despising of pleasure is pleasurable, when we are habituated to it" (*Lives of Eminent Philosophers* 6.2.70 (Loeb Classical Library, trans. R. D. Hicks [New York: Putnam, 1925]).

4. For example, John Climacus, *The Ladder of Divine Ascent* (Boston: Holy Transfiguration Monastery, 1978), pp. 13–14.

5. See, for example, Thomas Aquinas's discussion "Of the Contemplative Life," in the *Summa Theologiae,* quoted in *An Anthology of Devotional Literature,* ed. Thomas Kepler (Grand Rapids, MI: Baker Book House, 1947), p. 144.

6. For example, Robert Ornstein writes of the senses as "data-reduction agencies," in *The Psychology of Consciousness* (New York: Penguin, 1972), p. 61.

7. *The Sayings of the Fathers,* in *Western Asceticism,* ed. Owen Chadwick (Philadelphia: Westminster Press, 1958), p. 109.

8. Elaine Scarry, *The Body in Pain* (New York: Oxford University Press, 1985), p. 34.

9. Chapter 9 will discuss an exception to this generalization: Erasmus's *Enchiridion,* which seems preoccupied with counseling the avoidance of sexuality.

10. Augustine *Confessions* 8.7 (trans. Rex Warner [New York: New American Library, 1963]).

11. Clement of Alexandria *Stromateis* 3 (in *Alexandrian Christianity,* ed. Henry Chadwick [Philadelphia: Westminster Press, 1954], p. 138).

12. Martin Luther, *An Exhortation to the Knights of the Teutonic Order* 1523: "Physicians are not amiss when they say: if this natural function [sexual intercourse] is forcibly restrained it necessarily strikes into the flesh and blood and becomes a poison, whence the body becomes unhealthy, enervated, sweaty and foul-smelling" (in *Luther's Works,* vol. 45, ed. Walter I. Brandt [Philadelphia: Muhlenberg, 1962]).

13. Among contemporary writings that deal with sexual relationship as central to spirituality: Carter Heyward, *The Redemption of God: A Theology of Mutual Relation* (Washington, DC: University Press of America, 1982); Mary Daly, *Pure Lust: Elemental Feminist Philosophy* (Boston: Beacon, 1984); Dorothy Donnelly, "The Sexual Mystic," in *The Feminist Mystic,* ed. Mary Giles (New York: Crossroad, 1982); and *Radical Love: An Approach to Sexual Spirituality* (Minneapolis, MN: Winston, 1984); Martin S. Laird, O.S.A., "Contemplation and Sexuality," *Studia Mystica* 8, no. 1 (Spring 1985): 49–57; James Nelson, *Embodiment* (Minneapolis, MN: Augsburg, 1978).

14. Rosemary Radford Ruether, *Sexism and God-Talk* (Boston: Beacon, 1983), pp. 79–80.

15. Mary Daly, *Pure Lust,* pp. 67–68.

16. For an alternative interpretation of female food asceticism, see Caroline Walker Bynum, *Holy Feast and Holy Fast: The Religious Significance of Food to Medieval Women* (Berkeley: University of California Press, 1987).

17. Julian of Norwich, *Showings,* Long Text, trans. Edmund Colledge, O.S.A. and James Walsh, S.J. (New York: Paulist, Classics of Western Spirituality, 1978), pp. 297–98.

18. For an exposition of this position, see Robert Bellah, *Habits of the Heart: Individualism and Commitment in American Life* (San Francisco: Harper & Row, 1986).

19. Carol Gilligan, *In a Different Voice* (Cambridge: Harvard University Press, 1982).

20. Rosemary Radford Ruether, *Womenguides* (Boston: Beacon, 1985).

21. For a discussion of men in relation to feminism, see *Men in Feminism,* ed. Alice Jardine and Paul Smith (New York: Methuen, 1987).

22. This conclusion represents a change of mind from my earlier attempt to rehabilitate the idea and practice of asceticism, by reading historical texts treating the methods and goals of asceticism in the best possible light and apart from their social effects (*Fullness of Life: Historical Foundations for a New Asceticism* [Philadelphia: Westminster Press, 1979])

## Chapter 6   The Word Made Flesh

1. Julian of Norwich, *Showings,* Long Text, chap. 6 (New York: Paulist, Classics of Western Spirituality, 1978), p. 186.

2. For a discussion of the centrality of food practices to the piety of medieval mystics, see Caroline Walker Bynum, *Holy Feast and Holy Fast: The Religious Significance of Food to Medieval Women* (Berkeley: University of California Press, 1987), pp. 31–72 and passim.

3. *Oxford Dictionary of the Christian Church,* 2nd ed., ed. F. L. Cross and E. A. Livingstone (Oxford: Oxford University Press, 1974).

4.
> Verbum caro panem verum verbo carnem efficit;
> Fitque sanguis Christi merum; et si sensus deficit,
> Ad firmandum cor sincerum sola fides sufficit.

[quoted by Bynum, *Holy Feast,* pp. 51–52]

5. Thomas à Kempis, *The Imitation of Christ,* trans. Betty I. Knott (London: Collins, 1963), pp. 213ff.

6. Francis de Sales, *Introduction to the Devout Life,* trans. John K. Ryan (New York: Doubleday, Image, 1972), p. 119.

7. Ibid., pp. 107–8.

8. John Calvin *Institutes of the Christian Religion* 4.14.1 (ed. John T. McNeill [Philadelphia: Westminster Press, Library of Christian Classics, 1970]); for an illuminating discussion of Calvin's life and thought, see William J. Bouwsma, *John Calvin: A Sixteenth Century Portrait* (New York: Oxford University Press, 1988).

9. *Institutes* 4.14.3.

10. *Institutes* 4.14.6.

11. *Institutes* 4.14.8–9.

12. *Institutes* 4.14.17.

13. *Institutes* 4.17.3.

14. *Institutes* 4.17.5.

15. *Institutes* 4.17.5.

16. *Institutes* 4.17.10.

17. *Institutes* 4.17.3

18. See my discussion of differences in visual experience in Protestant and Roman Catholic worship in the sixteenth century in *Image as Insight: Visual Understanding in Historical Christianity and Secular Culture* (Boston: Beacon, 1985), chap. 5.

19. Johann Arndt, *True Christianity,* trans. Peter Erb (New York: Paulist, Classics of Western Spirituality, 1979), p. 110.

20. Ibid., p. 111 (italics mine).

21. *The Imitation,* p. 219.

22. Ibid., p. 223.

23. Rudolf Arnheim, *Art and Visual Perception* (Berkeley: University of California Press, 1954), p. v.

## Chapter 7   Gratitude and Responsibility

1. "New Every Morning Is the Love," words written by John Keble, 1822, in *The Hymnal of the Protestant Episcopal Church* (New York: Church Pension Fund, 1940).

2. Martin Luther, *The Freedom of the Christian,* in *Martin Luther: Selections from His Writings,* ed. John Dillenberger (New York: Doubleday, Anchor, 1961).

3. Ibid., p. 300.

4. Ibid., p. 304.

5. Luther, "Preface to the Epistle of St. Paul to the Romans," in *Martin Luther,* ed. J. Dillenberger, pp. 19ff.

6. *The Freedom of the Christian,* in *Martin Luther,* ed. J. Dillenberger, p. 61.

7. Ibid., p. 58.

8. Ibid., p. 72.

9. Keith Thomas describes an increasing concern about cruelty to animals that began to be common in the eighteenth century, a sensitivity previously missing in the Christian West (*Man and the Natural World* [New York: Pantheon, 1983], pp. 143ff).

10. Washington Gladden, *The Christian Way,* in *An Anthology of Devotional Literature,* ed. Thomas Kepler (Grand Rapids, MI: Baker Book House, 1947), pp. 577–78.

11. Walter Rauschenbusch, *A Theology for the Social Gospel* (Nashville, TN: Abingdon, 1981), p. 5.

12. Ibid., p. 12.

13. Ibid.

14. Ibid., p. 103.

15. Ibid., p. 108; Rauschenbusch's book, *Prayers of the Social Awakening,* (Boston: Pilgrim Press, 1910), makes it clear that his use of "man" for humankind includes women as well as minorities; see especially his prayer, "For Women Who Toil," pp. 55–56.

16. Rauschenbusch, *A Theology for the Social Gospel,* p. 145.

17. Augustine *City of God* 19.15.

18. 1John 4:16.

19. See Paula J. Caplan's argument that it is not accurate to say that because they are willing to act in self-sacrificial ways women are masochistic. Masochism requires enjoyment of suffering for its own sake, and this does not accurately characterize women's roles. In fact, women are highly *rewarded* for being nurturant, charitable, supportive, etc. ("The Myth of Women's Masochism," in *The Psychology of Women: On-going Debate,* ed. Mary Roth Walsh [New Haven: Yale University Press, 1987], p. 93).

20. Edwin Hubbell Chapin, *Duties of Young Women* (Boston: George W. Briggs, 1848), p. 23.

21. Ibid., p. 160.

22. Ibid., p. 53.

23. Ibid., p. 13.

24. Ibid., p. 12.

25. Phoebe Palmer, *The Promise of the Father* (Salem, OR: Schmul Publishers, 1859), p. 115.

26. Ibid., p. 116.

## Chapter 8   An Appetite for Prayer

1. Alice Munro, *The Progress of Love* (New York: Alfred A. Knopf, 1986), p. 4.

2. *The Westminster Dictionary of Christian Spirituality,* ed. Gordon S. Wakefield (Philadelphia: Westminster Press, 1983), p. 95.

3. A. R. Burn, "Hic Breve Vivitur," *Past and Present* 4 (1953): 2–31.

4. John Donne, "Thoughts on Death," in *An Anthology of Devotional Literature,* ed. Thomas Kepler (Grand Rapids, MI: Baker Book House, 1947), p. 324.

5. Anonymous, *The Way of a Pilgrim,* trans. Helen Bacovcin (New York: Doubleday, Image, 1978), pp. 142–43.

6. Ibid., p. 26.

7. Ibid., p. 24.

8. Ibid., p. 34.

9. Ibid., p. 157.

10. Ibid.

11. *The Way of a Pilgrim,* pp. 162–63; See also Thomas Aquinas on the role of "appetite" in contemplative practice: "Although the contemplative life consists chiefly in an act of the intellect, it has its beginning in the appetite. . . . And since the end corresponds to the beginning, it follows that the term also and the end of the contemplative life is found in the appetite, since one delights in seeing the object loved, and the very delight in the object seen arouses a yet greater love" ("Of the Contemplative Life," in *An Anthology of Devotional Literature,* p. 151).

12. Washington Gladden, *The Christian Way,* in *An Anthology of Devotional Literature,* p. 581.

13. Martin Luther, "A Simple Way to Pray," in *Luther's Works*, vol. 43, ed. Jaroslav Pelikan (St. Louis, MO: Concordia, 1968): 193.

14. Jean Nicholas Grou, *The Hidden Life of the Soul*, in *An Anthology of Devotional Literature*, p. 528.

15. Francis de Sales, *Introduction to the Devout Life*, trans. John K. Ryan (New York: Doubleday, Image, 1972), p. 95.

16. Quoted by Keith Thomas, *Man and the Natural World: A History of the Modern Sensibility* (New York: Pantheon, 1983), p. 38.

17. See also Teresa of Avila's *The Way of Perfection*, in *An Anthology of Devotional Literature*, p. 283: "A helpful means to keep you in the presence of our Lord would be to have with you a favorite image or picture of him. Do not be content merely to carry it without looking at it. Use it as a means of inspiring you to speak to him."

18. The few suggestions by medieval texts from Gregory the Great forward, that religious paintings were tolerated for the purpose of instructing the illiterate—the "books of the illiterate"—have been overinterpreted by art historians and historical theologians as accounting for all religious art. Historical texts describe many other reasons for the use of visual imagery, reasons that center on their religious use as meditative objects. See my discussion of the functions of religious images in *Image as Insight: Visual Understanding in Western Christianity and Secular Culture* (Boston: Beacon, 1985), esp. chap. 4.

19. John of Damascus *The Orthodox Faith* 4.16 (trans. Constantine Cavarnos, *Orthodox Iconography* [Institute for Byzantine and Greek Studies, 1977], p. 51).

20. *Meditations on the Life of Christ: An Illustrated Manuscript of the Fourteenth Century*, ed. Isa Ragusa and Rosalie B. Green (Princeton, NJ: Princeton University Press, 1961): "Even those who ascend to greater contemplation ought not to renounce it [visual images] at the right time and place. Otherwise it will seem to be condemned as vile, which would show great pride. Remember . . . that the blessed Bernard [of Clairvaux] the highest contemplator, never renounced it. As appears in his sermons, he esteemed and praised it beyond measure" (p. 387).

21. William Hood, "St. Dominic's Manners of Praying: Gestures in Fra Angelico's Cell Frescoes at San Marco," *Art Bulletin* 68, No. 2 (June 1986): 194–206.

22. *Meditations*, Prologue, p. 5.

23. Hood, "St. Dominic's Manners of Praying," p. 198.

24. Painting scenes from the life of Christ was also considered a devotional exercise. This is well known in Eastern Orthodox churches, but it was also practiced as meditation in the West. Vasari described the fifteenth-century monk-painter Fra Angelico as living an ascetic life that informed his painting. A modern reviewer commented: "One is tempted to interpret Vasari's sentence characterizing the ascetic life of the painter—'Si esercito continuamente nella pittura, ne mai volle lavorare altre cosa che si santo'—as implying that for Fra Ancelico the imitation of Christ in art was actually a form of personal devotional exercise" (Colin Eisler, "The Athelete of Virtue: The Iconography of Asceticism," *De Artibus Opuscula: Essays in Honor of Erwin Panofsky* [New York University Press, 1961], p. 88).

25. Quoted by Michael Baxandall, *Painting and Experience in Fifteenth-Century Italy* (Oxford: Oxford University Press, 1972), p. 46.

26. *Introduction to the Devout Life*, p. 87; Jean Nicholas Grou concurred: "Those who are beginners cannot do better than use *The Imitation of Christ*, pausing on each sentence and meditating upon it" (in *An Anthology of Devotional Literature*, p. 528).

27. Jean Leclercq, O.S.B., *The Love of Learning and the Desire for God*, trans. Catherine Misraki (New York: Fordham University Press, 1974), p. 19; see also the *Ancrene Riwle*, an

early thirteenth-century rule for female recluses: "The remedy for sloth is spiritual joy and the comfort of joyful hope, which comes from reading. . . . Often, dear sisters, you ought to say fewer fixed prayers so that you may do more reading. Reading is good prayer. Reading teaches us how to pray and what to pray for, and then prayer achieves it. In the course of reading, when the heart is pleased, there arises a spirit of devotion which is worth many prayers" (ed. and trans. M. B. Salu [London: Burns and Oates, 1955]).

28. LeClercq, *The Love of Learning*, pp. 20–22.

29. François Fénelon, in *An Anthology of Devotional Literature*, p. 461.

30. Isaac of Syria, *Directions on Spiritual Training*, in *Readings in Christian Theology*, ed. Peter C. Hodgson and Robert H. King (Philadelphia: Fortress, 1980), p. 296.

31. Philippe Ariès, *The Hour of Our Death*, trans. Helen Weaver (New York: Alfred A. Knopf, 1981); and *Images of Man and Death* (Cambridge: Harvard University Press, 1985), p. 31. See also A. Gregory Schneider, "The Ritual of Happy Dying among Early American Methodists," *Church History* 56, no. 3 (September 1987): 348–63.

32. See Elaine Scarry's important suggestion that the reason for many old people's ceaseless talk is their awareness of imminent death. "The voice becomes a final source of self-extension: so long as one is speaking, the self extends out beyond the boundaries of the body, occupies a space much larger than the body. . . . Their ceaseless talk articulates their unspoken understanding that only in silence do the edges of the self become coterminous with the edges of the body it will die with" (*The Body in Pain*, [New York: Oxford University Press, 1985], p. 32). This describes one of the few options provided in a secular culture for differentiating "self" from body in the frightening prospect of death. The formation of a religious center of subjectivity, as urged by devotional manuals of the Christian West, provide another alternative, an alternative that seems less pitiful than that of "ceaseless talk."

33. Jeremy Taylor, *The Rule and Exercises of Holy Dying*, in *An Anthology of Devotional Literature*, p. 360.

34. Thomas Aquinas, in *An Anthology of Devotional Literature*, p. 145.

35. Isaac of Syria, in *Readings in Christian Theology*, p. 107.

36. Thomas Aquinas, in *An Anthology of Devotional Literature*, p. 148.

37. For a historical example, see my article, "Infancy, Parenting, and Nourishment in Augustine's *Confessions*," *Journal of the American Academy of Religion* 50, no. 3 (September 1982): 349–64.

38. St. Teresa, in *An Anthology of Devotional Literature*, p. 283.

39. Alice Miller, *For Your Own Good* (New York: Farrar, Straus & Giroux, 1984).

40. Francisco de Osuna, *The Third Spiritual Alphabet*, Fourteenth Treatise, (New York: Paulist, Classics of Western Spirituality, 1976), p. 363.

41. Ibid., pp. 360–61.

42. Ibid., pp. 362–63.

43. For example, St. Jerome *Epistula* 14.2: "Should your mother with ashes on her hair and garments show you the breast at which she nursed you, heed her not; should your father prostrate himself on the threshold, trample him underfoot and go your way. With dry eyes fly to the standard of the cross. In such cases, cruelty is the only affection" (trans. in *A Select Library of the Nicene and Post-Nicene Fathers*, second series, vol. 6 [New York: Christian Literature Co., 1893], p. 14). See also Clarissa W. Atkinson, " 'My Mother, Your Servant,' " in *Immaculate and Powerful: The Female in Sacred Image and Secular Culture* (Boston: Beacon, 1985), pp. 139–72.

44. Miguel de Molinos, *Spiritual Guide*, in *An Anthology of Devotional Literature*, p. 446.

## Chapter 9    Loving the Neighbor in God

1. Aelred of Rievaulx, *Spiritual Friendship,* trans. Mary Eugenia Laker (Washington, DC: Cistercian, 1974), 17.

2. Nothing, of course, forbids similar friendships among women, but although Aelred wrote for women as well as men monastics, he used no female models. In the twentieth century, Virginia Woolf pointed out that there are no great female friendships in the literature of the Christian West. In religious visual images, however, the friendship of Mary and Elizabeth as depicted in Visitation scenes was available as a model of love between women. The Visitation was, of course, occasioned by the impending birth of sons who would be closely related in their lives and work; it is difficult to say to what extent this modified and weakened an otherwise powerful model of female friendship.

3. *Spiritual Friendship,* p. 72.

4. Ibid., p. 73.

5. Ibid., pp. 74–75.

6. The history of interpretation by which "Platonic love" came to be understood as nonsexual is too complicated to trace here; it is, however, approximately opposite to Plato's description of eros as attraction that may include, but is not limited to, physical attraction.

7. *Spiritual Friendship,* p. 77; see also p. 87.

8. Plato's *Symposium* presents several scenarios for the role of physical attraction in eros. Although ambiguous in its conclusion, it seems to imply that in the case of a very advanced "self-master" such as Socrates, physical attraction is never disengaged but, precisely because it is not consummated, produces a continuous intense eros that is productive of great intellectual achievement. In the *Symposium,* for example, Socrates lay all night with Alcibiades, the young man to whom he was attracted, without sexual contact.

9. *Spiritual Friendship,* pp. 78–79.

10. Francis de Sales, *Introduction to the Devout Life,* trans. John K. Ryan (NY: Doubleday, Image, 1972), p. 181.

11. Ibid., p. 17.

12. Ibid., pp. 177f.

13. Thomas à Kempis, *The Imitation of Christ,* trans. Betty I. Knotts (London: Collins, 1963), p. 93.

14. John of Damascus, *The Ladder of Divine Ascent* (Boston: Holy Transfiguration Monastery, 1978), p. 12.

15. See also chapter 3 for a discussion of Augustine's idea of "loving the neighbor in God."

16. Augustine *Confessions* 6.15 (trans. Rex Warner [New York: New American Library, 1963]).

17. I will use these terms to refer to Christian lifestyles that exclude sexual intercourse, not to indicate a physical state in which genital sexuality has never been experienced. On changing historical ideas of virginity, see Clarissa W. Atkinson, "Precious Balsam in a Fragile Glass: Ideology of Virginity in the Middle Ages," *Journal of Family History,* Summer 1983, pp. 131–43.

18. For a discussion of rationales for and practices of celibacy in the Greek and Roman culture in which Christianity emerged, see Michel Foucault, *The Use of Pleasure* (New York: Pantheon, 1985), and *The Care of the Self* (New York: Pantheon, 1986).

19. The primary literature is voluminous; I will only cite here two secondary works that identify primary sources and discuss celibacy in Christian tradition: Henry C. Lea, *History*

*of Sacerdotal Celibacy in the Christian Church,* 3rd ed., 2 vols. (London, 1907); John Bugge, *Virginitas: An Essay in the History of a Medieval Ideal* (The Hague: Martinus Nijhoff, 1975).

20. Epiphanius *Expositio fidei catholicae* 21, in Migne, PG 823–24.

21. Athanasius, *On the Incarnation,* in *Christology of the Later Fathers,* ed. Edward R. Hardy (Philadelphia: Westminster Press, 1954), p. 104.

22. Among many others, Gregory of Nyssa *On the Making of Man* 17–18 (trans. in *A Select Library of the Nicene and Post-Nicene Fathers,* second series [New York: Christian Literature Co., 1893], 6:387f).

23. Samuel Laeuchli, in *Power and Sexuality* (Philadelphia: Temple, 1972), has demonstrated that the legislation of what constituted acceptable and unacceptable sexuality was one of the primary means for asserting ecclesiastical control by Christian churches in the first centuries of Christianity.

24. William E. Phipps, "The Plight of the Song of Songs," *Journal of the American Academy of Religion,* March 1974, pp. 82–100.

25. For example, Origen's formula came to be a commonplace of devotional literature: "If you have despised all bodily things . . . then you can acquire spiritual love" (*Homilies on the Song of Songs* 1.2; quoted in Phipps, "The Plight of the Song of Songs," p. 88).

26. John Bugge, *Virginitas* (The Hague: Martinus Nijhoff, 1975); for a description of gender-specific interpretations of virginity during the medieval period, see Jane Tibbetts Schulenberg, "The Heroics of Virginity: Brides of Christ and Sacrificial Mutilation," in *Women of the Middle Ages and the Renaissance,* ed. M. B. Rose (Syracuse, 1986), pp. 29–72.

27. Although marriage has been stoutly defended by many Christian authors, there is also a considerable tradition of ascetic authors who did their best to disparage marriage, thereby aligning themselves with a persistent gnostic strain within Christianity. Jerome is one of the most blatant maligners of marriage, but his views are, unfortunately, not idiosyncratic: "Men marry, indeed, so as to get a manager for the house, to solace weariness, to banish solitude; but a faithful slave is a far better manager, more submissive to the master, more observant of his ways, than a wife who thinks she proves herself mistress if she acts in opposition to her husband, that is, if she does what pleases her, not what she is commanded" (*Against Jovinian* 1.47; trans. in *A Select Library of Nicene and Post-Nicene Fathers,* second series, 6:393).

28. For example, Francis de Sales's *Introduction to the Devout Life,* trans. John K. Ryan (New York: Doubleday, Image, 1972), is typical of devotional manuals in finding sexual activity legitimate only within marriage: "It is never licit to derive shameful pleasure from our bodies in any way whatsoever except in lawful marriage, whose sanctity by just compensation can repair damage received in such pleasure" (p. 156).

29. Quoting Seneca, the first-century Stoic, Jerome wrote that "a wise man ought to love his wife with judgment, not affection. Let him control his impulses and not be borne headlong into copulation. Nothing is fouler than to love a wife like an adulteress. . . . Let them show themselves to their wives not as lovers, but as husbands" (*Against Jovinian* 1.49, trans. in *A Select Library of Nicene and Post-Nicene Fathers,* second series, 6:386).

30. Jean-Louis Flandrin, "Contraception, Marriage, and Sexual Relations in the Christian West," in *The Biology of Man in History,* Selections from the *Annales* (Baltimore, MD: Johns Hopkins University Press, 1975), pp. 23–47; see also Vern L. Bullough, *Sexual Variance in Society and History* (Chicago: University of Chicago Press, 1976).

31. See Augustine's treatises, *On the Good of Marriage* and *On Virginity,* for his formulation of the step beyond Paul's "It is better to marry than to burn," a scriptural text admired by devotional texts throughout the Christian centuries.

32. Clement of Alexandria, "On Spiritual Perfection," in *Alexandrian Christianity,* ed. Henry Chadwick (Philadelphia: Westminster Press, 1954), p. 38.

33. See Augustine *City of God* 22.30, for a discussion of influential theologians' evaluation of human bodies; also Margaret R. Miles, *Augustine on the Body* (Missoula, MT: Scholars Press, 1979); "Theology, Anthropology, and the Human Body in Calvin's *Institutes of the Christian Religion,*" *Harvard Theological Review* 74, no. 3 (July 1981): 303–23; " 'The Rope Breaks When It Is Tightest': Luther on the Body, Consciousness, and the Word," *Harvard Theological Review* 77, no. 3/4 (1984): 239–58; John Giles Milhaven, "Thomas Aquinas on Sexual Pleasure," *Journal of Religious Education* 5, no. 2 (1977): 157–81.

34. *Treatise to the Knights of the Teutonic Order,* passim, *Luther's Works,* vol. 45, ed. Walter I. Brandt (Philadelphia: Muhlenberg, 1962); however, Luther's statement that he himself married in order to please his father and spite the pope is also not indicative to modern readers of a deep understanding of the possibility for spiritual growth contained in loving sexual relationship; see also Calvin's statement, made before he had seriously considered marriage: "I have never taken a wife, and I do not know if I shall ever marry. If I did so it would be to free myself from trivial worries so that I could devote myself to the Lord" (quoted in William J. Bouwsma, *John Calvin: A Sixteenth Century Portrait* [New York: Oxford University Press, 1988], p. 22).

35. *The Enchiridion of Erasmus,* trans. Raymond Himelick (Bloomington, IN: Indiana University Press, 1963), p. 178.

36. Ibid., p. 79.

37. Ibid., p. 83; see also Erasmus's treatise *Christiani matrimonii institutio,* in *Desiderii Erasmi Opera Omnia* vol. 5, ed. Jean Leclerc (Leiden, 1703–6), col. 696E.

38. *Enchiridion of Erasmus,* p. 177.

39. Ibid.

40. Ibid., p. 179; readers familiar with Erasmus's *Enchiridion* will remember the gender imagery which is the vehicle for his "reasonable" conclusion that sexual pleasure is an unmitigated evil. Women are repeatedly characterized as "deadly sirens," "silly women," "strumpets," and other locutions in the same vein. Moreover, he moves imperceptibly from discussing the need for spiritual love in marriage to discussing sexual relationships outside marriage without distinguishing sexual pleasure in loving relationships from casual or promiscuous sex. In any relationship, sex spoils and exploits the man who indulges in it: "It drains away one's patrimony. It destroys at the same time the vigor and attractiveness of the body. It damages health and produces countless ailments, all of them disgusting. It deforms the flowering of youth and hastens a repulsive old age" (p. 178).

41. Ibid., p. 184.

42. Ibid., p. 389.

43. Ibid., p. 80.

44. Ibid., p. 179.

45. Augustine *City of God* 22.17 (ed. David Knowles, trans. Henry Bettenson [Middlesex, England: Penguin, 1972]).

46. Curiously, although women are regularly accused of receiving great sexual gratification through exploiting men, men are seldom berated for "using" women, perhaps since women's bodies were understood to exist for "use," i.e., for reproduction; indeed, in canon law, rape was not considered one of the most serious of sexual offenses; "the great crimes were sodomy, bestiality, incest, and adultery" (Jean-Louis Flandrine, "Contraception, Marriage, and Sexual Relations in the Christian West," in *Biology of Man in History,* Selections from the *Annales* [Baltimore: Johns Hopkins University Press, 1975], p. 32).

47. Sigmund Freud, *Civilization and Its Discontents,* trans. Joan Riviere (New York:

Doubleday, Anchor, 1958); see also Herbert Marcuse, *Eros and Civilization: A Philosophical Inquiry into Freud* (Boston: Beacon, 1974).

48. See especially Michel Foucault, "Sexuality and Solitude," in *On Signs,* ed. Marshall Blonsky (Baltimore, MD: Johns Hopkins University Press, 1985), pp. 365–72.

49. For an important account of the process by which a West German women's collective analyzed "female sexualization" as a central aspect of "the ways individuals reproduce society," see *Female Sexualization,* ed. Frigga Haug (London: Verso, 1987), p. 50.

50. Ibid., p. 13.


## Chapter 10    Dying Happily

1. Dietrich Bonhoeffer, *Letters and Papers from Prison* (New York: Macmillan, 1972), p. 103.

2. Ignatius of Antioch, "Letter to the Romans," in *Early Christian Fathers,* ed. Cyril Richardson (New York: Macmillan, 1970), p. 105.

3. Ibid., p. 104.

4. *The Sayings of the Fathers,* in *Western Asceticism,* ed. Owen Chadwick (Philadelphia: Westminster Press, 1958).

5. Evagrius, *Praktikos and Chapters on Prayer,* ed. John E. Bamberger (Kalamazoo, MI: Cistercian Publications, 1970).

6. Augustine *Sermon* 306.3.

7. Augustine *Confessions* VI.6 (trans. Rex Warner [New York: New American Library, 1963]).

8. Thomas à Kempis, *The Imitation of Christ,* trans. Betty I. Knott (London: Collins, 1963), p. 70.

9. Ibid., p. 73.

10. Ibid., p. 71: "As long as we wear this feeble body, we cannot be free from sin, or live without weariness and suffering. . . . So we must hold on in patience, and wait for God's mercy, until the storms pass by and our mortal nature is swallowed up in life."

11. Horace Bushnell, *Sermons for the New Life* (New York: Scribner, 1858), p. 242; see also *The Enchiridion of Erasmus,* trans. Raymond Himelick (Bloomington, IN: Indiana University Press, 1963), p. 133: "Christ alone embodies every principle of living happily."

12. Henry Suso, *Selected Maxims,* in *An Anthology of Devotional Literature,* ed. Thomas Kepler (Grand Rapids, MI: Baker House Books, 1947), p. 184: "Where the sensual appetite is the moving principle of a man's actions, there is toil, suffering, and mental darkness."

13. John Welsey, *Christian Behavior,* in *An Anthology of Devotional Literature,* pp. 517–18.

14. Kierkegaard, *Journals,* in *An Anthology of Devotional Literature,* p. 543.

15. Michel Foucault, "Sexuality and Solitude," in *On Signs,* ed. Marshall Blonsky, (Baltimore, MD: Johns Hopkins University Press, 1985), p. 367.

16. Augustine *Confessions* 8.7 (trans. Rex Warner [New York: New American Library, 1963]).

17. Anonymous, *The Cloud of Unknowing,* trans. Clifton Wolters (Middlesex, England: Penguin, 1961), p. 60.

18. Jeremy Taylor gives the following reasons for humility: "1. The spirit of man is light and troublesome. 2. His body is brutish and sickly. 3. He is constant in his folly and error, and inconstant in his manners and good purposes. 4. His labours are vain, intricate, and endless. 5. His fortune is changeable, but seldom pleasing, never perfect. 6. His

wisdom comes not till he be ready to die, that is, till he be past using it. 7. His death is certain, always ready at the door, but never far off" (*The Rule and Exercises of Holy Living*, in *An Anthology of Devotional Literature*, p. 352.

19. Ibid., p. 351.

20. Ibid., p. 352.

21. Ibid., p. 355.

22. August Hermann Franke, *Following Christ*, in *Pietists—Selected Writings*, ed. Peter C. Erb (New York: Paulist, Classics of Western Spirituality, 1983), p. 143.

23. Simeon the New Theologian, *The Discourses*, "Self-Examination on the Beatitudes," (New York: Paulist, Classics of Western Spirituality, 1980), p. 329.

24. Ibid., p. 331.

25. Miguel de Molinos, *The Spiritual Guide*, in *An Anthology of Devotional Literature*, p. 444.

26. John Calvin *Institutes of the Christian Religion* 3.6.1 (ed. John T. McNeill [Philadelphia: Westminster Press, n.d.], 1:689).

27. Calvin *Institutes* 3.7.2 (ed. John T. McNeill, 1:692).

28. Julian of Norwich, *Showings*, Long Text, chap. 2 (New York: Paulist, Classics of Western Spirituality, 1978), p. 178.

## Chapter 11   Conclusion

1. Quoted by William J. Bouwsma, *John Calvin: A Sixteenth Century Portrait* (New York: Oxford University Press, 1988), p. 191.

2. For an argument from a behavioral science perspective on the impossibility that rational thought can actually transcend embodiment, social location, and the concrete circumstances of one's life, see George Lakoff, *Women, Fire, and Dangerous Things* (Chicago: University of Chicago Press, 1987).

3. Walker Percy, *The Second Coming* (New York: Washington Square Press, 1980), p. 31.

4. Michel Foucault, "Powers and Strategies," in *Power/Knowledge* (New York: Pantheon, 1972), p. 134.

5. The literature is so huge and multidisciplinary that it cannot be fully cited here: Jürgen Habermas's *Knowledge and Human Interests* (Boston: Beacon, 1976) was an early exploration of the inevitability of perspective in knowledge; the "sociology of knowledge" has been demonstrated not only in the humanities and social sciences but also in the sciences; see, for example, *Discovering Reality: Feminist Perspectives on Epistomology, Metaphysics, Methodology, and Philosophy of Science*, ed. Sandra Harding (London: D. Reidel, 1983); and George Lakoff, *Women, Fires, and Dangerous Things;* Richard Rorty's *Philosophy and the Mirror of Nature* (Princeton, 1979) was an important statement concerning the impossibility of getting beneath hermeneutics to foundational metaphysical statements; and Fergus Kerr's *Theology After Wittgenstein* (Oxford: Basil Blackwell, 1986) explores theological repercussions of the contemporary realization that claims to objectivity must be relinquished.

# Index